DISCOVERING

the

MEANING

of

SCRIPTURE

How to Read, Understand,
and Apply Your Bible

R. W. Hamilton III

To my mentor and true friend, Dr. Richard Fulton.

I know no other more committed to the gospel of Jesus Christ.

TABLE OF CONTENTS

APPRECIATION

Having now finished my second publication, it has become quite obvious to me that writing and publishing a book takes a village. It is therefore with sincere appreciation that I make mention of some of those who have collaborated with me in this project. First, I should like to thank my team of advisors who have heeded the call in assisting me in writing this manuscript: Dr. Randal Lyle, Dr. Robert "Bob" Williams, Ernest Hopkins, Dr. James "Jim" Hughes, Matthew Linde, and Hannah Foster. All of you made suggestions and provided insights that were so helpful to me along the way. Next, I wish to express my heartfelt gratitude to Jack Watson and Johnn Hudson. Jack, your encouragement and prayers for me and this project have been sorely needed and immensely appreciated. Johnn, your adroitness for being a valuable sounding board and your technical knowledge has made this process so much easier.

Furthermore, I would be remiss not to call attention to the authors and the works that I have strongly leaned on while writing this book: Grant R. Osborn: *The Hermeneutical Spiral: A Comprehensive Introduction to Biblical Interpretation*; William W. Klein, Craig L. Blomberg, and Robert L. Hubbard Jr.: *Introduction to Biblical Interpretation*; Gordon D. Fee and Douglas Stuart: *How to Read the Bible for All Its Worth: A Guide to Understanding the Bible*; Robert H. Stein: *A Basic Guide to Interpreting the*

1

Bible: Playing by the Rules; Dan McCartney and Charles Clayton: *Let The Reader Understand: A Guide to Interpreting and Applying the Bible*; Henry A. Virkler and Karelynne Gerber Ayayo: *Hermeneutics: Principles and Processes of Biblical Interpretation*; Roy B. Zuck: *Basic Biblical Interpretation: A Practical Guide to Discovering Biblical Truth*. The contribution these authors have made to this book should be obvious to anyone who knows them well.

Finally, I am so very grateful for my godly, loving wife Amber and our delightful son Elan. Hopefully, the latter will one day grow up to love God and desire to know Him through the preserved and inspired text that we call the Bible. I hope this book will help him, and anyone else, in that endeavor!

FOREWORD

By way of introduction, I am Robert Lee Williams, Ph.D. in New Testament and Early Christian Literature (University of Chicago, 1983). I am privileged to have taught my first love of Bible and theology for the past forty years at a variety of post-secondary school levels, community college, Bible college, Christian liberal arts college, theological seminary, and graduate theological institute. In addition, I have from other strong inclinations served as pastor and inner-city minister in multicultural communities.

It is an honor and privilege to have the opportunity to recommend to you *Discovering the Meaning of Scripture: How to Read, Understand, and Apply Your Bible*. The author, R. W. Hamilton III, "Trey," will emerge as a wonderful surprise for you not yet acquainted with him. In his twenty years of Christian life, Trey has combined his love for the Bible and his aptitude in medical work. His biblical training has extended from ABS (2002) to BTh (2009) into MDiv work by 2011. This commitment and training have led him into pastoral work, most recently planting a church in Burleson, TX, in 2015. Indicative of his combination of scholarly and pastoral motivations, Trey published his first work last year, *God's Word to Us: The Story of How We Got Our Bible*, an eminently readable and careful historical exposition of the transmission of our Bible, concluding a valuable theological chapter on its inspiration and preservation.

3

I have known Trey since that first publication saw the light of day, at which time providentially he and his family became a part of Meadowridge Community Baptist Church and most fortunately the life group of which I am a part. He was immediately a valued contributor and consequently became part of the teacher rotation. His deep knowledge and clear way of communicating, indeed with energy, endeared him to the group. Consistent with his holistic understanding of the Christian life, Trey is a devoted husband to his lovely wife Amber and father to his bright son Elan. He, in the meantime, has occupied a position as a Respiratory Therapist with Medical City of Fort Worth since 2007.

Now, in rapid succession, he has completed another substantial book, this one on a more complex topic and happily couched in terms accessible to the Christian committed to his faith but not formally trained in it. The academic area is hermeneutics, but his title resists using the abstruse term, knowing that the Christian reader understands the importance of reading his or her Bible intelligently and applying it carefully. Those two skills are what this study will enable the reader to do, indeed to improve in doing. Equally, Trey insists, it will enable the reader to detect, and to circumvent, ways that we often read our Bibles innocently but erroneously. I do not know of a more important book to read in order to check, and improve, one's understanding of his or her Bible. I have taught hermeneutics in seminary with other books, the best there were at the time. This is the best one I have seen for orienting a reader how to think correctly about the "science" of interpreting the Scriptures. Yes, it is a scientific set of principles that should not be left to guesswork or simply to well-meaning instincts, even the Spirit-guided instincts of the Christian reader. Even they are sometimes deficient. You may have noticed!

Trey Hamilton provides the reader a logical and easy-to-follow presentation. The book contains five major sections, progressing from the "need" to the "rules" to particulars of "literary analysis" and patterns of "theological analysis" to conclude with "practical use."

"Part 1: The Need for Hermeneutics" introduces the area of study with a motivational pair of chapters. "The Goal of Interpretation" (Chapter 1) explains why one needs to "learn" how to interpret. "The Task of the Interpreter" (Chapter 2) then itemizes what the issues involves. Then "Part 2: The Rules of Interpretation" differentiates the three broad areas of principles important for sound interpreting of the Scriptures (in fact, for any written document). "Contextual Analysis" (Chapter 3) explores what the surrounding verses and the book as a whole are discussing. Trey is at pains to insist that a verse will only mean what makes sense in its textual environment. Then outside the text itself "Historical-Cultural Analysis" (Chapter 4) shows what people were doing at the time and how they lived, noting differences from us today. Finally, "Lexical-Syntactical Analysis" (Chapter 5) explains within the passage the importance of the writer's particular word usage and why he put sentences together as he did. These guidelines are indispensable, and complete, for gaining an overall grasp of what one is reading, sometimes in contrast to one's first impressions, and at other times deepening correct senses one has of the text.

Such broad perspectives usually leave one, however, in need of particular understanding of the kind of literature one is studying in his or her Bible. So follows "Part 3: Language and Meaning: The Literary Analysis of Scripture" with six detailed chapters on kinds of literature we encounter in God's Word. Trey discusses each chapter in a threefold way: introducing the kind of literature, then listing characteristics of it, and finally specifying principles of the particular kind with clarification of each principle. This section is replete with well-chosen examples. The discussions become a virtual reference book on interpreting the kinds of literature.

He explains first in "Historical Narratives" (Chapter 6) the most common kind of literature in biblical "genres" have particular features that can misguide us. For example, narrative records historical activity without specifying whether we should follow the examples recorded. Next, in "Law" (Chapter 7) we find that phenomenon is given by God to his people but, surprisingly, is not always to be followed by us today. Trey enables us to make critical distinctions here. Then in "Poetry" (Chapter 8) comes the question of what is literal and what is figurative. The principles make sound interpretation surprisingly predictable, not just guesswork. "Prophecy" (Chapter 9), a genre overlapping with poetry, also involves some clear, illuminating distinctions, most notably that of forthtelling and foretelling, a common area of stumbling and ambiguity for the diligent reader. Then "Apocalyptic Literature" (Chapter 10) takes us from ambiguity to mystery. Trey masterfully clarifies how apocalyptic, while a subset of prophetic literature, is at the same time to be interpreted in some ways distinct from prophecy. Finally, in "Parables" (Chapter 11), the curious little stories told most famously by Jesus are explained with nuance. They are not simple and certainly not all to be interpreted by the same principles. Trey makes clear this tricky distinction.

"Part 4: Seeing the Big Picture: The Theological Analysis of Scripture" brings the reader to what to make of the details. Many will never have known anything but vague impressions of these topics. "The Pattern of Revelation" (Chapter 12 and continued in chapter 13) is a wonderful summary of God's inspiring words and humans' usually regrettable responses in the sweep of the Bible. Trey is truly in his element here with his emphasis on God's Kingdom, God's activity on earth, as it is manifested throughout the sixty-six books. He deals with what is termed "canonical criticism" in the academic world and does so in a lucid way for the range of readers. Then in "Doing Theology" (Chapter 14) he continues the kingdom theme with his other favorite concept, related to kingdom, "already not yet" eschatology. This chapter in fact includes much more, orienting the reader to areas of theological pursuits and explaining the value of each.

Mr. Hamilton concludes with "Part 5: The Practical Use of Scripture," providing some insightful guidelines on extending one's now heightened understanding of the Bible to employing it in one's life. In "Using the Bible for Spiritual Growth" (Chapter 15) Trey surveys the multiple areas of life, individually and corporately, in which we desire, indeed we are called, to apply the Bible appropriately. We are reminded of how we should live out our learning in every area of life. We all know that James insists, "So faith by itself, if it has no works, is dead" (2:17). Trey itemizes areas of our lives calling for application of the Bible for ourselves and others, noting in the process pitfalls for us to beware. Similarly, in "Applying the Biblical Message" (Chapter 16) he marshals concepts from his preceding chapters to warn us against major deficiencies of interpretation, in Paul's words, "rightly handling the word of truth" (2 Tim. 2:15b). Trey encourages our use of principles in applying our Scriptures, which he memorably terms "principlizing" the Scripture.

In conclusion, the reader may well sense now why it is to me an honor and privilege to be invited to write this foreword and why I enthusiastically recommend it to him and her as a "must read" in being the informed Christian that we all wish to be, both in understanding our sacred Scriptures and in living them out to the fullest. This book will guide the reader thoroughly and will do so in an easily readable way.

Robert Lee Williams, Ph.D.
Distinguished Fellow
Doctoral Supervisor, New Testament and Historical Theology
B. H. Carroll Theological Institute
Fort Worth, 2019

PART 1

THE NEED FOR HERMENEUTICS

In his preface to the book, *Rightly Divided: Readings in Biblical Hermeneutics*, Roy B. Zuck provides the following imaginary, yet often real-life, scenario. He asks his readers to imagine themselves as part of a small-group Bible study that meets each week in a person's home. The group, other than the host or hostess, has no designated leader to lead the study. Each Thursday evening the group gathers to discuss a passage in the book of Romans. When the group comes to a difficult verse or group of verses, each person gives their own opinion on what it means. The views differ and even contradict each other. Having no way of determining which view is correct, they move on to another passage in the chapter and again voice differing opinions. This so-called Bible study concludes with each having discussed various ideas but with no sense of whether the verses mean all those things shared, or if any of them. Why do informal Bible study groups face this problem? The truth is, they unfortunately lack some basic hermeneutical guidelines—rules that help us interpret the Bible.

The word "hermeneutics" is said to have its origin in the name Hermes, the Greek god who served as the emissary and messenger of the gods, delivering and interpreting their delightful or dreadful messages. By the first century, the verb form *hermeneuo* was used to mean "interpret" or "translate." The verb appears three times in the New Testament, each time with the sense of translating from one language to another (John 1:42; 9:7; Hebrews 7:2). In a more technical sense, hermeneutics is often defined as the science and art of biblical interpretation. Hermeneutics is considered a science because it has rules that can be classified in an organized system. It is considered an art because communication is flexible, and a rigid application of rules will sometimes distort the intended meaning of a communication. To be a good interpreter one must learn the rules of hermeneutics as well as the art of applying those rules.

When we hear someone speak or we read what someone has written, our understanding of what is being communicated is usually spontaneous and the rules by which we interpret meaning occur automatically and unconsciously. When something complicates that spontaneous understanding, we become much more cognitive of the processes we use to understand (for example, when translating from one language to another). "Hermeneutics is essentially a codification of the processes we normally use at an unconscious level to understand the meaning of a communication. The more obstacles to spontaneous understanding, the more aware we must become of the processes of interpretation and the need for hermeneutics."[1]

The difficulty in interpreting the Bible usually stems from the fact that it was written so long ago. The Old Testament books were written approximately between 1400 BC and 400 BC, while the New Testament books were written roughly between AD 45 and AD 95. Thus, some of the books (Genesis–Deuteronomy) were written about 3,400 years ago, and the last book of the Bible (the book of Revelation) was written about 1,900 years ago. This means that in order to properly understand what we are reading in our Bible, we must bridge several gaps posed by having such an ancient book in our hands:[2]

Time Gap: Since we cannot talk with the authors and with the initial hearers or readers to discover firsthand the meaning of what they wrote, due to the extensive time gap between us and them, a huge chasm exists. What was known and clearly understood to the original recipients of Scripture is often less clear or uncertain to us today.

Geographical Gap: Today, most Bible readers live thousands of miles from the places where Bible events occurred. The Middle East and the surrounding Mediterranean regions of present-day Europe and North Africa were the places where Bible people lived and traveled. These extend from Babylon in present-day Iraq to Rome, with many different types of geographical landscapes and features in between. Since the Bible often makes important references to many of these geographical places, our unfamiliarity with them puts us at a major disadvantage.

Cultural Gap: There are great differences between the way people in Bible times lived and thought and the way people of today think and behave. Therefore, it is important to know the cultures and customs of the various people-groups mentioned in our Bible. More often than not, a faulty interpretation of Scripture stems from our ignorance of the culture and customs of peoples.

Language Gap: Besides gaps in time, geography, and culture, there is also a chasm between our way of speaking and the way people in Bible times spoke and wrote. The languages in which the Bible was written— Hebrew, Aramaic, and Greek—have unusual or obscure expressions, difficult to comprehend in English. Today we seldom speak in proverbs and parables, yet a good portion of the Bible is proverbial and parabolic. Figurative language, frequently used throughout Scripture, will sometimes obscure our understanding of a text.

Spiritual Gap: It is also important to note that a gap exists between our way of thinking and the way God thinks and acts. The fact that the Bible is written about God puts the Bible in a unique category. God, being infinite, is not fully comprehensible by the finite mind of man. The Bible speaks of God's performing miracles and making predictions about the future. The Bible also speaks of difficult-to-comprehend truths such as the

Trinity, the dual nature of Christ (being both man and God), God's sovereignty in relation to man's free will. All these and others contribute to our difficulty in understanding fully all that is in the Bible.

These five gaps pose serious problems when a person seeks to understand the Bible. Even the Ethiopian in Acts 8 faced several of these gaps, including the time gap, language gap, and spiritual gap.[3] While much of the Bible is straightforward and easy to understand, admittedly, other parts are more difficult. Even Peter wrote, "Our beloved brother Paul, according to the wisdom given to him, has written to you, as also in all his epistles, speaking in them . . . some things hard to understand" (2 Peter 3:15–16). Some Bible verses remain a mystery even to the most skilled interpreters. Thus, if we are going to bridge these gaps and discover the correct meaning of Scripture, we will need to develop an approach and establish methods that are appropriate for such a task. When we consciously set out to discover and employ such principles, we engage with hermeneutics. The basic goal of this book, therefore, will be to establish, explain, and demonstrate guidelines and methods that will help guide those who desire to understand Scripture correctly, and more completely.

1

THE GOAL OF INTERPRETATION

In all communication three distinct components must be present: the Author (or sender), the Text (or message), and the Reader (or receiver), or, as it is sometimes defined, the Encoder, the Code, and the Decoder. Unless all three elements are present, communication is impossible. So, when it comes to "Bible" communication, each author takes the role as "encoder," who sends the message ("code") they wish to convey, and we the readers must "decode" their message by ascertaining its meaning. The main goal, or at least the initial goal, of interpreting the Bible, then, is to discover the meaning of the message being sent—what does the text "mean"? But where does meaning come from? While some interpreters will argue that it comes from one component, others will argue that it comes from another.

The Text (or Code) as the Determiner of Meaning

There are those who would argue that meaning is a property of the text itself, which is to say, it is the text that determines what a writing means. They would claim that a literary text is "autonomous" in the sense that its meaning is completely independent of what the author meant when he wrote the text. In other words, what the biblical author was intending to convey by the text is quite irrelevant with respect to the meaning of the text. As a result, reading a related work such as Galatians in order to help us understand what Paul meant when he wrote Romans would make little or no sense—one could just as well read *Moby Dick*. So then, according to this view, the text is autonomous and has no connection with its author. It possesses its own meaning.

We often hear preachers say something like, "Our text tells us" or "The Bible says." But for most preachers, their use of the phrase "the Bible says" is intended to be understood as "the writer means." However, those who argue that the text possesses its own meaning, these two phrases are not in any way the same. Every text is an independent work of art that is to be interpreted independently of its author—the normal rules of communication no longer apply. Because it is "art," the original composer no longer possesses control of it; the art itself possesses its own meaning independent from its creator.[1] If in some way Paul could appear before those who argue for a semantic autonomy of the text and say, "What I meant when I wrote this was . . ." the response would essentially be, "What you say, Paul, is interesting but quite irrelevant."[2] Paul's willed meaning of his text, what he sought to communicate in his writing, is no more authoritative than any other person's interpretation. Thus, it is illegitimate to place any authorial control over the meaning of a text. This is a very popular approach among modern literary critics.

Perhaps the biggest problem with this view, that the text itself is the determiner of meaning, is that it distorts what a text is and what a text can do. A written text is simply a collection of letters or symbols. They can be Hebrew, Greek, or English letters; Chinese or Japanese symbols; or even Egyptian hieroglyphics. They may be written right to left, left to right, or up and down. They can be written on papyrus, parchment, stone, or metal. Yet the letters and the material upon which they are written are inanimate objects. They cannot reason or think for themselves. Meaning, however, is the result of deliberate thought and reasoning. Whereas a text can convey meaning, it cannot produce meaning, because it cannot think. Only the author and reader of the text can think. Thus, meaning can only come from either the author or the reader.

The Reader (or Decoder) as the Determiner of Meaning

Some interpreters have also claimed that the meaning of a text is determined by the reader. In other words, the person who reads the text gives (or creates) its meaning. According to this view, sometimes called reception theory, if different readers come up with different meanings (as with our imaginary Bible study above), this is simply due to the fact that a text permits the reader to discern multiple meanings. This view not only assumes that there are many legitimate meanings of a text, but allows for each interpreter to contribute his or her meaning to the text. Today it is common to hear someone say something such as, "What this passage means to me is . . ." or, "The verse may mean something different to you, but for me it means . . ." Such statements may legitimately describe the many different applications, or implications, of the author's intended meaning, but we should be careful our interpretations are not made apart from the intended meaning that the author originally meant to convey.

A reader-determined meaning is sometimes called a reader-response approach in literature. That is, each reader responds to a work of literature as the creator of meaning. These reader-created meanings are at times self-consciously driven by various philosophical or social concerns. Other times the reader may simply appeal to his or her idiosyncratic view without any reference to a broader social agenda. We would note that the reader-response approach is not the reader discovering the author's meaning or the application of the author's meaning in the reader's life (discussed below). The reader is the actual determiner or creator of meaning, with the exclusion of any validation from the text. Such an interpretive approach, of course, inevitably results in readers proposing a variety of contradictory meanings. Adherents of the reader-response approach to Scripture would rather affirm various irreconcilable interpretations than suggest that one interpretation is more valid than another.

The Author (or Encoder) as the Determiner of Meaning

The more traditional approach in determining the meaning of a text has been to see its meaning as being determined by the author (called author-centered meaning). According to this view, the meaning of a biblical text is what the author consciously intended to communicate to his readers when he wrote his letter. This view argues that if Paul were alive and told us what he meant to convey in writing Romans, the issue would be settled. The text means what Paul says it means. Similarly, the meaning of the Gospel of Luke is what Luke purposely willed to convey to Theophilus when he wrote his Gospel. Consequently, this view contends that "the Bible and other great works of literature are not to be treated as unique works of art possessing distinct rules supposedly appropriate only to art. On the contrary, they are to be interpreted in the same way that we normally interpret other forms of written or verbal communication. This is essentially the common-sense approach to communication."[3] All normal conversation assumes that the goal of interpretation is to understand what the speaker or writer means by the words he or she is using. For instance, in your attempt to understand this paragraph, are you not seeking to understand what I mean to communicate by my choice of words?

Several objections have been raised against the view that the meaning of a text is determined by the author. One of the most common of these objections is called the "intentional fallacy." This objection, made famous by William K. Wimsatt, Jr. and Monroe Beardsley, argues that it is impossible to climb inside the mind of an author, such as Paul, and experience everything that was going through his mind as he wrote. His innermost feelings and emotions are simply not accessible to the reader, unless he chose to reveal them in his text. As a result, it is argued that the meaning Paul willed is inaccessible.

But when reading a biblical text, the primary goal is not to experience or duplicate the writer's mental and emotional experiences when they wrote. Rather, the goal is to understand what they meant when they consciously sought to communicate to their readers through writing. A careful distinction must be made between what Paul wished to convey in his text and the psychological experiences he went through while writing. What Paul sought to convey by his text has been made available to the reader in the text itself. On the other hand, the inner mental and emotional experiences of Paul are private and not accessible to the reader unless Paul explicitly revealed them in his text. For instance, you the reader are incapable of knowing the mental state of myself (the writer) as I currently write this book. (Am I tired, hungry, sad, or happy?) But in no way does that prevent you (the reader) from understanding what I wish to convey. The goal of interpreting a book such as Romans, then, is not to relive Paul's psychological state, but to understand what he meant by the written text he gave us. The intentional fallacy appears to confuse this objective. A text means what an author such as Paul wished to convey by his words, and having access to his words, we have access to Paul's intended meaning.

The intentional fallacy also argues that an author at times may fail to adequately convey the thoughts he wishes to communicate, or the writer may be what some have called "linguistically incompetent." As Stein comments,

> All of us at some time or another have realized that we may not have expressed adequately what we wish to communicate. Even very capable communicators can at times fail to express correctly or accurately what they meant. It is therefore quite possible that an author could fail to express in an understandable way what he or she sought to communicate. Authors could even mislead the reader by a poor or wrong choice of words. This objection, however, tends to be more hypothetical than real. Most writers, such as Paul, possess sufficient literary competence to express their thoughts adequately. In fact, those who articulate this position usually do so believing they are sufficiently competent to express their own thoughts quite adequately. If they did not,

why would they write them? Why then deny this competence to other writers?[4]

Furthermore, the notion that the biblical writers could have been at times incapable of adequately expressing their thoughts is in direct opposition to the Christian doctrine of the inspiration of Scripture. For the Christian, "the belief that the Bible is inspired introduces a component of divine enabling into the situation. If in the writing of Scripture the authors were 'moved by the Holy Spirit' (2 Peter 1:21), then it would appear that the authors of the Bible were given a divine competence in writing. This 'competence' enabled them to express adequately the revelatory matters they wanted to communicate in their writing."[5]

Finally, a related objection is that modern readers are incapable of understanding the meaning of an ancient author such as Paul. The radical differences between the present situation of the reader and that of an ancient author is simply too vast. How can today's reader, familiar with modern conveniences (television, computers, smart phones, etc.), understand an ancient author writing thousands of years ago in a time of sandals, togas, and mudbrick houses?[6] Admittedly, the difference between the time and place of an ancient author and the modern reader is very real, and should not be minimized. Again, Stein rightly argues,

> Far too often we tend to modernize ancient writers and assume that they thought exactly like twenty-first-century Americans. Consequently we misunderstand them. On the other hand, we can also overemphasize these differences. After all, we are not trying to understand the thoughts of worms or toads. The common humanity we share with the authors of the past and the fact that we both have been created in the image of God facilitate bridging the gap of time. The basic needs for food, clothing, warmth, security, love, forgiveness and hope of life after death that the ancients had are still the basic needs we have today.

Thus, while difficult, understanding an ancient author is not impossible.[7]

The Role of the Author. Texts do not simply appear out of nowhere. For us to have them, someone at some point had to write them. They are the result of someone desiring to write something meaningful and have others read it. If this were not so, these texts would not exist. Since this took place in time past, "What the author willed to convey by the linguistic symbols used (whether the symbols were Hebrew, Aramaic, Greek, Latin, or Chinese is immaterial) possesses a meaning that can never change. What a biblical author willed by his text is anchored in history. It was composed in the past, and being part of the past, it can no more change than any other event of the past can change."[8] Consequently, the meaning of a text is forever fixed.

Yet what an author such as Paul consciously willed to say in the past may also have implications that go beyond his original intent, of which he was not necessarily aware. Those implications are also part of the meaning of the text. When, for instance, Paul wrote in Ephesians 5:18, "Be not drunk with wine," he was consciously thinking that the Ephesian Christians should not become intoxicated with "wine" within a first-century context (a drink usually mixed as three parts water and one-part wine). This mandate, however, undoubtedly has implications that go beyond what Paul was consciously thinking. Paul gave a principal of meaning that has implications about not becoming drunk with alcohol, whether that alcohol be beer, whiskey, rum, vodka, or champagne. Paul, although he was not consciously thinking of these alcoholic beverages, clearly intended for Christians not to become drunk by using them as well. Certainly no one in Ephesus would have thought, "Paul in his letter forbids becoming drunk with wine, but I guess it would not be wrong to become drunk with beer." Thus, Paul's text has implications that go beyond his own particular conscious meaning at the time.

These implications do not in any way contradict Paul's original meaning. Rather, they are perfectly included in the principles Paul wished to communicate in this verse. Thus, what an author of Scripture stated in the past frequently has implications with respect to things of which he was not always aware or did not even exist at the time the text was written. The purpose of biblical interpretation involves understanding the specific conscious meaning of the author, as well as the principles he sought to communicate. If Paul did in fact prohibit becoming drunk with modern-day alcoholic beverages, does he not also forbid in Ephesians 5:18 the unnecessary use and abuse of narcotics? Other statements of Scripture clearly forbid the abuse of the human body in such a manner. But does this specific passage forbid the illicit use and/or abuse of narcotics? If we understand Paul's command as a principle of meaning, then it would appear that this passage does indeed prohibit the illicit use of narcotics. If the principle of meaning willed by Paul in this saying is something like "Do not take into your body substances that will cause you to lose control of your senses and natural inhibitions," then the use of narcotics is likewise prohibited by this verse. If we were able to ask Paul about this latter instance, would he not reply, "I was not consciously thinking of narcotics when I wrote this passage, but that is exactly the point I was meaning to convey"? The fact is, many passages have implications or unconscious meaning its author was not aware of but nevertheless fit the principle of meaning willed in the text. More often than not, the main concern of interpretation is determining what legitimate implications can be deduced from an author's intended meaning (more on the topic of application will be discussed in chapter 16).

The Role of the Text. As already stated, a text consists of a collection of verbal symbols. These symbols can be various kinds of letters, punctuation marks, accents (Greek), or vowel points (Hebrew). An author can use any combination of symbols he wants in order to write his text. In fact, he can invent a language that only he and whomever else he wishes would know. However, if an author wants to convey meaning to as many people as possible, as the biblical authors did, then he or she will choose a code which the readers will understand. This code, conveyed through the use of words and grammar that the author and his readers have in common, gives "shareability" to a text. According to Stein,

> Shareability is the common understanding of a text's words and grammar possessed by both author and reader. Apart from this, a reader cannot understand what an author wills to say. As a result, an author purposely submits himself or herself to the conventions and understanding of language possessed by the readers. Thus, if we understand how the author's intended audience would have understood the text . . . we, as readers today, can also understand the meaning of that same text. Because we can learn how a contemporary of Paul would have understood the Greek words (vocabulary), grammatical construction (syntax), and context of the text, we can also understand Paul's meaning, for the apostle purposely [submitted himself to the norms of the language of his readers].[9]

For the sake of understanding, an author will abide by the common use of words and grammar that is shared among his intended audience. However, within the norms of language, words possess a range of possible meanings. We can find this range of meaning in a dictionary or lexicon. An author is aware, if he wants to be understood, that the words he uses must possess one of these meanings. By the context they are placed in, the reader can usually narrow down the possible meanings of words to just one. For example, the word "love" can be understood to mean a number of things.[10] It can mean passionate affection, personal attachment, sexual intercourse, a strong preference for or liking, a score of zero in tennis, a salutation in a letter. In the sentence, "He lost six love," however, it can only mean a score of zero in a tennis match. The sentence "Let us love one another," on the other hand, is quite ambiguous. It can mean one thing when found in the context of Jesus's teaching and quite another thing in the context of a romantic poem. Through the specific context an author provides—the sentences and paragraphs in which he places his verbal symbols—he reveals the specific meaning of his words.

Furthermore, by reading a text, we may learn all sorts of historical, sociological, cultural, and geographical information. The subject matter of a text can often provide a wealth of information for the reader to investigate. For example, we can read the Gospels to learn about the historical and cultural setting of first-century Palestine. We can study the book of Joshua to learn about the geography of ancient Canaan or second-millennium military strategy. We can study the Psalms to learn about ancient Hebrew poetry or Israelite worship. All of this is both possible and often worthwhile, but when this is done, we should always be aware of the fact that this is not the study of the text's meaning. The meaning of these texts is what the authors of the Gospels, Joshua, and the Psalms willed to teach their readers by recounting history, culture, geography, and poetry.

The Role of the Reader. Using the verbal symbols of the author, that is, the text, the reader seeks to understand what the author meant by these symbols. Knowing that the author intentionally used shareable symbols, the reader begins with the knowledge that the individual building blocks of the text, the words, fit within the norms of the language of the original readers. Seeing how the words are used in phrases and sentences, and how the sentences are used within paragraphs, and how paragraphs are used in chapters, and how chapters are used in the entire work, the reader seeks to understand the author's intent in writing his text. This process is called the "hermeneutical cycle." This expression refers to the fact that the whole text helps the reader understand each individual word or part of the text, while at the same time, the individual words and parts help us understand the meaning of the text as a whole. This sounds complicated, yet all of this goes on simultaneously (and often subconsciously) in the mind of the interpreter. The mind is able to switch back and forth from the meaning of the individual words and the general understanding of the whole text until it comes to a successful resolution of the text's meaning.

If a reader is truly interested in what a biblical author meant by his text, he or she will be interested in his other writings as well, for these are especially helpful in providing clues to the meaning of the words and phrases in the text.[11] After considering its surrounding context, and the context of the entire book, when it comes to understand what Paul meant in a particular verse in Romans, we should afterward consult the book of Galatians (which is the Pauline writing most similar to Romans), then 1 and 2 Corinthians (which were written in close proximity to the time when he penned Romans), and then finally his other epistles. After having worked through the Pauline material, the reader can also look elsewhere through the New Testament, and then the Old Testament, for other supporting texts.

After consulting the passages that pertain to our text throughout the Bible, it might be beneficial to consult with appropriate non-biblical literature as well—such as, the intertestamental literature, rabbinic literature, the writings of the early church fathers, and contemporary Greek literature. The order of importance would be determined by which of these best reflect the way Paul thought, and the subject matter in question. For example, familiarizing ourselves with Jewish teaching (found in Rabbinic literature) at the time of Paul may help us better understand Paul's argument against Judaistic ideology in Romans 3, whereas contemporary Greek literature may help us gain a more exact meaning to the Greek terms he chose to use in a given text. In a similar way, a verse in the Gospel of Luke is best interpreted by the verses surrounding it, the paragraphs in chapters surrounding that verse, the rest of the Gospel of Luke, and then the book of Acts (which was also written by Luke). Acts would reveal better how Luke thought than Matthew, Mark, or John, but other Gospels would be better than Isaiah, which in turn would be better than Josephus, a Jewish historian of the first century.

Once the reader knows the meaning of the author, he or she will need to seek out those implications of that meaning that are especially relevant. Although the meaning of a text can never change—its meaning is locked in past history—its significance is always changing. This is why some people claim that a particular Scripture may have different "meanings." Yet a text does not have different "meanings," for an author like Paul willed a single specific pattern of meaning when he wrote. A text, however, has different "significances" for different readers. For example, the words of Jesus, "And you will be my witnesses in Jerusalem, and in all Judea and Samaria, and into the ends of the earth" (Acts 1:8), have a single meaning. Jesus wanted to see the Gospel message spread throughout the entire world. Yet the various implications, the significance of Jesus's words, will no doubt vary a great deal for each reader. For some it involves pastoring a local church; but for others, it may involve going overseas to a foreign land to work among an unreached people, or it may simply involve witnessing for Christ within one's inner city. There is one meaning of a text, the meaning consciously willed by the author, but the particular way that meaning affects certain readers, its significance, will at times be quite different.

In summary, every passage of Scripture are the result of an author who deliberately chose a sequence of words in order to communicate a certain meaning; and, having access to their words, we have access to their intended meaning. These words were written in the past and, therefore, their meaning is forever fixed in history. However, what an author willed to communicate in the past might have implications that go beyond their original intent. These implications are discovered by identifying the principle of meaning the author wished to convey within the text itself. Furthermore, a text might also have significance for some that differs considerably for others. This does not imply that a text can have multiple meanings. Rather, certain text, in relation to its original meaning, might apply differently to different interpreters according to their unique situations. The goal, then, of every interpreter is to first discover the intended meaning of a text (what the author meant by the words they used), and secondly, to appropriately apply that meaning to our current situations. In the following chapter we will look more generally at the task involved with interpreting a biblical text.

2

THE TASK OF THE INTERPRETER

The Qualifications of the Interpreter[1]

All understanding requires some frame of reference from which we can interpret. Thus, to understand a lecture about the properties of molecular matter, one must have at least some knowledge of chemistry (atoms, protons, electrons, etc.). The more knowledge the listener has about chemistry, the more understanding he or she will gain from the lecture. Likewise, if the Bible is God's self-revelation to His people, then the essential qualifications for a full understanding of this book is to know the revealing God. To know God is to have a relationship with Him. The Bible uses the term "faith" to describe the essential requirement for such a relationship: "And without faith it is impossible to please God, because anyone who comes to Him must first believe that He exists and that He rewards those who earnestly seek Him" (Hebrews 11:6). Only the one who seeks God in faith can truly understand what God has spoken in His Word.

1 Corinthians 2:13–15 make it clear that the ability to apprehend God's truth in its fullest sense belongs only to the "spiritual person." Since the subject matter of Scripture is spiritual in nature, in that it concerns God who is spirit, the reader must engage with God on a spiritual level—through

the aid of the Holy Spirit. So while excellence in methodology is a necessary qualification, excellence alone can never result in a full understanding of the Bible. Such understanding comes only through possessing the spiritual sensitivity that God gives to those who have faith in Him—to those who believe. Thus, faith is foundational for a correct interpretation.

This is not to mean, however, that one who does not believe cannot understand the Bible in all points. Both unbelievers and skeptics alike can often grasp much of its meaning. They are mentally capable of recognizing the Bible's general claims even when their own beliefs or values lead them to deny those claims. But an unbelieving person will never fully comprehend the true significance of the Bible's message, for he or she is not ultimately committed to the Bible as divine revelation. So while we do not assert that a believing interpreter will always be right in an interpretation or that an unbelieving interpreter will necessarily be wrong, we nevertheless argue that even when scholars apply the same methodology, their differing presuppositions will ultimately lead them to different conclusions. For example, when it comes to the biblical accounts of demonic possession, an unbelieving scholar might say, "The passage states that a man was possessed by a demon, though we now know demons do not exist and there is psychological explanation for his behavior." On the other hand, those who accept the Bible as God's revelation expect it to provide factual information, and thus they would not utter such a statement. They may be bemused over what the Bible teaches, they may disobey its instructions, but they are bound to acknowledge it as the true Word of God.

While a "faith-relationship" with God is foundational to gaining a proper understanding of Scripture, it is not the only requirement. A reverence for God and His Word are also essential to interpreting the Bible correctly. A lackadaisical attitude toward the Bible will not lend itself to a proper understanding of God's Word. The Scriptures are called "holy" and must be treated as such (2 Timothy 3:15). Furthermore, the Scriptures should also be approached with a willingness to obey them—a willingness to put into practice what has been learned in the Word. When one sees how the Lord has worked in the lives of people in the Bible who obeyed or disobeyed Him, and when he comprehends the precepts and instructions given in the Bible for one's life, he should willingly follow those instructions.

Finally, the interpreter must also depend on the Holy Spirit. As Moule wrote, "The Blessed Spirit is not only the true Author of the written Word, but also the Supreme and true Expositor."[2] The Bible tells us in John 16:13 that the Holy Spirit guides us into all truth. The word "guide" means "to lead or guide along the way of a path." Jesus's promise to the disciples was that when the Holy Spirit came, He would both magnify and clarify His teachings to them and His provision for them. On the Day of Pentecost, after Christ ascended to the Father, the Holy Spirit came to indwell believers. As a result, the disciples came to understand the significance of Jesus's words regarding Himself and His death and resurrection. Though verse 13 was addressed specifically to the Twelve (v. 12), all believers receive the indwelling of the Spirit (1 Corinthians 12:13) and thus may be similarly guided into the same truth about Christ.

Only by the Holy Spirit can believers appropriately apply and assess the significance of Scripture. Believers, however, are not automatically guided by the Spirit to comprehend the truth of Scripture because, as already stated, obedience is necessary. Guidance implies obedience to the guide, and a willingness to be "led." The Holy Spirit's role, however, even with a willingness to be "led," does not mean that our interpretations will be infallible. Inerrancy and infallibility are characteristics of the Bible's original manuscripts, but not the Bible's interpreters. Thus, the result of our interpretation may not always be accurate. Nor does He give some interpreters a "hidden" meaning divergent from the normal, grammatical meaning of the passage, or even sudden intuitive flashes of insight into the meaning of Scripture. Many passages are readily understood, but the meaning of others may come to light only gradually as the result of careful study. The Spirit's part in hermeneutics does not suggest some mysterious work that is unexplainable and unverifiable.

So then, these spiritual qualifications do not automatically mean that an individual's interpretation of the Bible will always be correct. These are prerequisites, not guarantees. Besides these spiritual qualifications, a willingness to study is essential. As Ramm has explained, "Matters of fact cannot be settled solely by spiritual means. One cannot pray to God for information about the authorship of Hebrews and expect a distinct reply. Nor is it proper to pray for information with reference to other matters of biblical introduction expecting a revelation about the revelation."[3] The Bible student must also seek to be as objective in his approach to the Bible as possible, without coming to the Scriptures with prejudice or preconceived notions (discussed further below).

Interpretation and Presuppositions

Interpretation depends not only on the methods and qualifications of interpreters, but also upon their presuppositions. Thus, our approach to hermeneutics requires two essential components: (1) a set of presuppositions that both constitutes and facilitates a necessary starting point, and (2) a deliberate strategy involving methods and procedures that will help determine and verify viable interpretations.[4] Although our preunderstandings may at times hinder us from understanding a text, they nevertheless provide a preparatory starting point for any understanding. Indeed, certain preunderstandings are desirable and even essential. Therefore, we present here the assumptions or presuppositions that we believe are necessary for an accurate interpretation of the Bible.

Presuppositions about the Nature of the Bible. Our view of the nature of the Bible, more often than not, will determine the meaning we derive from it. "If the Bible owes its origin to a divine all-powerful being who has revealed His message via human writers, then the objective of interpretation will be to understand the meaning communicated through the divinely-inspired document. If the interpreter adopts an alternative explanation of the Bible's origin, then he or she will prescribe other goals in interpreting the text."[5] The Bible as God's divinely inspired, written revelation to

His people has been the church's universal creed throughout its history. For most Christians, the Bible is a trustworthy communication by Spirit-guided writers and is true in all it intends to teach. Its writers not only intended to convey what is factual, their record does actually convey that which is factual and reliable. This includes all the individual parts as well as its overall message. This is not the place for an exhaustive defense of the Bible's trustworthiness, but several New Testament texts assume this conclusion (e.g., Matthew 5:18; John 10:35; 17:17; 2 Timothy 3:16; Titus 1:2; 2 Peter 1:20–21). The psalmist likewise affirms that God's commands are entirely perfect (Psalm 119:96). We thus believe that this presupposition alone does justice to the Bible's character in its claims of truthfulness.

How, then, do we handle apparent contradictions or errors? Following our supposition of faith (that the Bible is true), we are bound to look for viable solutions. When responsible exegesis provides a possible explanation, we claim such as a vindication, even if we cannot be sure that our proposed solution is certain. It means that the charge of "error" is not mandated. And when every possible solution seems contrived or contentious, we frankly admit that at present we do not know the best way to solve the problem. This does not mean that no solution exists; it simply means that we do not have a solution at this time. In fact, in the vast majority of alleged contradictions and errors, viable solutions do exist so that our withholding judgment in certain instances is not simply "special pleading." This is no more presumptuous than the postmodern scholar who assumes a critical omniscience about such questions. Our presupposition of truthfulness means that we must reject the position that the Bible errs and assume, rather, in cases of uncertainty that our knowledge, or our theory to explain the evidence, remains deficient.

Furthermore, as a divine revelation from God, the Bible manifests unparalleled spiritual worth and the unique power to change lives. This makes the Bible useful in ways unlike any other book. With the Spirit's aid we come to know the Scriptures and find life-giving and life-changing meaning. As we respond in faithful obedience, we grow in maturity; our thoughts and lives are directed by the Spirit-energized reading of Scripture. To treat the Bible in any other way robs it of its central purpose as God's revelation to His creatures.

Finally, we must affirm that the Bible is an understandable and accessible book. It presents a clear message to anyone willing to read it. But if the Bible is clear, then why do we need rules and methods to interpret it? To say that the Bible is clear, however, is not to say that the Bible is simple or that anyone may easily grasp all that it contains. The doctrine of the perspicuity (or clarity) of the Scriptures, championed by the Protestant Reformation, always referred to that which was essential for right doctrine or living—not to every sentence of the Bible. Granted, some passages of the Bible, as already stated, are difficult to understand. Yet, the Bible is not a puzzle or book of secrets and riddles given in obscured communication that only an elite group can understand. Written so that common people could understand its truth, the Bible's central message is accessible and apprehensible by all Christians throughout all ages.

Presuppositions about the Methodology of Bible Interpretation. Many books on the interpretation of the Bible stress that the reader should interpret the Bible "like any other book." On one hand this is true, because, as we have argued, the Bible was written in ordinary human language, and we should therefore go about understanding its content in the same way we would any other book. But on the other hand, by arguing for divine authorship, we also determined that the Bible is unlike any other book. The only way to understand the Bible properly is to submit to it as the Word of God.

Although God is its ultimate author, the Bible is still genuinely human speech. Thus, we must seek to understand the content of the Bible in the same way we would attempt to understand any other human speech. As McCartney and Clayton put it, "What the human author said in his original context must be intrinsically linked to what God intends to say for all time—they must be organically related. Otherwise, we would have no means of understanding the speech, no [interpretive] framework in which to arrive at [its meaning]."[6] So if we wish to obtain a sound understanding of what God is saying in a text, we must seek to understand what the human author was saying in his original context, both textual and historical. We cannot simply assume that our subjective impression of a text is the meaning that God intends for us. The task of grammatical-historical exegesis (understanding a text in its historical and grammatical context), which will be explained further in chapters three through five, is the first step to understanding God's Word. Nevertheless, as divine speech, the Bible is categorically different from ordinary human speech in its effectual power, its absolute trustworthiness, and its applicability to all God's people at all times.[7] Grammatical-historical exegesis may exhaust the accessible meaning of an ancient inscription on a potsherd or piece of parchment, but the limits imposed by this method cannot entirely do justice to Scripture.[8] Thus, in chapters 12–14 we will look closer at how we can learn more from the Bible than what grammatical-historical exegesis alone will allow.

Preunderstandings of the Interpreter. No one comes to a text without a background. This means that our interpretations will inevitably be influenced in some way by the preunderstandings that we bring to the process of interpretation. In the past, the discipline of hermeneutics concentrated on methods for understanding what the ancient text meant to the ancient world from which it came. Now it is recognized that far more attention must be given to what the interpreter brings to the interpretive process. We need to know ourselves, as well as the procedures that are necessary for interpreting an ancient book.

The term "preunderstanding" describes what each interpreter brings to the task of interpretation. Every interpreter approaches Bible study with preconceptions and prior dispositions. Our preunderstandings consist of our prior experiences, conditioning, and training: political, social, cultural, psychological, and religious—in short, every aspect of our lives up to this point. All these influence, and in many instances determine, how we view the world. Although we inevitably bring presuppositions to the text we seek to interpret, we are nevertheless capable of reaching an objective interpretation that is free of our own predisposed bias. Every interpreter begins with a preunderstanding. After an initial study of a biblical text, his or her preunderstanding is no longer what it was. Then, as the interpreter proceeds to question the text further, out of their newly formed understanding, different answers emerge—new understandings result. This scenario is often referred to as the hermeneutical cycle, or better, the hermeneutical spiral. The interpreter does not merely go around in circles in a kind of vicious cycle, but rather a progressive spiral of development. Thus, the prerequisite of faith enables the Christian in studying the Bible to come to a deeper understanding of God and what the Scriptures say. As we learn more from our study of Scripture, we alter and enlarge our pre-understanding in hopes of learning more from our study of Scripture. In essence, this process describes the nature of all learning: it is an interactive, ongoing process. So then, as we study the Bible, we are interacting with its text (and with its divine Author), and, as a result, over time we enlarge our understanding.

The hermeneutical spiral can be very positive as God through His Holy Spirit brings a new and more adequate understanding of His truth, as well as a proper application to believers' lives. If the Bible is true, which brings us back to our presuppositions, then subscribing to its truth constitutes the most adequate starting point for interpreting its content. But alone that would be insufficient to comprehend the Bible. Understanding the Bible's message adequately demands appropriate methodology and study, as well as the willingness of interpreters to allow the Bible to alter and clarify their preunderstandings. The metaphor of a spiral describes the healthy upward process an interpreter should hope to make toward an adequate comprehension of the Bible.

PART 2

THE RULES OF INTERPRETATION

Having established that the fundamental goal of interpretation is to discover the meaning of a text as it was intended by its author, we now move to identify and explain the principles and procedures that are necessary to discern accurately that meaning. For its useful insights, this section borrows the basic outline and overall thoughts found on pages 213–319 of *Introduction to Biblical Interpretation,* by William W. Klein, Craig L. Blomberg, and Robert L. Hubbard, Jr.

To know what the biblical authors meant by the words they used, we have to understand their message consistent with the way people ordinarily use language to communicate ideas.[1] It should seem obvious to any unbiased reader that the biblical writers intended for their original audience to understand what they wrote. They did not use secret or cryptic codes to convey their thoughts. Though they occasionally used riddles, parables, and apocalyptic symbols that might be challenging for the reader to comprehend, they nevertheless intended to communicate clearly even through these. Like most writers, the authors wrote in a straightforward and direct manner so that readers would understand their message and appropriately respond to it.

In normal conversation we usually understand what we hear immediately without a second thought. A lifetime of experiences has programmed the memory bank of our minds to process the meaning of words and sentences almost unconsciously. However, when confronted with an ancient book, like our Bible, this does not necessarily hold true. Statements that were quite clear to the initial readers of Scripture may not communicate clearly to us at all. What was almost automatic comprehension for them takes considerably more effort for us. So whenever we encounter a passage we do not automatically understand, we have to stop and think about it. Hence, we must deliberately analyze the unclear statement according to the principles of verbal and written communication that normally function unconsciously. This basic premise underlies most of the guidelines of biblical interpretation that we will present in this book. Each hermeneutical principle addresses some essential need and provides the necessary steps for overcoming the barriers that prevent modern readers from understanding the Bible.

The complex skill of biblical interpretation and its application is divided into six steps:

1. Contextual analysis (discussed in chapter 3) considers the relationship of a given passage to the entire passage surrounding it, since a better understanding of an author's intended meaning results from an acquaintance with the larger context.

2. Historical-cultural analysis (discussed in chapter 4) considers the historical–cultural milieu in which an author wrote in order to understand his references and purpose.

3. Lexical-syntactical analysis (discussed in chapter 5) develops an understanding of the definition of words (lexicology) and their relationship to one another (syntax) in order to understand more accurately the meaning the author intended to convey.

4. Literary analysis (discussed in chapters 6–11) identifies the literary form (genre) in a given passage or body of work, such as historical narrative, law, prophecy, poetry, or apocalyptic literature. Each has its unique mode of expression and interpretation. Furthermore, figures of speech and other literary devices such as metaphors and similes, allegories, hyperbole, and parables are also examined under literary analysis.

5. Theological analysis (which we will discuss in chapters 12–14) studies the level of theological understanding at the time the revelation was given in order to ascertain the meaning of the text for its original recipients. It also takes into account related Scriptures, whether given before or after the passage being studied, in order to assess the theological contribution a passage might have on Scripture as a whole.

6. Application of text (which we will be examined in chapters 15 and 16) is the important step of determining what significance a biblical text might have on readers today that live in a different time and culture. In some instances, the transfer is accomplished fairly easily; in other instances, such as biblical commands that were obviously influenced by cultural factors (e.g., greeting with a holy kiss), the transmission across cultures becomes more complex.

In these six analyzations, steps one through three belongs to general hermeneutics—the general principles which are applicable to the interpretation of all languages and writing. Steps four and five constitutes special hermeneutics—the specific principles that apply to particular types of literature which often complement or even supersede the general principles. Step 6—the application of a biblical message from one time and culture to another—is not always considered to be an integral part of hermeneutics, per se, but is included here as an important step in interpretation because of its obvious relevance for the twenty-first-century believer so widely separated by both time and culture from the original recipients of Scripture.

3

CONTEXTUAL ANALYSIS

One of the most basic and fundamental principles of biblical interpretation is that the intended meaning of any passage must be consistent with the literary context in which it occurs. In literature, the context of any specific passage is the text that comes immediately before and after it. The context of a sentence is its paragraph, the context of a paragraph is the surrounding paragraphs within the chapter (and sometimes outside the chapter), and the context of a chapter is the surrounding chapters in the book. Ultimately, then, the whole book in which a passage appears is its controlling context.

Words taken out of context will usually misrepresent their intent. To use a common example, public officials will often complain how the news media unfairly represented their views by taking something they had said "out of context." While their protest may be nothing more than an attempt to cover up an embarrassing slip of the tongue, the point remains valid. Misunderstandings arise when people hear only part of what was said and base their understanding on it. The same is true of the Bible. Undoubtedly, were the biblical writers alive today, they would loudly protest against the many Christians who frequently quote individual Bible verses and apply them to their lives in violation of their underlying context. Misconstruing the context of a biblical passage has serious consequences. We must interpret every passage consistent with its context for three main reasons:

Context Provides Continuity of Thought

First, taking a passage out of context violates the writer's continuity of thought. A writer's continuity of thought consists of a chain of related ideas that have been linked together in a certain way in order to communicate a specific idea. Most meaningful communication involves some level of logical thought flow in which one thought leads naturally to the next. A preceding statement prepares for the one that comes after it, and the statement that follows builds upon the one that came before it. People communicate, not with a sequence of randomly selected ideas, but with related ideas linked together in a logical pattern. For example, consider the confusing account:

> While working the night shift, a security guard spotted two thieves. A tire on the left side was blown out. The stock market had dropped considerably by the end of the day. Of course, the food was overcooked and the home team hit the winning shot at the buzzer.

Grammatically, these sentences can occur together, but they are completely unrelated; they present no logical connection. People who wish to make a point do not usually communicate ideas this way. Normally all sentences in a paragraph strive to develop a common theme. Each sentence carries or builds on the thought expressed in the previous sentence. Taken together, the sentences provide a continuity of subject matter that unifies the whole. Since we normally communicate ideas through a progression of related statements, each sentence must be understood in light of the other sentences in the text—as it relates to the writer's main idea. Any interpretation of a text that is most likely to be correct must not ignore nor contradict the point of its overall context.

Context Provides Accurate Meaning of Words

Second, an interpretation of a text must be consistent with its context due to the nature of words. Since most words have more than one meaning, the literary context is essential for determining the most likely meaning of a word within a sentence. Usually the mind automatically understands the correct meaning of words based entirely on the subject matter that is being communicated. Confusion or misunderstanding occurs when the subject matter is vague or when several meanings fit equally well. A person must then deliberately stop and think about the words and their various possible meanings and analyze the context more carefully to select the word meaning most likely intended by the writer. For example, if we hear only the exclamation, "That was the largest trunk I have ever seen!" we do not possess enough literary context to know what kind of "trunk" is meant (in fact we have none).[1] Does it refer to the trunk of a tree, the trunk of a car, or the trunk of an elephant? Suppose, however, we read the statement in a book about animals at the zoo. Then we automatically picture an elephant's trunk. Given an article about the engineering of various automobiles, the image of a car storage compartment would emerge. Yet neither of these meanings will come to mind if we are reading about the largest trunk seen in a California redwood forest. The literary context defines the meaning of the word. Interpreters are not free to simply pick whichever meaning is most desirable to them. We must understand each term according to the meaning that is consistent with the main idea expressed in its literary context. This is how we ensure successful communication.

Context Keeps the Overarching Themes of a Text in Focus

The third reason why correct interpretation must agree with context is that since most biblical books were written as complete documents, their writers intended them to be read and understood as an entire unit.[2] Despite the look of many Bibles, the biblical writers did not intend for their statements to be taken as independent or stand-alone concepts. The sentences and paragraphs comprise individual units of a larger literary work, and interpreters must understand them according to their relationship to the whole argument of the book. While chapter and verse divisions in our Bible have proven helpful in many ways, they also present one of the biggest hurdles for Bible interpretation. We must keep in mind that they were not in the original documents. Although some verse divisions were in place in the early centuries AD, it was not until the ninth and tenth centuries that divisions began to appear in the Hebrew Bible. F. F. Bruce says, "The standard division of the Old Testament into verses which has come down to our own day and is found in most translations as well as in the Hebrew original was fixed by the Masoretic family of Ben Asher about AD 900."[3] The division into chapters, on the other hand, is much later. Most attributed the first chapter divisions as the work of Stephen Langton, professor at the University of Paris and later Archbishop of Canterbury, in 1228. Three centuries later, in 1560, Robert Estienne (also known as Stephanus), a Persian painter and publisher modernized many of the chapter divisions and added the current verse numbering in his fourth edition of the Greek New Testament. The Geneva Bible (1560) was the first English version to incorporate both the modern chapter and verse divisions. Although these divisions were meant to be helpful, even a casual reading of the Bible reveals that some of these are poorly placed; chapter changes occasionally interrupt the thought flow of a passage, and new verse divisions will even begin at times in the middle of a sentence.

The chapter and verse divisions do help identify and locate passages quickly, but, unfortunately, they have also contributed to the widespread practice of isolating individual versus and elevating them as complete units of thought. Each verse is treated as an independent expression of truth—a "quote for the day"—without any connection to its wider context. There is simply no justification for interpreting individual versus as independent thought units that contain autonomous expressions of truth. Readers must understand biblical statements as integral parts of the larger units from which they occur. Detached from their context, individual versus may take on meanings never intended by the writers. To qualify as the text's intended meaning, then, an interpretation must be compatible with the specific intention of the immediate context, as well as the total thought (or context) of the book.[4]

In closing, an important principle must guide our practice of interpretation: a text taken out of context is a pretext. Here we define a "pretext" as an alleged interpretation that only appears to be valid but in reality obscures the real intent and meaning of a text. This principle serves as a warning against the popular tendency to engage in invalid proof-texting: quoting biblical passages to prove a doctrine or standard for Christian living without regard for the literary context. As a ridiculous example, one could string along three verses to prove that Jesus promoted suicide: "Then he . . . went and hanged himself" (Matthew 27:5); "Jesus said to him, 'Go and do likewise'" (Luke 10:37), and "What you do, do quickly" (John 13:27). The blatant disregard for context is obvious. Unfortunately, other "proof-texting" does not appear so ridiculous but is equally invalid. Such proof-texts are merely "pretexts" when the interpreter fails to implement this hermeneutical principle. There is nothing wrong with quoting verses to prove a point provided we understand them according to their contextual meaning (under the correct circumstances proof-texting can be valid). However, before citing any verse in support of a position, we should first check to ensure that the passage is about the same subject and really does have the meaning that proves our point. Otherwise the interpretation is only a pretext, using a passage that seems on the surface to prove some point when in actuality it does not. Such a pretext carries no divine authority, but rather it subverts what the authoritative text really means.

Only by concentrating on the main idea of a paragraph (its theme) and knowing how each sentence contributes to the development of that idea can one discern the real meaning and significance of the individual sentences. This is probably the single-most important principle of hermeneutics, since literary context is at the heart of all communication. It affects the reader's understanding of both the meaning of individual words and the meaning of the overall statement. This requires an interpreter not just to focus on the words of a passage (which unfortunately is the emphasis of many Bible teachers), but also to consider carefully the contribution of the passage to the literary work as a whole. It requires taking into account what the author is seeking to accomplish by writing his text. It seeks to preserve the integrity of the line of thought being developed throughout the text.

The Circular Study of Literary Context

When it comes to interpreting a passage in its literary context, we will need to examine the passage in relation to the three major contextual domains (or circles of context) in which it exists: (1) the immediate context; (2) the book context; (3) the entire Bible context (especially the writings of the same author where available). While each of these contextual domains often provide significant insight into the intended meaning of the passage, a decreasing level of certainty exists as one moves outwardly from the immediate context to the context of the entire Bible. Thus, each domain must be applied in a definite order of priority.

Immediate Context. The immediate context plays the most crucial role in determining the meaning of a specific passage. The immediate context is defined as the surrounding material that is directly related to a particular passage. In some instances, this will be the preceding and succeeding sentences and paragraphs; in others it may be a subsection or a major division of a book. The practice of outlining a book helps the interpreter to discern its natural divisions and to establish the immediate context in which a passage occurs. As the interpreter moves from one verse to the next, he or she should notice how the author's individual ideas come together to reveal the main idea of the passage. The main idea (or theme) of the immediate context regulates the meaning of the individual words, phrases, and sentences within the specific passage.

As with any skill, learning how to recognize the main theme of a passage takes practice. The following steps illustrate the process. First, carefully read the surrounding material of the passage to determine the dominant subject. That is, find the topic to which everything in that paragraph or section refers. Second, write a topic sentence in your own words describing the main idea of the passage. A good topic sentence is both precise and concise. It is not enough to say that the theme of a passage is "love." Obviously, one passage does not tell us everything there is to know about love. A precise topic sentence contains a brief summary (preferably one line) of what the passage says about love. For example, a good topic sentence for 1 John 3:16–23 would be: Love is demonstrated by our actions. Repeat this process for each of the major divisions of the book. These division breaks provide the immediate context for each passage and collectively an outline for determining the overall theme of the entire book.

Furthermore, passages are linked not only by a common theme, but also by structure. A thorough interpreter investigates not only what a text says, but also how the writer organizes his thoughts. Just as one must understand each sentence in the given passage consistent with the general theme of the immediate context, so also one must interpret the sentence according to the paragraph's structural relationship with its surrounding material.

When arranging passages in a particular order, writers may employ many different structural relationships. In some sections paragraphs are arranged chronologically. Historical narratives, for instance, typically proceed in this way, reporting events in the order in which they occurred. Writers normally indicate such secessions of events by temporal adverbs and conjunctions that indicate continuation: now, then, later, afterward, etc. Other material may be grouped together based on its thematic continuity. For example, the Gospel writers sometimes group together events or teachings that were of a familiar nature even though they did not happen in the order they are placed (i.e., how the writer of Matthew grouped together the parables in chapter thirteen to exemplify Jesus's teaching ministry).

In some instances, the relationship between adjoining paragraphs may be confusing and seem entirely random. The student may discern no "logical" reason for the sequence of ideas, whether chronological or thematic. Such apparent "jumps" in thought between successive passages may be described as psychological transfer. As Klein, Bloomberg, and Hubbard explain,

> This occurs when one subject triggers a psychological switch to a different subject. In the mind of the writer there is a connection between the thoughts but it is more psychological than logical. The relationship was clear to the writer but may not be immediately apparent to the reader. Before accusing the writer of a mental lapse in writing, the student should attempt to discover the writers frame of reference and the likely connection.[5]

An example of this may occur at 2 Corinthians 6:13. Following a heartfelt plea for his readers to "open wide [their] hearts" (11–13), Paul appears to interject a seemingly unrelated section, 6:14–7:1, which begins, "Do not be unequally yoked together with unbelievers." Then at 7:2 he resumes where he left off at 6:13, repeating, "Open your hearts to us." The connection between sections may be psychological in nature and intend to convey something like, "If you are to open your hearts to us, you cannot, likewise, open your hearts to those who are unbelievers." If so, Paul must have felt that their current unholy associations were in some way responsible for undoing the genuine relationship between him and the Corinthians.

Finally, we may also encounter an abrupt transition from one paragraph to another when a writer introduces a new topic. Sometimes the writer prepares the reader for the transition (break in thought flow); at other times there is no warning. Thus, in interpreting a passage in a way that is consistent with its context, an interpreter should look for any possibility of an abrupt transition either before or after the text. Doing so will protect the interpreter from creating forced contextual insights where the writer intended none.[6]

Context of the Entire Book. After considering the immediate context of the surrounding passage, the next important literary context for determining the author's intended meaning belongs to the book in which the passage occurs. A few helpful guidelines for developing a better understanding of the controlling context of any book are as follows: (1) read through books in one setting, more than once if possible (especially shorter books); (2) develop an outline that summarizes the book's content; (3) from this outline seek to understand the book's purpose(s) or controlling theme(s); and (4) list any parallel passages within the book that deal with the same subject matter.

It is often helpful, before studying any passage, to understand the purpose of the book or the author's aim in writing. Knowing why the writer composed the book sets important limitations on the meaning of its individual parts. We can rightfully assume that the individual statements or sections contributed in some way to the writer's main goal.[7] Sometimes the writer takes out the guesswork by explicitly stating the purpose for the book. For example, at the beginning of his Gospel, Luke precisely states his purpose for writing:

> *Inasmuch as many have taken in hand to set in order a narrative of those things which have been fulfilled among us, just as those who from the beginning were eyewitnesses and ministers of the word delivered them to us, it seemed good to me also, having had perfect understanding of all things from the very first, to write to you an orderly account, most excellent Theophilus.* (Luke 1:1–3)

Luke lived in a day when multiple conflicting written records and oral reports were being circulated and, consequently, were creating confusion about the details of Jesus's life. Thus, he intended to confirm for Theophilus a credible and carefully investigated account of Jesus's life and ministry. In contrast to Luke, John, the author of the fourth Gospel, waited until near the end of his book to indicate that his purpose in writing was to present the necessary evidence for a sustaining belief in Jesus, which results in eternal life (John 20:30–31). Other books like Romans and 1

Corinthians may have multiple purpose statements at various places in the book, but even so they still present to the reader a primary goal that underlines the entire book. For example, the book of Romans was written for the purpose of proclaiming God's imputed righteousness through the gospel (1:15). 1 Corinthians, on the other hand, was written for the purpose of resolving disunity within the congregation (1:10–11). So then, although many minor purpose statements may occur throughout these two books, it is important that we do not lose sight of the book's primary purpose.

For many Old Testament books, explicit purpose statements are more difficult to discover (if we can discover them at all). When we encounter books that lack formal purpose statements, interpreters must infer them from its content. They must observe what the author accomplishes in the book, and then deduce the purpose from that information. While this approach may prove reasonably accurate in finding the writer's goal, it remains conjectural. Rather than speculate about questionable, inferred purposes, we suggest that in such cases interpreters identify the book's dominant theme by noting those topics the author emphasizes in the book. For example, in a short book like Esther, the dominant theme of God's providence and protection over His people is easily discernible. For the book of Judges, the author reveals to us that his book is about a period in which there was a leadership crisis in Israel (1:1–2). Joshua had died, and no leader had been appointed to take his place. This point is further emphasized in the concluding summary of the book where the author points out that "in those days there was no king in Israel; everyone did what was right in his own eyes" (21:25; cf. 17:6).

The basic outline of the book is another important part of its literary context. How each major division contributes to the total message of a book depends primarily on the writer's general train of thought. Once an interpreter understands how the various topics of a book relate to its central idea, they will be better prepared to answer how the specific train of thought of a section relates to a passage under study. In summary, an interpretation is more likely to be the correct one when it explains the passage in a way that is consistent with the theme of the section in which the passage occurs. Moreover, the likely interpretation shows how the section contributes to the overall progress of the book itself.

The final item to consider for studying the literary context of an entire book concerns parallel passages. Parallel passages are those that deal with the same subject matter as the specific passage under study. When a writer refers to a subject more than once in a book, one or more of the passages may clarify the meaning of vague or difficult passages found in other sections. By quickly skimming through a book, the interpreter may locate other passages that deal with the same subject matter as the passage under investigation. Once discovered, they can be studied to see if they contribute in some way to the understanding of the passage. So, for example, to understand the Day of the Lord in Joel 2:31 (a passage that Peter references on the Day of Pentecost in Acts 2:20), the student must investigate what else Joel says about the Day of the Lord in his prophecy (e.g., 1:15; 2:1, 11; 3:14), as well as other places where the theme emerges even though the specific wording ("Day of the Lord") does not occur.[8] Likewise, for insight into what the writer of Hebrews meant by "perfection" in the section that starts with 6:1, the student must gain insight from other references that relate to the word "perfect" found in the letter (2:10; 5:9, 14; 7:19, 28; 9:9; 10:1, 14; 11:40; 12:23).

But a word of caution is in order. Before we allow any passage to interpret another, we must be sure that they are indeed parallel passages. Sometimes passages use identical words but with different meanings for those words. This would be only an apparent parallel. Even when both passages are true parallels, one cannot simply read the ideas of one passage into the other without proper justification. "We become liable to serious errors when we interpret a passage in light of another while ignoring the immediate context of each passage. As a precaution, always interpret each parallel passage according to its own immediate context and the entire book context before comparing the passages."[9] Only after we know the contextually valid meaning for each parallel passage can we compare the passages to see if any of them sheds light on specific details in the passage under study.

Context of the Entire Bible. As we observed earlier, the Bible's divine inspiration gives continuity of thought and an overall unity to all its sixty-six books despite its diversity of human authors. Because of this unity, the entire Bible provides a literary context for all passages in it. While we should not expect all biblical writers to have the same perspective on every concept or present their views in the same way—they will have different insights and distinct emphases depending upon their purpose for writing—due to the Holy Spirit's inspiration of the entire Bible, we can be sure that the correct meaning of every portion of Scripture will be consistent with the rest of the teaching of the Bible on that subject. In other words, one passage will not contradict the clear teaching of the rest of the Bible on that subject.

Three groupings of biblical books should be consulted in interpreting a passage according to the context of the entire Bible:[10] First, we should study parallels in other books attributed to the same author. As Klein, Bloomberg, and Hubbard noted,

> These writings come from the same mind energized by the Holy Spirit, thus promising the highest level of linguistic and conceptual continuity. There is the highest degree of probability that the same person talking about the same subject in a similar way means the same thing. Furthermore, each biblical writer has a personal understanding of and fairly consistent pattern for articulating an aspect of God's truth. Thus, to comprehend Paul's understanding of faith in Romans 3:22, the interpreter is wiser to consult passages in Galatians (e.g., 2:16; 3:8, 11, 24) than passages in James. This applies not merely to the words used, but even more to the ideas they represent.[11]

Parallels in books by different writers in the same Testament follow second in order of significance. Writers from the same Testament share a greater commonality than with those writing under a different Testament. Old Testament writers used the Hebrew (or Aramaic) language and reflected a Semitic culture in what was primarily an Israelite setting. They shared a focus on the nation of Israel as God's special people, on exclusive loyalty to Yahweh as an expression of that relationship, and on the prophetic promises of future blessings—giving them, diverse as they were, a unique camaraderie. New Testament writers, by contrast, spoke Greek and resided in a predominantly Hellenistic culture (the Roman Empire). They lived in the age of Messianic fulfillment and proclaimed the good news of God's grace made available to all through the death and resurrection of Jesus.[12] Writings of the same Testament that were likely known by a later author take precedence over later writings not yet known to that author.

Since the writings of the Old Testament cover a span of about a thousand years, personal relationships among its writers were rare. This means that the help that Old Testament books can provide for interpreting individual passages will often be considerably less than what can be expected from the New Testament. Not only did the New Testament writers compose their books over a brief period of fifty or so years, they often had close interpersonal relationships with each other. Of course, this does not mean they always agreed with each other, as Galatians 2:11–14 shows. However, even allowing for diverse expressions of Christian doctrine, interpreters can expect a high degree of continuity in the way these early Christians communicated their faith.

The final type of parallel passage consists of those from the other Testament. Despite its time gap, Old Testament parallels for New Testament studies often prove highly valuable. Because most New Testament writers knew the Old Testament well, they borrowed theological language and concepts from it. After all, the Bible of the early church was the Old Testament. Furthermore, their entire thought-world, especially the religious ideology in which they formulated their belief systems—monotheism, covenant, election, people of God, atonement, and sin, to name a few—derived from Old Testament theological convictions.[13] New Testament parallels to Old Testament texts will often help readers establish a more complete viewpoint of a particular subject by drawing out further implications and intended meanings. For example, in Luke 4:18–21, Jesus explicitly identifies His ministry as the fulfillment of Isaiah 61:1–2. Passages such as these demonstrate the relevance of New Testament revelation for Old Testament interpretation. At the same time, interpreters must exercise extreme caution to avoid overly reading New Testament concepts back into Old Testament passages. As with any passage of Scripture, our first task is always to understand each text on its own terms—as its writer and readers would have understood it. Only after we understand the meaning of the Old Testament text can we address the issue of how the two Testaments complement each other in understanding a biblical concept or the Bible as a whole.

Many Christians have failed to realize that God's message for us today in the Old Testament must grow out of the intended meaning of the text itself. Its significance for our lives may differ greatly from its significance to the original readers, but not its essential meaning.[14] Unfortunately, well-meaning but misguided belief that every part of the Bible must convey New Testament doctrine has kept many people from discovering the great truths about God's character and His relationship with His people that are revealed to us in the Old Testament. It is important, however, that we allow the Old Testament to stand on its own merits. Which is to say, we must interpret its passages in keeping with the intention of its texts; that constitutes the essential goal of Old Testament interpretation.[15] While the careful use of parallels give the Bible student an ability to appreciate the overall contribution a text makes in understanding the Bible as a whole, interpreting passages in light of their context places important restrictions for determining its meaning. More on this matter will be discussed in chapter 14 (under Biblical Theology).

In summary, the following steps are involved in the contextual analysis of a passage:

1. Carefully read the surrounding material of the passage to determine the dominant subject. Pay particularly close attention to how the author's individual ideas come together to reveal the main idea of the passage. Remember, the main idea (or theme) of the immediate context regulates the meaning of the individual words, phrases, and sentences within the specific passage.

2. Write a topic sentence in your own words, describing the main idea of the passage. Remember, a good topic sentence is both precise and concise.

3. Repeat this process for each of the major divisions of the book. Remember, these division breaks provide the immediate context for each passage. Collectively they establish an outline for determining the overall theme of the entire book. Once an interpreter understands how the various topics of a book relates to its central idea, they will be better prepared to answer how the specific train of thought of a section relates to a passage under study.

4. Finally, we should look for other parallel passages that might shed light on the passage under study. Parallel passages should first be considered from within the book that the passage originates. Second, passages from other books from the same author should be considered; and finally, passages from other books with different authors. Remember, the Bible's divine inspiration gives continuity of thought and an overall unity to all its sixty-six books despite its diversity of human authors. Because of this unity, the entire Bible provides a literary context for all passages in it. However, as the interpreter moves away from the immediate context, a decreasing level of certainty results.

4

HISTORICAL-CULTURAL ANALYSIS

Biblical passages not only express a writer's train of thought, they also reflect the writer's way of life—one that in many ways differs radically from that of our present day.[1] The biblical writers wrote their message to an ancient world that lived and thought very differently than we do today. Consequently, every time we study Scripture, we must be mindful of the vast time span and cultural gap that exists between us and the original readers. Each passage was God's Word to other people before it became God's Word to us. The fact that the Bible always comes to us secondhand, through others who lived at different times and in different places, means that an interpreter must seek to understand the historical and cultural setting of a passage as accurately as possible, and must interpret the meaning of the passage consistent with that understanding.

Any interpretation of a passage that would have been inconsistent with the historical and cultural setting of the author and recipients cannot be valid. Fortunately, archaeological findings, historical research, and sociological and cultural studies have provided a wealth of information that can be used as resources for gaining insight into the historical-cultural background of the Bible. So impressive is the material available that Russell Spittler boasted, "Advances in lexicography and archeology have put us in a place to know more about the ancient world than it knew about itself."[2] While this statement carries much validity, others would caution us as to not overestimate our knowledge of the ancient world of our Bible. One author noted, "Despite of all the detailed insights gained by these studies [anthropology, sociology, linguistics, history, and psychology], our knowledge of some of the details of the interrelated components of each Bible story remains extremely limited. What we do not know and cannot find out far exceeds the valuable information available to us; consequently, we must always make modest and realistic claims for any of our historical-cultural reconstructions—and the interpretations that depend on them."[3]

Principles for Historical-Cultural Interpretation

Several principles guide the interpreter in understanding each passage according to its historical background. First, we must determine how the biblical setting was like ours and how it differed from ours. There will always be some similarities between our lives and the lives of those who lived during biblical times. These commonalities provide reference points that help today's reader understand the meaning of many passages of Scripture. Differences, on the other hand, must be studied carefully to provide the interpreter with information that helps clarify historical-cultural ambiguities. The letter to the church at Laodicea (Revelation 3:14–22) provides an intriguing example. In the Lord's description of this church, He condemns it for being "neither cold nor hot." He continues to say, "I could wish you were cold or hot!" (v. 15). He finds no reason to commend the people of this church; they are completely useless—neither like hot water (as in a comfortable bath) nor like cold water (as in a refreshing drink). Apart from insight gained from archaeological studies, interpreters might seriously misunderstand the purpose for the Lord's rebuke. That is, we must interpret hot and cold in light of the historical context of Laodicea, which was located close to hot springs (Hierapolis to its north) and cold streams (Colossae to its south). Now both hot and cold water are desirable; both are useful for distinct purposes. But the spiritual state of this church more closely resembled the tepid lukewarm water of Laodicea that was stored in aqueducts. By the time the water made its way to the city (piped in from the north and the south), it was no longer "hot" or "cold." Neither hot nor cold—it was putrid and emetic and therefore useless if left as is. Jesus is not saying that active opposition to Him or willful unbelief (an incorrect interpretation of "cold") is better than being a complacent ("luke-warm") Christian.[4]

The second principle moves from the objective information regarding the historical-cultural setting of a passage to the subjective factor of mind-set: we must determine the psychological impact that the biblical message would have had on its original audience. Mind-set describes the common mental attitude or social outlook among a particular people group. When determining the meaning of any passage, interpreters should seek to know, where possible, how the original recipients would have reacted to what was written or spoken. Obviously, we will not always know this with any degree of certainty. Nevertheless, to the extent that we are able (through our research of the historical data), we should always seek to discover how a text would have impacted the value systems of the original audience and to identify whether their feelings would resemble or differ from ours. The Parable of the Good Samaritan provides an excellent example. To most present-day readers, the phrase "Good Samaritan" is understood to be positive (i.e., we have "Good Samaritan" hospitals). To Jesus's Jewish listeners, however, Samaritans were anything but good; they were despised. Yet Jesus, a Jew, makes a despised Samaritan the hero of His story about true neighborliness—in contrast to the religious leaders whom the Jews respected. With little imagination, one can sense the discomfort and shock of the audience. From this emotive angle a fuller appreciation of the passage's intended meaning emerges. It gives us a deeper insight into the meaning of Jesus's words and a basis for understanding them.

A final principle for interpreting a passage according to its historical-cultural setting is presented here as a negative warning: interpreters must not become so preoccupied with the historical–cultural insight of a text that they lose sight of the main task of understanding the text consistent with its context. While the understanding of the historical and cultural details of a text allows us to better understand the text's intended meaning, we must always allow the words of the text to provide the context for determining what historical details are significant for the interpretation of the passage. A fitting example is found in the way certain interpreters explain the meaning of 1 Timothy 2:12. This passage has troubled many Christians since Paul appears to value men over women in regard to serving in the church. Viewing this understanding as a contradiction to passages that express both men and women as having equality in the body of Christ (i.e., Galatians 3:28), some suggest that this portion of Scripture was only applicable to the time and culture of Paul's day. One or more of the following reasons are usually given: 1) Jews held a higher regard for men than women, and Paul was only wanting to keep peace in the church. 2) Women were typically less educated at this time, so men were logically more suited for leadership. 3) Ephesian women (Ephesus was the residence of Timothy at the time Paul had written the letter) were seen as unruly and thus would have caused a distraction for the Ephesian church. While it is generally accepted that the culture of Paul's day held men in higher esteem than women and that women were typically less educated than men (Ephesian women being unruly is less certain), none of these reasons are given to us in the text. In fact, there is no hint whatsoever that Paul is motivated by a cultural precedent. Rather, Paul specifically appeals to the order of creation for his rationale, not the influence of culture. So then, while knowledge of the historical-cultural setting is important for discovering the intended meaning, it should always serve the supportive role of aiding one's understanding of the text and must never supplement the plain meaning of the text itself. Background material should help us understand the meaning of the text; it must not become an additional message that contravenes that meaning.

Retrieving the Historical-Cultural Background

Retrieving the historical-cultural background of the Bible involves two distinct studies: (1) studying the historical-cultural background of an entire book and (2) studying the historical-cultural background of specific passages within a book. Understanding the historical setting of the entire book gives insight into the individual passages and sections within the book. But each individual passage also requires careful analysis for understanding the historical-cultural factors that are pertinent to it.

Exploring the general background of the book. Before studying a particular passage, the Bible student should become as familiar as possible with the historical-cultural background of the book in which it occurs. This includes any pertinent information pertaining to the writer(s), recipient(s), date of writing or setting, and purpose of the book. Important resources that Bible students will want to consult include Bible-survey and introduction books, commentaries, Bible dictionaries, and encyclopedias. At times even the brief introductions in many study Bibles can provide a helpful start.

When using secondary sources such as these, it is always important for students to look up the biblical references. Doing so will not only give us a better understanding of the references that have been cited, but it will also allow us an opportunity to confirm the validity of each reference. Along with insight regarding the introductory material of a book, good reference works also include valuable facts drawn from ancient, non-biblical literary sources, and archaeology. When time permits, students should read through the book at one sitting (perhaps several times) and record everything they find about the writer, recipient(s), date, and purpose of the book on separate sheets of paper. After they analyze and review this material (preferably prior to consulting other sources), they will find the information in the reference works more meaningful.

When it comes to research concerning a book's author(s), students should focus primarily on matters of identity, characteristics, the relationship they have with their audience, and pertinent circumstances at the time of writing. This information will help the student understand the book from the perspective of the writer. Of course, such material may be more accessible for some books than others. We cannot obtain information about who wrote some of the books of the Bible due to them being anonymous or having uncertain authorship. In such cases, the inductive insight we gain from reading the book itself may be all we can learn about the writer. Furthermore, knowing about the recipients—their location and circumstances (both internally and externally)—may help explain an author's subject matter, as well as their purpose for writing the book. Unfortunately, little information is available concerning the recipients of many books in our Bible. In some prophetic books the situation is complex in that the audience addressed by the prophet may differ from the city or nation about whom the prophecy is made. For example, Obadiah prophesied about God's judgment against Edom, though He addressed the book to Israel as both an encouragement and warning.

Date is another key factor for establishing the historical-cultural background of a book. Knowing when a book was written is important because it may give us a clue as to the circumstances out of which the author is writing. Furthermore, it may also provide the backdrop for understanding the significance (i.e., its cause or effect in history) of an event referenced in our Bible. For some biblical books there is not enough evidence to determine a precise or reliable date. The historical facts included in the book may fit several periods equally well. Or we may be able to set a book only within a given century at best. In such situations the main emphasis should be on the general circumstances in that period of time and in that part of the world. For example, Jonah's prophecy is set in the eighth century BC during the reign of the oppressive Assyrians. Thus, the brutal militarism of these hated pagans explains Jonah's reluctance to go to Nineveh to prophesy. For interpretive purposes, knowing the characteristics of a given period of time provides more insight than knowing a specific date.

For most of the New Testament we can be fairly confident in knowing the dates in which the books were written, at least within a ten-year period. Knowing the dates of the epistles adds both color and commentary to many passages. For example, knowing that Paul wrote the book of Romans in AD 56 provides a deeper perspective for his exhortation to believers in submitting to governing authorities (Romans 13:1–5). When Paul wrote these words, the infamous emperor, Nero, was ruling the Roman Empire, who would, within just a few years after Paul had penned his charge, commit unimaginable atrocities against Christians. Furthermore, knowing the dates of many epistles helps us identify more accurately the error or heresy the author is refuting (i.e., 1 John). In Psalms, Proverbs, and some historical and prophetic books, interpreters may need to distinguish, if possible, between the time when the material was composed and the time when a writer or redactor (final editor) organized the book into its final shape. This may help the interpreter understand the structural arrangement of a book in light of the cultural-historical setting in which it was organized.

Examining the historical-cultural factors of a specific passage. Knowing the historical-cultural background of a biblical book provides the initial framework for determining the meaning of the specific passages within that book. Thus, each passage must be interpreted consistent with its specific, original situation—that is, what the writer most likely meant by these words to those recipients in the given set of circumstances.[5] We must determine whether the historical information learned about the book as a whole applies in any particular way to the specific passage under examination. Any interpretation of a passage must agree with the historical-cultural background of the whole book. However, knowing the general background and setting of a book may not be enough in deciphering the historical-cultural meaning of a given text. Individual passages within the book may contain special historical-cultural features that are specific to the meaning of that passage. Though a student may know much about the historical background of the book of Amos, all that insight will not help interpret the meaning of the words found in Amos 5:26: "You also carried

Sikkuth your king And Chiun, your idols, The star of your gods, Which you made for yourselves." The student may understand a great deal about the historical background of the Gospels without having any idea about the wide phylacteries worn by the Pharisees (Matthew 23:5). Along with the general historical background and setting of a book, students of Scripture must also research the specific historical-cultural details, including geographical features, political-economic structures, social customs, and religious practices that are mentioned in individual passages.

Of course, the first resource to consult is the Bible itself. It contains valuable data concerning many historical-cultural references. Beyond the Bible, other sources provide the necessary means for securing reliable background information. Bible introductions, Bible dictionaries, encyclopedias, commentaries, and many specialized works provide helpful material for clarifying historical and cultural references.

In summary, when it comes to retrieving the historical-cultural background of a passage or an entire book, unfortunately, we are not always in a position to discover all we would like to know about certain features. But where possible, our goal is to comprehend the following:

1. The historical background and situation of the writer, particularly anything that helps explain why he wrote this passage.

2. The historical background and situation of the people involved in the text and/or the recipients of the book that can help explain the occasion or purpose for the author's writing.

3. The relationship between the writer and audience or the people involved in the text that may shed light on the book's subject matter.

4. The cultural or historical references mentioned in the text.

With this knowledge at hand, we seek next to explain the meaning and importance of the text in light of the historical-cultural setting. To the extent that we are able to enter the world of the biblical setting, we can grasp the meaning of the passage. An interpretation of a passage that accurately reflects a book's original setting and is consistent with its historical circumstances has a better claim of validity than one that does not.

5

LEXICAL-SYNTACTICAL ANALYSIS

Lexical-syntactical analysis is the study of the meaning of individual words (lexicology) and the way those words are combined (syntax) in order to determine more accurately the author's intended meaning. It is necessary because the biblical author's intended meaning is communicated through words arranged in a particular way. Any communication that involves writing words underscores the importance of the lexical principle of hermeneutics: the correct interpretation of Scripture will be consistent with the normal meaning of words in a given context.

On the surface words seem so simple. They make up such a routine part of our lives that we seldom stop to consider their complexity. To appreciate fully what is involved in the normal meaning of words, we must first understand several characteristics of words: their nature, range and nuance of meaning, and their change of meaning over time.

Crucial Issues about the Nature of Words

Words, in the most basic sense, are a combination of sounds or symbols that represent an idea. The idea a word represents can be communicated either orally or visibly. But why a word means what it does is mostly a matter of convention—it's just the way it is![1]

Throughout the development of a language, users of that language arbitrarily assign meanings to the words they use. By common practice English speakers associate certain words with a certain meaning. When English speakers hear a word such as "oak," their minds will automatically identify a certain species of tree. But replace the word with *eiche*, most English speakers would be puzzled. Why? Because English speakers have not assigned a meaning to the word "eiche." To the average English speaker, the word means nothing. This illustrates the most fundamental fact about words: each word comes to represent a given idea (or ideas) only by its repeated use within a language. Thus, if two people wish to communicate, they both must use and understand words in the same way. So then, from the standpoint of hermeneutics, accurate interpretation requires that we understand a word in the same way the writer used it. To illustrate this further, American English makes use of the words "pants" and "trousers" with only minor differences.[2] However, in British English these two words refer to two entirely different garments. Trousers indicate their American counterparts while pants denote an undergarment (underpants). To successfully purchase an outer garment that extends from the waist to the ankles in Manchester, England, a wise American purchaser would ask the clerk for trousers, not pants. Understanding and using words the way other speakers of the language use them is critical for effective communication.

This, of course, complicates the task of interpretation for most Bible students. Since the original writers wrote in ancient languages that are foreign to us, we do not know innately the meanings of the terms they used. Thus, we need translators to interpret the meaning of the biblical text into English. Fortunately, scholars carefully study the biblical languages and do their best to convey the intended meaning of the words in English. Accordingly, interpreters must seek to understand what the original words of a passage meant at the time they were written, and in the context in which they occur. Recovering the correct meaning of the words the writer used, not simply what we think they should mean, is the chief objective for word studies. We must always remember that the biblical writers chose specific words to express their ideas, and it is our goal as interpreters to understand those thoughts by properly interpreting the words they have selected.

Words Have a Range of Meanings. To complicate matters even further, words often have more than one meaning. In fact, most words have several possible meanings. Take for example the word "ball." The "ball" that is round and used for playing a sport is not at all like the "ball" of your foot, or the "ball" that is a large social event where people go to dance, or even the idea expressed by the phrase, "you're on the ball!" In each of these examples the word is the same, yet the meanings are quite different. Each of the meanings represents at least part of the range of meanings of the word "ball." Normally words used with multiple meanings do not cause us any confusion or misunderstanding. When aided by the context, native speakers can usually sense the right meaning without any trouble. The ideas expressed in the larger message of the literary context will usually clarify the intended meaning.

This fact also holds true for biblical languages. Both the Hebrew word "*shalom*" and the Greek word "*eirene*," often translated as "peace" in English, according to most Bible dictionaries have several meanings. For the Hebrew *shalom* the range includes "absence of strife" in the sense of "peace and harmony," a sense of well-being and wholeness, as well as the eschatological state of eternal peace, much like our concept of "heaven." The range of meaning for the Greek *eirene* also includes an external absence of hostility, an eternal tranquility, as well as a sense of well-being. To understand what a biblical author means by "peace" in a specific text, one must determine which of these potential meanings best fits the context. The reader cannot just pick arbitrarily whichever meaning they prefer. One has only to return to the word "ball" to see how silly it would be to assign the wrong meaning in a specific context. No less is true in our study of biblical words.

Multiple times throughout the Upper Room Discourse (John 13–17) Jesus promises His disciples "peace." Certainly Jesus did not mean "absence of hostility" or trouble-free lives, for He concludes His discourse with the words, "These things I have spoken to you, that in Me you may have peace. In the world you will have tribulation; but be of good cheer, I have overcome the world" (John 16:33). The statement "be of good cheer" perfectly insinuates that though His disciples would encounter considerable hostility in the world, He would nevertheless give them an inward tranquility—an ultimate sense of their own well-being. So, the fact that many words have a range of meanings complicates biblical interpretation. To understand the meaning intended by the speaker or writer, interpreters must determine the word meaning that makes the best sense in its context.

Of course, word meanings may overlap. Often we call these words synonyms. Two or more words are considered synonyms when at least one of the meanings of one word overlaps with at least one of the meanings of another word. As an example, hit is synonymous with punched in the sentence, "Bobby ____ Mike in the nose," but not in the sentence "That song was a big ____ last year." They are synonyms only within the range of meanings they share in common. Many Bible students often draw up fairly rigid distinctions between words that have similar but not exactly equivalent meanings. For instance, the beginning Greek student is often taught to distinguish between two Greek words for love: *agapao* and *phileo*. Many scholars have maintained that *agapao* always speaks of a divine, perfect love, while *phileo* is reserved to speak of human, brotherly love. Thus, when analyzing John 21:15–17, some have observed that when Jesus twice asks Peter if he loves Him, using the verb *agapao*, Peter responds that he loves Him with the verb *phileo*. In the third exchange, both use the verb *phileo*. More than one preacher has presented this passage, arguing that Peter was unable to love (*agapao*) Jesus with a perfect, godly love but could only love (*phileo*) him with a lesser human affection. D. A. Carson, however, skillfully argues that although these two words do not have an identical range of meaning, they do have considerable semantic overlap, and one should take great caution before building an interpretation based solely on contrasts between words that may have (in certain contexts) synonymous meanings.[3] Considering the semantic range of words helps the interpreter recognize the specific nuances of a word that distinguishes or overlaps its meaning with other terms.

Word Meanings Change Over Time. Word meanings do not remain fixed; they change over time. New meanings develop, and old ones become obsolete. The King James Version of the Bible readily illustrates this phenomenon. Revered for numerous qualities, including its poetic beauty and scholarship, the praiseworthy translation frequently shows how English words today have considerably different meanings from when they were used in 1611. One example is the KJV's use of the word "conversation" (2 Corinthians 1:12; Galatians 1:13; Ephesians 2:3; 4:22; Philippians 1:27). These texts have little to do with what we think of when we use the word "conversation" today; so modern translations replace "conversation" with "conduct" or "way of life" to convey the Greek text's original intent, since the meaning of the English word has changed over time. Another well-known example is found in 1 Thessalonians 4:15, which promises that Christians will be raptured to meet Christ at His second coming. The KJV renders the passage, "We which are alive and remain until the coming of the Lord shall not prevent them which are asleep" (emphasis added). In 1611, "prevent" more closely followed its Latin derivation and conveyed the idea "to go before."[4] Today it means "to stop" or "to hinder." Because the meaning of the English word has changed, what served as a good translation in the seventeenth century no longer communicates Paul's original meaning. Hence, most modern versions substitute the word "precede" for the KJV's "prevent."

The same principle holds true for the original languages of Scripture. As Klein, Blomberg, and Hubbard well state,

> The original meaning of a word or the meaning derived from a word's etymology or root may be of no more than historical interest to the interpreter. Past meanings may be interesting and even colorful, but we must always resist the temptation to believe

that past meanings exert some residual influence on current usage. One may not simply discover a meaning for a word that exists in classical Greek, for example, and assume that meaning could occur at the time of the New Testament.[5]

The Bible student must determine the range of meanings that were in common use at the time a book was written.

Modern linguistics has almost universally accepted the dictum that a distinction be made between the development of a language (diachrony) and the contemporary use of a language (synchrony). This linguistic principle contends that the meaning projected by a speaker or author should be strictly governed by the state of the language at the time of their speaking or writing. The process by which the language came into that state (diachrony) may be interesting and may at times inform the lexical-analysis (the meaning of the words used), but users of a language are rarely conscious of how words or phrases took on the meaning(s) they currently have. Hence, with respect to lexical-syntactical analysis, the only thing that matters is the ordinary usage of words or phrases at the time the writer or speaker was using them. However, a biblical writer may at times adopt a meaning or make reference to a word spoken in the past by an earlier writer. For example, the Greek word translated in the New Testament as "covenant" or "testament" was more commonly understood in contemporary Hellenistic Greek (the time the New Testament was being written) to mean "will" (as in last will and testament). Yet the word was used in the Greek Old Testament (LXX) to translate the Hebrew word *berith*, which meant covenant (note how the author of Hebrews plays on the two meanings of the Greek word ["will" and "covenant"] Hebrews 9:15–22). Consequently, since the Greek term ("covenant") is used in the New Testament in reference to its "Old" Testament usage, the word can only be understood in light of its historical use in the Old Testament. So then, in cases where the biblical authors are clearly conscious of the historical use of a term, diachronic analysis must be used in addition to synchronic study. In other words, when a biblical writer picks up on a certain word which earlier Scripture has given a specialized meaning, we must go back to the earlier use of the word to see what content that word had for the later writer.[6]

A similar approach to diachrony is etymology, the study of the origin and historical development of words. Understanding the origin of a word and the way in which the meaning of a word has changed over time can sometimes be helpful in establishing the meaning of rare words. But etymology is extremely dangerous when used to read more meaning into words that are readily known. Users of a language are hardly ever conscious of the etymological origin of words when they use them, and hence etymology has very little use in establishing meaning. Few English speakers, when they use the word "nice," are conscious of its derivation from the Latin word *nescius*, meaning ignorant. In spite of all this, a recent trend in biblical word studies has focused on the etymology of Greek and Hebrew terms. Out of this focus has come the fallacious argument that the root of words should be the bearer of its basic meaning. Take, for example, the Greek word *hyperetes* found in 1 Corinthians 4:1, "Let a man so consider us, as servants (*hyperetes*) of Christ and stewards of the mysteries of God." From this passage many have argued that since *hyperetes* derives from the verb *eresso* (meaning to row); the basic meaning is "rower." Others have argued further that *hyperetes* should be understood to mean "under rower," since *hyperetes* derives morphologically from *hypo* (meaning under) and *eretes* (rower). Yet the fact remains that there is very little evidence that *hyperetes* was ever used for "rowers" from classical Greek literature, and it was certainly never used that way in the New Testament. As Louw remarks, to derive the meaning of *hypertes* from *hypo* and *eretes* is no more intrinsically realistic than deriving the meaning of butterfly from "butter" and "fly."[7]

Furthermore, some etymologizing has even been done with English words. How many times has the meaning of the word "atonement" been interpreted in reference to its English etymology, "at-one-ment"? This may illustrate a certain aspect of the meaning but hardly helps us identify what the biblical writers meant by it. Another kind of English etymologizing tries to define Greek words by reference to English words that are etymologically derived from them. This is unfortunately common even among some of the best Bible teachers. The Greek word for "power" (*dynamos*) is the source for the English dynamite, so preachers love to talk about God's dynamite power. This may add color to the concept, but the apostles did not conceive of God's power as something that blows things up.

Words Have Connotative and Denotative Meanings. Another characteristic of words is that they may convey significance outside of their normal denotative meaning. One of the more obvious examples of this is how the Bible uses the word "dog." Most naturally, the word "dog" denotes a four-legged, hairy animal. But when used of a person (as in, "You dog!") it usually communicates an emotive sense of disapproval. In this specific use, "dog" figuratively stands for a person and, therefore, has a connotative meaning outside of its usual denotative use (as in, "Sadie is our family dog."). So then, when Paul warns the Christians at Philippi to "Beware of dogs, beware of evil workers, beware of the mutilation" (Philippians 3:2), the word carries a noticeable derogatory force. First-century Jews, which considered dogs to be reprehensible creatures, often expressed their disdain for Gentiles by equating them with "dogs." Paul, likewise, throws back at some Jewish troublemakers their own derisive use of the term "dog." This connotative slant is not always intended in other uses of the word "dog" in the New Testament. In the parable of the rich man and Lazarus, for example, the word "dog" is clearly meant to convey its more common, natural meaning (Luke 16:21). Words with connotative meanings are not always easy to identify. Interpreters, therefore, must study words carefully to discern not only their denotative meaning, but also any connotative subtlety that the original recipients would have sensed.

The Grammatical-Structural Relationship of Words

Important as it is to study the meanings of words, apart from a larger context we cannot always be certain what a word means. People communicate by combining words together in a specific way. The grammatical and structural relationships of words within a text make up the final component we must analyze to properly understand a writer's meaning—how an author has chosen to combine his words so that he can communicate his point effectively.

While grammar consists of many rules, those rules can be divided into two basic categories: morphology and syntax. Morphology concerns the forms of individual words—typically how words are inflected (manipulated) to indicate their function in a language. To use a simple example, in English we may put an -s on the end of some nouns to indicate more than one. The -s is a morpheme designating "plural" in English. So, we say, "John has one ball, but Joe has two balls." Functioning like the English -s, Hebrew employs îm, ê, or ôt at the end of its words to make plurals. Greek is more complex, with different plural indicators (morphemes) often associated with each case—similar to how in English we add -ed at the end of some verbs to indicate past tense: "Today I will play one game, though yesterday I played two games."

Since Greek is a highly inflected language (more so than English), most Greek words undergo changes in keeping with their function in the sentence in which they occur. For example, end markings (called case endings) are added to nouns to indicate whether a noun is nominative, vocative, genitive, dative, and accusative. These cases inform the reader of gender (feminine, masculine, or neuter), if the noun is singular or plural, and whether the writer is speaking in first, second, or third person, to give a few examples. Because word order in Greek can vary, case becomes the primary means of identifying the function of a noun in a sentence. Likewise, end markings are added to verbs to indicate mood. The mood of the verb in each main clause indicates whether the writer was making a statement (indicative), giving a command (imperative), expressing a possibility (subjunctive), or making a wish (optative). Since it makes a big difference whether a sentence asserts a fact, expresses a possibility, or gives a command, the interpreter must understand each sentence consistent with the mood expressed.

Another grammatical impact the main verb has on a sentence is tense. Although tense in English mainly concerns time (past, present, future), in other languages—such as Hebrew and Greek—the tense of a verb also indicates the kind of action from the perspective of the writer. It indicates whether the writer or speaker regards the action of the verb as an act occurring in the past (aoristic), an act currently occurring (present), an act progressively unfolding (imperfect), a past completed action with present-day results (perfect), or a past completed action with future implications (future perfect). English typically employs perfect or simple past tense to convey a completed action: I have graduated from college, or I graduated from college. The Greek verb tense, however, often specifies how the writer views the nature of the action. In other words, the implication the action has in the present (perfect), had in the past (pluperfect or past perfect), or will have in the future (future perfect).

In addition to morphology, syntax describes the method (or rules) each language has for combining words in order to communicate. Word order is a crucial element for understanding the English language. The statement "John hit the ball" means something completely different from the statement "The ball hit John." Because the words John and ball are not marked in any particular way, their function in each sentence is determined entirely by word order. Word order is less fixed for languages like Hebrew and Greek, but even so, some conventions still apply.

Language consists of combining various elements, as building blocks, to construct meaningful communication. Combining morphemes (minimal elements of meaning, like the plural marker -s in English) produces words; putting words together produces phrases, clauses, and sentences; and combining sentences results in paragraphs, passages, or discourses. Furthermore, the relationship that exists between the words that make up a sentence may be indicated by word order, the form of words, and the use of connecting words (conjunctions, prepositions, etc.). This underscores the absolute necessity of interpreting every biblical passage consistent with its grammar. "Since grammar is a basic component of how writers organize words to express their thoughts and how audiences decipher the meaning from the words, grammatical analysis is an essential aspect of correct interpretation."[8]

Finally, grammatical studies are necessary for a correct interpretation of Scripture because the biblical languages will sometimes convey nuances that are not clearly presented in an English translation. As an example, the First Epistle of John begins with an explicit declaration of the reality of Christ's physical body. Attempting to counteract the Gnostic teaching that Jesus only "appeared" to have a physical body, the author affirms that his message about Jesus is based upon "That which was from the beginning, which we have heard, which we have seen with our eyes . . ." (1:1, emphasis added). Both verbs occur in the Greek perfect tense, which expresses that a completed action (what was seen and heard) has ongoing results (a new state of affairs). Thus, by using the perfect tense, the author relates that his experience of Jesus produced a new state of affairs in which he now lives. His intentions go well beyond the reporting of mere past events. Similarly, the command in 1 John 4:1, "Beloved, do not believe every spirit, but test the spirits, whether they are of God" (emphasis added), uses a present imperative of prohibition, "a grammatical construction often employed to forbid the continuation of something already happening. In this context, 'Stop Believing every spirit' might well express the grammar more precisely."[9] The grammatical construction used here suggests that Christians were gullibly accepting some allegedly "spirit-induced" utterances and needed to stop!

Hebrew, while employing features that appear similar to those we find in English—nouns, adjectives, verbs, and prepositions to name a few—will also exhibit features that function quite differently from either English or Greek. One example of such a feature is how Hebrew employs an infinitive before a finite verb (e.g., Isaiah 6:9 is literally translated as "hear (infinitive) and hear (finite verb)" and "see (infinitive) and see (finite verb)," as it is in the RSV). This feature of Hebrew grammar is always to indicate certainty of continuation. Thus, "hear and hear" may be a direct translation, but it obscures the meaning. It is better translated (as it is in the ESV): "Keep on hearing, but do not understand; keep on seeing, but do not perceive." Another common grammatical feature in Hebrew is "the construct state," which consists of two words—either of which can be a noun or adjective—with the word "of" between them (as in the "king of Israel," or even a longer construction such as the "son of the king of Israel"). The relation between the two is a matter of interpretation since the construction may indicate various ideas. For example, the phrase "wisdom of Solomon" (1 Kings 4:30) stands for the wisdom that Solomon displays. On the other hand, "mourning of an only son" (Amos 8:10) in context clearly indicates the mourning for an only son, and not the morning that the son does. Or the construct state may be descriptive, as in "scales of righteousness" (Leviticus 19:36), meaning "just balances" as the ESV translates, while at other times the relationship is one of apposition—where the second word defines the first as in "the land of Canaan" (Numbers 34:2) or "daughters of Zion" (Isaiah 1:8).

These brief examples illustrate that English versions do not always clarify certain nuances of the biblical languages or how much a translation is the result of the interpretive decisions by the translators. One translation may be more direct in its wording of the original text, but another may capture the original nuance more precisely. Therefore, accurate interpretation requires careful evaluation of the grammatical nuances found in the biblical languages (the Hebrew and Aramaic in the Old Testament and Greek in New Testament). Ideally, every interpreter should have at least a basic knowledge of these biblical languages, since even the best translations do not (and probably should not) always bring out the many grammatical features of the original languages. Where good modern translations do express clearly some grammatical nuances, they involve a greater or lesser degree of interpretation, for scholars do not always agree on the significance of certain grammatical constructions in a given passage. Knowing the biblical languages equips the interpreter to weigh the contextual evidence that is necessary for interpreting each grammatical nuance in a way that best fits the text. Every interpreter who aspires to become a biblical scholar must become competent in the biblical languages, and people who do not know Hebrew or Greek must always remember that they are at a disadvantage.

However, it is unrealistic to expect all interpreters to be proficient in Hebrew and Greek—stages of life, the pressures and responsibilities of living, access to a program of instruction, etc. make this ideal impossible for many Bible readers. Therefore, serious Bible students must compensate for their limitation of not knowing the biblical languages by having a good grasp of English grammar, by using the best direct English translations (a translation that follows closer to the original language) of the Bible (such as the KJV, NKJV, ASV, NASB, and ESV), and by using reliable commentaries and other resources written by scholars who can explain the grammar. While some grammatical insights cannot be discovered apart from reading the text in its original language, the willing student can uncover a surprising amount of important grammatical information by using the right resources and by carefully analyzing the English text. This is especially true of the structure. Analyzing the structure for meaningful grammatical insight requires an English translation that carefully preserves the original language sentence pattern. Many modern translations break up longer complex sentences in the original languages into several brief sentences in English, providing smoother reading. However, the gain in readability in some modern translations (such as the NIV and NLT) comes with a price tag: some original meaning, not to mention nuances, is lost, and one may fail to appreciate the text's original structure relationships. Most often and for most people, paraphrases are worth the price. But for serious study, more direct versions have their evident value. Studying a passage from a translation that more closely parallels the original language enables the interpreter to interact with the text's actual sentence structures. In return, this allows the student to determine how a subordinate clause and phrase relate to the main statement of the sentence and/or to each other. For this level of study, the more direct the English translation, the better.

Steps for Discovering Structural Relationships

Outside of some basic rules, many of us rarely consider all that is grammatically and linguistically required to ensure effective communication. Thus, even when studying a text in English, it requires conscious effort. Explaining the thought flow of a given passage often requires paying attention to and thinking carefully about the significance of the obvious. Sometimes the relationships that exist in a passage are so obvious that we ignore their contribution to its total meaning.

Usually the interpreter seeks to understand one passage at a time. So our first step involves tracing the flow of thought in the passage under study. How does the writer's logic develop in the passage? To begin, one must isolate, where appropriate, the individual paragraphs that make up the unit of thought or natural division within the text. Paragraphs typically develop a unit of thought, often incorporating a topic sentence that the paragraph develops. Next, the interpreter proceeds to analyze the building blocks of the paragraphs—each sentence—and how their assertions or propositions develop the writer's argument or narration. Placing proper proportionate weight on each element in a sentence involves distinguishing the main statement (independent clause) or statements from any subordinate (dependent) clause or clauses that qualify it. As an example, the main clause in James 1:2 is the sentence: "count it all joy." The three subordinate statements that follow (in the original Greek) qualify this statement. (1) "my brethren," (2) "when you fall into various trials," and (3) "knowing that the testing of your faith produces patience." For each subordinate (dependent) clause or phrase the student must determine (1) what word it modifies, (2) what type of clause or phrase it is (adverbial, noun, adjectival), and (3) how this affects the meaning of the sentence.

Most of the time, subordinate clauses answer one of the six well-known journalistic questions: who, what, why, when, where, or how. The first subordinate phrase, "my brethren," indicates who is to "count it all joy"; the second clause, "when you fall into various trials," shows when this is to be done; and the final one answers the question "why?" giving the reason for "counting it all joy." In the second sentence of the passage, verse four, two subordinate clauses follow the main statement, "But let patience have its perfect work." The first clause, introduced with "that you . . ." modifies the verb, "let have," and expresses the purpose (why) for allowing patients [perseverance] to "have its perfect work." The second clause ends with the phrase, "lacking nothing," which modifies the words "perfect and complete" at the end of the subordinate clause—answering the question, "What?" This phrase further explains the meaning of being "perfect and complete" by describing it negatively.

The third sentence in verse five presents a more complicated structure. It begins with a subordinate clause followed by a compound main clause that is broken up by another subordinate clause. The compound main clause reads, "Let him ask of God and it [wisdom] will be given to him." The opening subordinate clause, "if any of you lacks wisdom," is a conditional clause that qualifies the verb "ask." It indicates the specific condition in which one should offer this prayer. The subordinate clause that divides the main clause, "who gives to all liberally and without reproach," is a descriptive adjective clause that modifies "God." This reminder of God's benevolent character encourages the reader to pray for wisdom in times of trial. While an analysis of the structure of the remaining sentence in this paragraph would further illustrate the process and value of this approach, we leave that for the reader.

While all of this may seem like a lot of work, analyzing structural relationships within a sentence will enable the interpreter to identify the flow of the text's argument, recognize word associations, and discover the interrelationships that would not be otherwise evident. The interpreter is able to perceive the logic of a writer's flow of thought, or breaks in thought, and the unique features and distinctions that readers easily miss without the time and effort spent to analyze the structures in these ways.

The next step of the grammatical study of a passage focuses on the importance of connectives, adjectives, adverbs, and pronouns in a passage. Connectives, also known as transitional words (usually conjunctions, but also relative pronouns) and phrases, connect and relate sentences and paragraphs. The previous discussion of the relationship between main and subordinate clauses already underscored the significance of connectives as indicators of how the different parts of a sentence fit together. Although connectives are often small and seemingly insignificant, they exert an influence on meaning that far exceeds their size. "Like joints and junctions in a plumbing system of pipes, they regulate the flow of a text's argument."[10]

Secondly, the interpreter must carefully note any usage of adjectives and/or adverbs. These modifiers qualify the sense of nouns or verbs in some significant way. Traditionally considered a single part of speech, adverbs perform a wide variety of functions, making it difficult to treat them as a single, unified category. Adverbs normally help paint a fuller picture by describing how something happens, such as where, when, how, and to what degree. Adjectives, on the other hand, provide additional color to the noun it modifies. Adjectives within the Hebrew grammar are similar to those used in English and Greek. Often, though, Hebrew performs the function of description through "construct phrases," as in "the royal seed" (2 Kings 25:25) and "the royal throne" (1 Kings 1:46), or even through apposition: "the deceitful tongue" (Psalm 120:2). In James 1:2 discussed above, the writer significantly strengthens his opening words with the inclusion of the Greek adjective "all," a Greek word that conveys to his readers that trials should be an occasion for "complete and unalloyed" joy (notice how the same Greek word is used in 1 Peter 2:18). To consider it "all joy whenever you fall into various trials" is far more demanding than just to "consider it joy." Without the adjective "all" this command would be somewhat ambiguous as to the extent of trials one should consider joy. Similarly, the adverb "liberally" in verse 5 adds a vital dimension to God's giving. He does not simply give, James asserts; God gives liberally to all who ask Him for wisdom.

Finally, students must not underestimate the significance of another seemingly routine grammatical feature: pronouns. First, it is important to determine the antecedents of all pronouns in order to know whom or to what they refer. Next, an effort should be made in determining whether a pronoun is singular or plural. This process is often clearer in Hebrew and Greek than in English.

Whereas the pronoun "you" in English may be either singular or plural, in Greek and Hebrew this is not the case. For example, Paul in 1 Corinthians twice identifies believers as the temple of the Holy Spirit (cf. 1 Corinthians 3:16–17; 6:18–19). In the latter case, it is clear that Paul is referring to believers individually. However, in his first use, Paul is referring to believers as a whole. The use of second-person plural pronouns makes this distinction clear. "Paul uses the same temple analogy in two distinct ways: to refer both to individuals and to the entire Church. Unfortunately, many sincere believers have missed the point of Paul's warning in chapter three not to destroy God's Temple. Thinking of their individual body as God's temple, they understand Paul's admonition as a call to personal piety; they do not perceive Paul's true intent—a plea not to allow divisions to destroy the church."[11] Furthermore, at the conclusion of both letters to Timothy, Paul writes, "Grace be with you" (emphasis added). We might mistakenly take these as Paul's concluding benedictions to an individual, namely Timothy. Actually, the Greek pronouns are plural, indicating a prayer of God's blessing upon the entire church at Ephesus (cf. 1 Timothy 1:3).

Hebrew marks personal pronouns as to number, person, and gender. It employs demonstrative pronouns (this, that), interrogative and indefinite pronouns (who, what, whoever, how, why, where), and relative pronouns (who, whom, which). Greek, likewise, employees a wide array of pronoun types: personal, relative, demonstrative, intensive (as in the same man or the man himself), possessive (his, her, my), reflexive (yourself), reciprocal (love one another), interrogative, and indefinite. The specific distinctions that Greek relative pronouns make between singular and plural, as well as between masculine, feminine, and neuter, provide a level of clarity not available in our general English "who" and "what." Direct English translations of Jesus's genealogy in Matthew do not clarify that Jesus is the child of only Mary, not Mary and Joseph. Matthew 1:16 reads, "And Jacob begot Joseph the husband of Mary, of whom was born Jesus who is called Christ." Yet, the Greek text uses a feminine singular relative pronoun that restricts "whom" to Mary alone.

Remember, many such grammatical details that exist in the biblical languages will not always appear in English translations—even the so-called "word-for-word translations" (what we have called direct translations). By their very nature translations are limited in their ability to bring out all nuances. After all, no two languages ever mirror each other. Thus, a thorough understanding demands that the student check all interpretations against the original languages to be certain they are consistent with the grammar of the text. As we have repeatedly urged, students must surround themselves, along with a good translation, Bible dictionaries/lexicons and key biblical commentaries that provide insight into the nuances of grammar. One resource highly recommended by this author (for beginners to Greek studies) is *The Complete Word Study New Testament*, by Spiros Zodhiates.

PART 3

LANGUAGE AND MEANING: THE LITERARY ANALYSIS OF SCRIPTURE

Chapters three through five primarily focused on the methods used in the interpretation of all texts, that is, general hermeneutics. This section will now focus on special hermeneutics, which considers the interpretation of special literary forms or genres. The books of the Bible represent several literary types. In the Old Testament, there are historical narratives, laws, lyric poetry, wisdom literature, and prophecy. In the New Testament, there are historical narratives (Gospels and Acts), epistles, and apocalyptic literature. Not only do the sixty-six books each represent a major genre, many of them incorporate other minor genres (usually called subgenres) as well. For example, Daniel, a book mostly representing apocalyptic literature, begins with a narrative section; and the Gospels make use of parables, a certain genre which conveys a relatable, didactic story in order to illustrate a moral lesson or a spiritual truth.

An appreciation for the diversity of genres within Scripture is critical to interpretation because different genres require different ways of reading them. In this overview, we cannot hope to cover all the genres that appear in the Bible, but we will look at a few of the more common genres such as historical narrative, law, poetry, and prophecy, as well as some of the specialty genres that are sometimes difficult to interpret, namely apocalyptic literature and parables.

6

HISTORICAL NARRATIVE

The majority of our Bible tells a story, the story of God's dealing with humankind. Most of the books from Genesis to Esther in the Old Testament, and the Gospels and Acts in the New Testament, are biblical history. When we claim that these books are history, however, we are not at all implying that these books should be looked at in the same way we view other modern history books. Most history writing has the legitimate goal of rendering a coherent account of human events which accurately reflects and interprets the significant experiences that relate to those events. What sets modern history apart is that it attempts to do so by focusing exclusively on the cause and effect of this world. As McCartney and Clayton write, "Modern history interprets the data according to a modern presuppositional framework, which assumes that God does not directly intervene in the course of human events. The history writing of the Bible, however, does not conform to either the goal or the limitation of modern history writing. Biblical writers constantly referred to supernatural causes, particularly God's plan and activities, and they not only reflect the sensate experiences of events, but also undergird the story with theological meaning and instruction, both explicit and implicit."[1]

Biblical history and modern history do, however, have two things in common. First, they both attempt to give factual information about real-life events which are relevant to the existential understanding of a people.[2] They make connections to other contemporaneous events, as well as to the past and future. Second, both biblical and modern history put forth viewpoints on the meaning of events. The major difference is, of course, that the biblical writers relate events from a transcendent position. They adopt a viewpoint outside of this world, a "heavenly" perspective that seeks to evaluate the supernatural purpose lying behind the natural events. They write from the standpoint of God. This is why much of the Bible reads like a novel, with dialogue between its characters, as well as insight into their inner thoughts and commentary regarding their motives. It is not because the biblical writers made up the events, but because the reporting style was more closely related to the story genre than is most modern history.[3]

All history writing, in both the Old Testament and New Testament, has at least three major purposes:[4] (1) it informs the reader of how God's activity and purpose in the past has been worked out through His people; that is, it tells a story, (2) it shows us how God's activity in the past has constituted a people for Himself; that is, it established an identity for His people, and (3), by magnifying God's power and care over His people, it teaches us that God's people today should trust and obey this same God; that is, it demands a faith response. Often the purpose of a historical narrative is explicit and imbedded in the text itself. Within the narrative of Elijah and the prophets of Baal, we hear Elijah ask the people, "How long will you falter between two different opinions" (1 Kings 18:21). The purpose of what took place, at least in part, is the same as the purpose of recording it for future generations—to demonstrate empirically who is the one and only true God, and to establish His sovereign rule over our lives. Even if the explicit instructions given to the original hearers no longer applies to us today, biblical history still generally concerns itself with what is universal and essential for the human experience. So then, biblical history relates both events and their meaning; it is both history and theology.

What Narratives Are

To appreciate biblical history, we need to know some basic things about narratives—what they are, and how they work. All narratives have three basic components: characters, plot, and plot resolution. That is, most narratives presuppose some kind of conflict or tension that needs resolving. In traditional literary terms, the characters are defined as either the "protagonist" (the primary person in the story), the "antagonist(s)" (the person/people who brings about the conflict or tension), or sometimes the "agonist" (the other major characters in the story who get involved in the struggle). In the biblical story God is the protagonist, Satan (or those under his influence) are the antagonist, and God's people are the agonist. The basic "plot" of the biblical story is that God has created people for His glory—in His own image—who as His image bearers were to have dominion and stewardship over the earth that He created for their good (Genesis 1:26–30). But an enemy comes along who persuades the people to bear his "image" instead and thus to become God's enemies (Genesis 3). The plot resolution is the long story of "redemption," how God rescues His people from the enemy's clutches and their impending destruction, restores them back into His image, and provides for them "a new heaven and a new earth" (Isaiah 65:17; 66:22; 2 Peter 3:13; Revelation 20:11; 22:1–2).

As we read and study the Old Testament narratives, it is important to recognize that the biblical story is being told, in effect, on two levels. On one level we have what has just been described, often called "redemptive history." This level has to do with the whole universal plan of God worked out through His creation. Key aspects of the plot at this level are the initial creation itself, the fall of humanity into sin, the devastation of living in a sin-cursed world, and our need and provision for a Savior. Central to the historical narratives is the story of God redeeming a people for His name. These people are constituted twice by a former covenant and a new covenant.[5] Our interest in the historical narratives of the Old Testament concern the story of the first covenant, the story of the people of Israel: the call of Abraham and the establishment of an Abrahamic lineage through the patriarchs (Genesis 12–50); the enslaving of Israelites in Egypt and God's delivering them from bondage (Exodus 1–18); His covenant with them at Sinai, followed by the conquest of the promised land of Canaan (Exodus 20–Joshua); the Israelites' frequent acts of rebellion and disloyalty, and God's patient protection of and pleading with them (Judges–2 Chronicles); the ultimate destruction of northern Israel and later captivity of southern Judah, and the final restoration of His holy people after the exile (Ezra–Nehemiah).

On the other level, we find all the hundreds of individual narratives that make up the first level. This includes both larger narratives—for example, the Genesis narratives of Abraham, Isaac, Jacob, or Joseph as a whole—and the smaller units (such as Abraham's call out of Ur, or Joseph's encounter with Potiphar's wife) that make up the larger narratives. When it comes to the practical matters of interpreting biblical history, the fact that it is both history and theology means that, first, we must respect the historical integrity of the text, and that, second, we must recognize a purpose deeper than telling what "actually happened" from a human standpoint. Both Old Testament and New Testament historical books interpret history, and they give us the divine viewpoint. In some cases, more than one historical vantage point is necessary for us to get the full meaning of events, which is why we have four Gospels and two accounts of the monarchical period in the Old Testament (2 Samuel–2 Kings overlaps with 1–2 Chronicles). Biblical history not only records the events of redemptive history, but will often explain the significance of those events in light of their redemptive-historical meaning (a key feature in the Psalms; e.g., Psalms 78; 105; 106; 135; 136). This means that, when dealing with an historical text, we must ask ourselves, how does the historical event (second level) in our text relate to the first level (redemptive history) of the biblical story? (This will be further emphasized in chapters 12 and 13.)

An awareness of the two levels of narratives should help us in our understanding and application of Old Testament history. Thus, when Jesus taught that the Scriptures "testify of Me" in John 5:39, he was speaking of the ultimate (first level) meaning of historical narratives, in which His death and resurrection serve both as its defining act and climax (the gospel), and His coming judgment and lordship over all the earth as its plot resolution. He obviously was not speaking about every short individual passage of the Old Testament, since messianic passages (or passages that are otherwise identified in the New Testament as typological of Christ; i.e., 1 Corinthians 10:4) constitute only a small portion of its total revelation. What Jesus was saying was that Scripture in their entirety bear witness and focus toward Him as Lord and Savior.

What Narratives Are Not

Because the Old Testament narratives have frequently been interpreted in some unfortunate ways, it is important that we establish how the Old Testament narratives are not to be understood as well. First, Old Testament narrative are not allegories or stories filled with hidden meaning. While there may be aspects of narratives that are not easily understood, we should always assume that they had meaning for their original hearers. Approximately 10 percent of the New Testament consists of direct quotations, paraphrases, or allusions to the Old Testament. Of the thirty-nine books of the Old Testament, only nine are not directly referred to in the New Testament. Consequently, there is a significant amount of biblical literature illustrating the interpretive methods of Jesus and the New Testament writers. Several general conclusions can be drawn from an examination of Jesus's use of the historical narratives: He consistently treated them as straightforward records of fact. His allusions to Adam, Abel, Noah, Abraham, and David, for example, are all intended to be understood as references to actual people and historical events. When Jesus applied the historical record, he drew from the literal, as opposed to the allegorical, meaning of the text. He showed no tendency to deviate from the literary meaning of the text for a "deeper truth" based on some derived mystical level.

The apostles followed their Lord in accepting the historical accuracy of the Old Testament (Acts 7:9–50; 13:16–22; Hebrews 11). While some of our New Testament text do modify the original, historical meaning of a few Old Testament passages—for example, Paul interprets a handful of Old Testament narratives allegorically (or typologically) (i.e., 1 Corinthians 10:4; Galatians 3:16; 4:22–31)—the vast majority of the New Testament's use of the Old Testament historical narratives present a literal interpretation; that is, according to the commonly accepted norms of interpreting all types of communication—history as history, poetry as poetry, and symbols as symbols. There is no attempt to separate the message from its literal meaning in order to establish an allegorical interpretation. The few cases where the New Testament writers seem to interpret the Old Testament unnaturally can usually be resolved in light of the bigger picture (the first level of narratives) of the Old Testament (i.e., how Paul interprets "seed" in Galatians 3), and as we understand more fully the interpretive methods of biblical times. For the few examples that cannot be resolved, we must trust that the Holy Spirit inspired its writer to see in these passages more than what is afforded by its original historical-contextual meaning. As far as we the interpreters are concerned, we must keep in mind, however, that we are not under the same endowment of "inspiration" as the apostles and other New Testament writers. We have not been given special insight to see hidden meaning. While much of the Old Testament can be used to illustrate or exemplify New Testament truths, they should not be used to establish New Testament truths. The New Testament has already been provided to identify and explain the "deeper meaning" of the Old Testament—it doesn't need our help!

Secondly, individual Old Testament narratives are not intended to teach moral lessons. The purpose of the various individual narratives is to tell what God did in the history of Israel, not to offer moral examples of right or wrong behavior. Very often you will hear someone say, "What we can learn from this story is that we are not to do . . ." But unless the biblical narrator makes that point (or another biblical author at a later point), on what grounds do we make it? While we may rightly recognize from the story of Jacob and Esau the negative results of parental favoritism, the morals for raising children are not the focus for the narrative in Genesis. Rather, it serves to tell us how Abraham's chosen lineage was carried on through Jacob, not Esau. It illustrates how God, outside of cultural norms, chose who would be the "firstborn" to carry on the family line. While the narrative may illustrate the outcome of parental rivalry, this has little to do with the reason for the narrative as such.

However, even though the Old Testament narratives do not necessarily teach morals directly, they often illustrate what is taught explicitly and categorically elsewhere. According to Fee and Stuart, "This represents an implicit kind of teaching by illustrating the corresponding explicit teachings of Scripture."[6] They provide the following example:

> In the narrative of David's adultery with Bathsheba (2 Samuel 11), you will not find any such statement as, "In committing adultery David did wrong." You are expected to know that adultery is wrong because this is taught explicitly already in the Bible (Exodus 20:14). The narrative illustrates the harmful consequences of adultery to the personal life of king David and to his ability to rule.[7]

The narrative does not systematically teach about the universal effects of adultery, and thus it could not be used as the sole basis for such teaching. But as one illustration of the negative consequences of adultery in a particular case, "it conveys a powerful message that can imprint itself on the mind of the careful reader in a way that direct, explicit teaching may not do."[8] So then, many historical narratives often illustrate or exemplify moral truths that are explicitly taught in other passages and thus can be powerful aids in exhorting the reader toward obedience. The interpretive rule here is this: historical narratives may complement explicit moral commands elsewhere in Scripture, but must never establish them, and at the same time, must never be what drives our purpose in interpreting them.

More often than not, the primary reason Christians interpret the Old Testament narratives so poorly, reading into passages what is not there, is their tendency to assume that everything God has said in His Word is a direct word to them. Thus, they wrongly expect that everything in the Bible applies directly as instruction for their own individual lives. The Bible is a great resource in providing all that is needed in terms of guidance for godly living. But this does not mean that each individual narrative is somehow to be understood as a direct word from God for teaching us moral lessons. According to Fee and Stuart,

> Perhaps the single most useful bit of caution we can give here, about reading and learning from narratives, is this: do not be a monkey-see-monkey-do reader of the Bible. No Bible narrative was written specifically about you. The Joseph narrative is about Joseph, and specifically about how God did things through him—it is not a narrative directly about you. The Ruth narrative glorifies God's protection [and care] for Ruth and the Bethlehemites—not you. You can always learn a great deal from these narratives, and from all the Bible's narratives, but you can never assume that God expects you to do exactly the same thing that Bible characters did or to [expect to] have the same things happen to you that happened to them [whether good or bad].[9]

Historical narratives inform us as to how God interacted in and through the lives of the many followers that went before us, and our task is to learn God's Word through them, not to try to do everything that was done by them. As Fee and Stuart further note, "Just because someone in the Bible story did something, it does not mean you have either permission or obligation to do it, too. What you can and should do is obey what God in Scripture actually commands Christian believers to do. Narratives are precious to us because they so vividly demonstrate God's involvement in the world, and illustrate His principles and calling. They thus teach us a lot—but what they directly teach us does not systematically include personal ethics. For this area of life, we must turn elsewhere in the Scriptures—to the various places where personal ethics are actually taught categorically and explicitly."[10]

Characteristics of a Hebrew Narrative

An important part of reading the historical narratives well is to recognize the distinctive features that are often part of Hebrew narration. Identifying these narrative characteristics can greatly enhance our ability to hear the story from the perspective of the divinely inspired narrator. To help us identify some of these, we will use the life of Joseph, a skillfully narrated story by Moses (Genesis 37–50).[11]

The Narrator. A proper understanding of any narrative begins by paying careful attention to the one person who is not mentioned directly in the unfolding of the biblical story: the narrator himself. The narrator, since he is the one who chooses what to say, is responsible for the "point of view" of the narrative, and thus he provides the divine perspective from which the story is told. Sometimes God's point of view is disclosed directly by the narrator; for example, how the narrator of Genesis repeats that "the LORD was with Joseph" (Genesis 39:2, 3, 21, 23). Notice how this four-fold repetition happens early on in the narrative when Joseph is first taken into Egypt. These clues are intentional in focusing the reader's attention on God's providence within the story.

Very often the point of view comes by way of one of the characters. You will notice, for example, how at the end of the narrative (50:20) it is Joseph who tells the reader the divine perspective for the whole narrative: "You meant evil against me, but God meant it for good, to bring it about that many people should be kept alive, as they are today." So as we read the various narratives, we must constantly be on the lookout for how the inspired narrator discloses the point of view from which we are to under-stand the story.[12]

The Scene(s). Rather than building the story around the "character" of any of the characters, Hebrew narration more commonly centers the story around strategically placed scenes. These series of "scenes" serve to move the story along to its intended conclusion—much like a movie or television drama tells a story.

While each scene has its own integrity, the progressive combination of individual scenes makes up the story as a whole. Note, for example, how this happens in the opening episode narrated in Genesis 37. In the opening scene Joseph reports to his father the evil of his brothers, after which you are informed of the basic reason his brothers hate him: parental favoritism (a recurring theme in Genesis). This scene, along with its following scene (vv. 5–11), in which Joseph recounts his dreams, are used to provide the context for his brothers' deplorable acts in the scene that follows after them (vv. 12–18). The timing of this scene is crucial—the arrival of Joseph, the plot to kill, and the arrival of the Midianites is ordered so as to make sure the reader realizes that it all has unfolded in a divinely ordained manner. Its climactic point comes in the last verse, where Joseph ends up in Egypt (at a pivotal time) as the well-placed servant of an Egyptian official (v. 36).[13] The grouping of these individual scenes is what makes the narrative work as a whole.

The Characters. Through the use of strategically placed scenes, the narrator establishes the important role and personal qualities of the characters within the narrative. When it comes to Hebrew narration, it is important to keep in mind that characterization has very little to do with physical appearance. Hebrew narrative is simply not interested in creating a visual image of the characters. More important are matters of status (wise, wealthy, etc.) or profession ("captain of the guard," Genesis 37:36; "cupbearer," "baker," chapter 40) or tribal designation (Midianites, 37:36).

Two important features of characterization that are commonly found in Hebrew narratives are: First, characters often appear either in contrast or in parallel. When they are contrasted, which is most often, they must be understood in relation to each other. The contrast between Joseph and his brothers that begins in chapter 37 lies at the heart of the unfolding subsequent narrative in chapters 42–45 (especially the change of heart that has taken place between Judah and Joseph in 50:15–21). Characters in parallel usually happen at the first level of narratives, so that, for example, Joseph's life can be viewed as a sort of "rehearsal" for the life of Christ. (Jesus also experienced a special love from His Father, was hated and rejected by His brothers, falsely accused of wrongdoing, suffered at the hands of foreigners, later to be the exalted Ruler and Savior of those of us who seek Him.)

Second, characterization predominantly occurs in conjunction with the characters' words and actions, not in the narrator's own descriptions. In our narrative in Genesis, this happens especially with the main character, Joseph, and with the most significant secondary character, Judah. Of note is how Joseph's moral character develops from negative to positive as a main theme. "At the beginning Joseph, as part of a notably dysfunctional family, is depicted as a spoiled brat, talebearer."[14] His moral character, however, "comes alive" in the incident with Potiphar's wife, where his stance against sexual immorality lands him in prison. It is further testified by the loving but firm way he handles his brothers in chapters 42–45: "He weeps for them but will not reveal himself to them until they are tested and proved to be changed themselves."[15] Likewise, the narrator shows special interest in Judah. Judah is the one who argues for selling rather than killing Joseph (37:26–27), yet his morality is highly questionable (ch. 38). But the narrator's primary interest in Judah is in his radical change of character that emerges in chapters 40–45.[16]

Dialogue. An important feature of Hebrew narrative is dialogue. "Indeed, a significantly large part of all narratives is carried on by the rhythm between narrative and dialogue."[17] Three things are important to consider when interpreting dialogue: first, the narrator's use of dialogue is often a significant clue both to the story plot, and to the character of the speaker. Notice, for example, how this happens in the brief scene at the beginning of the story of Joseph (Genesis 37:5–11). Joseph's narration of his dreams sets the stage for his Father's response, "What is this dream that you have dreamed? Shall I and your mother and your brothers indeed come to bow ourselves to the ground before you?" It is this dialogue that sets the plot itself into motion, which is expressly brought to a conclusion at the narratives end (50:18). Second, contrastive dialogue is one of the chief methods of characterization. Note, for example, the length of Joseph's reply (39:8–9) to the very brief invitation of Potiphar's wife (v. 7). This comparative dialogue serves to emphasize the moral character of Joseph over the wicked advances of Potiphar's wife. Furthermore, you will see a different kind of contrastive dialogue with the final speeches of Judah and Joseph in 44:18–34 and 45:4–13, which are given to accentuate the change of heart in Judah, and the compassionate and forgiving heart of Joseph. Third, the narrator will often emphasize the crucial parts of the narrative by having one of the characters repeat or summarize the narrative in a speech. This happens particularly in the speeches of the brothers in 42:30–34 and of Judah in 44:18–34. So then, we must refrain from going too fast through these repetitions; they often tell us very important things about the point of view of the narrative.

Plot. Every narrative, without exception, must have a plot and plot resolution. This means that the narrative must have a beginning, middle, and end, which together build up a dramatic tension and which finally leads to a climatic resolution. Usually the plot is thrust forward by some form of conflict, which generates interest in the resolution. Plots can be either simple (as the inserted story of Judah and Tamar in Genesis 38) or complex, as in the story of Joseph as a whole, where several subplots are used to unfold the major plot of the narrative. An example of this is how the conflict between Joseph and his brothers brought Israel to Egypt, which in turn prepares the way for the next major part of the story of Israel—the exodus from Egypt. Also, you will notice that the plot in Hebrew narrative moves at a much faster pace than most modern narration—much like the short-story genre. So, as you look for the major plot and its resolution in any narrative, also look for the various devices the narrator uses to slow the pace of his story. This usually happens by dialogue, the sudden elaboration of detail, or by other forms of repetition. Very often a slowed pace is a signal pointing to the narrator's focus or point of view.

Features of Structure. In ways that most modern readers often miss, Hebrew narrative uses numerous structural features "to catch the hearer's attention and keep him or her fastened on the narrative."[18] While some of these have already been mentioned, here we will deal with them in greater focus, along with others, in hopes of better preparing the interpreter for their recognition.

Repetition. Repetition, a common rhetoric in Hebrew narrative, can take several forms. Here we will briefly examine the most frequent types. The first, and probably most important, is repetition of keywords. As an example, you should notice how the conflict dimension of the plot in chapter 37 is carried forward by the repetition of the word "hate" (37:4, 5, 8). Another example of repetition often occurs as a way of resuming the narrative after an interruption or detour. A good example of this is how 37:36 is repeated at the resumption of the Joseph narrative in 39:1. At other times, repetition takes the form of circular patterns, as in the cycles of the judges (Israel turns from God and serves idols, God turns Israel over to the oppressive surrounding nations, Israel turns to God and cries out for help, God raises up a judge to deliver them, Israel turns from God and the cycle is repeated; see Judges 2:15–16). This structural feature provides an important key to understanding the theme of the book of Judges.

Inclusio. An inclusio is a form of repetition where the writer states a theme or idea at both the beginning and end of a narrative (what is sometimes described as bookends). The theme of Joseph's brothers bowing down to him in 37:6–8 and 50:18 forms an obvious and important inclusio in Genesis. But another important example occurs as part of the creation story. The narrative is introduced in Genesis 1:1: "In the beginning, God created the heavens and the earth," and concluded in Genesis 2:1: "Thus the heavens and the earth were finished, and all the host of them."

A special form of an inclusio, frequently used in Hebrew narration, is known as a *chiasm*. A chiasm is a literary device, occurring in narratives, and even whole books (e.g., the book of Deuteronomy) that forms a unique repetition pattern (usually an ABCBA pattern). A notable example, and one that is rather simplistic, is found in our Joseph story. The structure of Genesis 39:19–41:45 is as follows:

A (39:19–23): Joseph was put in charge of the prison

   B (40:1–19): Joseph interpreted the dream

      C (40:20–23): Chief cupbearer forgot Joseph

         D (41:1–8): Pharaoh's dream

      C (41:9–13): Chief cupbearer remembered Joseph

   B (41:14–36): Joseph interpreted the dream

A (41:37–45): Joseph was put in charge of Egypt

Chiasms serve four major purposes: (1) to give structure and poetic form, making text more digestible and memorable, (2) to set the scene and draw the reader into the flow of thought of a narrative, (3) to emphasize or clarify major points in a text, and (4) to connect the individual scenes or subunits of a narrative into one cohesive unit.

Irony. Irony is a literary device that expresses contrast for literary affect or impact. It usually involves surprise or the unexpected. The Old Testament narratives are full of ironic twists and reversals. For example, the ironic reversal of routines is an obvious motif throughout the book of Esther. To name a few, Haman was hanged on the gallows he had erected for Mordecai, and, previous to this, he was forced to honor Mordecai in ways he had expected Mordecai to honor him. Also, the Jews strike down their enemies on the very day their enemies had expected to strike them down. Besides the features we have included here, you will still find other, sometimes more complex, rhetorical features throughout the historical narratives.[19]

In conclusion of this section, we remind you that the one crucial element to keep in mind as you read any Hebrew narrative is the presence of God in the story. "In any biblical narrative, God is the ultimate character, the Supreme Hero of the story."[20] The narrator often reminds the reader of this with bold, explicit statements such as, "the Lord was with Joseph" (39:2, etc.), "interpretations [of dreams] belong to God" (40:8), "God sent me before you to preserve for you a remnant on earth, and to keep alive for you many survivors" (45:7), "God meant it for good" (50:20), "God will visit you and bring you up out of this land to the land that he swore to Abraham, to Isaac, and to Jacob." (50:24). "To miss this dimension of the narratives is to miss the perspective of the narrative altogether; and pre-cisely, because of these explicit statements about God's presence in the nar-rative, one should constantly be aware of God's presence in more implicit ways (e.g., the source of Joseph's dream in chapter 37; the timing in the narrative that brought Joseph, his brothers, and the Midianites together in 37:25–28; etc.)."[21]

Gospel Narratives

Many, if not most, of the rules that have been discussed in regard to interpreting Old Testament narratives often apply equally to New Testament narratives as well. So then, on the one hand, a designated study for Gospel narratives may seem redundant, but on the other hand, because they form a unique literary genre (the Gospel genre), a combination of the teachings of Jesus and the stories about Jesus, it is important for us to briefly consider some of the hermeneutical challenges that are unique to Gospel narratives.

First and foremost, interpreting the Gospels correctly begins by understanding what a Gospel is. The Gospels are selective, purposeful accounts of the life of Jesus. Each Gospel has a theological agenda that the author is defending to a particular audience. For Luke and John, these are explicitly spelled out (cf. Luke 1:1–4; John 20:30–31). Matthew and Mark, however, have no such clear thesis statement, and thus their core purpose must be inferred from the structural perspective the author provides (their own unique way of storytelling). As primarily theological treatises, Gospels carry a purpose well beyond a simple presentation of the facts; and the writers, therefore, are far from neutral, unbiased reporters. As each Gospel progresses, their writers develop themes and arguments that support their claims and purpose for writing. For example, Matthew extensively uses the Old Testament as proof of the fulfillment of Jesus's ministry and the validity of His teachings, while Luke emphasizes the historical accuracy and impact of Jesus's life.

Second, establishing some ground rules for interpreting Gospel narratives is essential. A good place to start is to recognize that the narrative accounts tend to function in more than one way in the Gospels. The miracle stories, for example, are not recorded to offer moral instruction or to serve as modern precedents. Rather, they function as vital illustrations of the power of the Kingdom of God that has been brought to us through Jesus's own ministry. By their very nature they may illustrate the power of God in a believer's life today, but this is not their primary function. They are not to serve as paradigms for all believers, or to mandate a certain expectation for today. Furthermore, other stories such as the rich young man (Mark 10:17–22) and the request to sit at Jesus's right hand (Mark 10:35–45) are placed in the context of Jesus's teaching, where the story itself serves as an illustration of what is being taught. Thus, the point of the story of the rich young man is not that all Jesus's disciples must sell all their possessions to follow Him. There are clear examples in the Gospels where that was not the case (cf. Mark 14:3–9). The story instead illustrates the point of how difficult it is for the rich to enter the Kingdom precisely because they are trusting in material wealth for their security in life. So then, narratives must be interpreted in light of their overall context, in relation to the major theme of the broader section of which it shares, and by noting the interplay between the narrative and any surrounding teaching or imperatives of Christ.

In our effort to understand any Gospel narrative, we should

1. *Read the entire Gospel, noting where the overall book breaks into distinctive sections (or units).* Such an overview will help us in discovering the Gospel's primary purpose, argument, and intended audience. Furthermore, sections may be identified by the author's use of similar terms. For example, notice how Matthew concludes each major section with a similar summary statement: "When Jesus had ended these sayings. . ." (7:28; 11:1; 13:53; 19:1; 26:1), or by the author's use of similar material (such as how Matthew groups parables of similar content together [Matthew 13; see Luke 15:1–32]).

2. *Determine the overall theme for each section break.* While much of the Gospel writings follow a chronological outline, authors often shuffle this order to accommodate a particular theme or emphasis they are developing. The best way to identify the theme of any section is to note any recurring words or statements in the section. Look for theological terms such as "Kingdom of God" or "Kingdom of heaven," "fulfilled," "believe," "life," etc. being repeated within a section. By comparing a list of these words and summarizing them, a clear emphasis is likely to emerge.

3. *Identify any significant or recurring themes.* The best way for determining a Gospel's overall theme or purpose is to look for repeated themes throughout the book. For instance, eternal life as a result of believing the gospel (the good news of Jesus's death and resurrection on behalf of sinners) is easily discernible as a major theme throughout the Gospel of John.

4. *Finally, interpret each individual story (or narrative) in light of the controlling context and unified theme of the section in which it is*

placed. Paying attention to the events, discourses, and themes of the passages that come before and after the one you are studying, gives you clues for determining the author's purpose for telling the story at hand. For example, Matthew concludes the Sermon on the Mount (Matthew 5–7) with the observation that Christ was teaching the people "as one having authority." Then we see in Matthew 8 and 9 that Jesus demonstrates His authority in a series of miracles. A further example is found in John 6. After the miracle of feeding the five thousand, Jesus gives a discourse on the spiritual reality and necessity of Him being the "bread of life."

7

LAW

Embedded in the story of redemptive history, particularly in the Old Testament (Exodus 20–40; Leviticus; various passages in Numbers and Deuteronomy) but also in the New Testament (i.e., The Sermon on the Mount), are several statements of ethical standards that God has set for His people. This arrangement of law and narrative works together to give context to the law and indicates clearly that the law is given by God as part of His redemptive activity. Thus, the law cannot be interpreted apart from its redemptive-historical context. Jesus's own teaching establishes the profound importance of the law in regard to redemptive history. In Matthew 5:17, He sharply refutes any notion that the gospel does away with the law, "Do not think that I have come to destroy the law and the prophets. I did not come to destroy, but to fulfill." And "One jot or one tittle will by no means pass from the law till all is fulfilled" (v. 18). The Greek word that is translated as destroy (*kataluo*) means to dissolve, demolish, undo, or invalidate. Conversely, "fulfill" means to "carry out;" "fulfill to the fullest measure of the intent and purpose." The nature of the law's fulfillment, then, rules out any notion of dissolving, abrogating, or invalidating the law; and that, the law being fulfilled, means that its purpose is not in and of itself, but rather in relation to that which fulfills it. So then, the law is not just a list of ethical standards, but a central part of God's story of redemption and His covenant with His people.

Divorced from the redemptive activity of God, the legal material becomes something other than redemptive.[1] This was the error that Jesus (Matthew 23:13–36), and later Paul (especially in Romans and Galatians), had to frequently combat. Thus, the first principle in interpreting a legal or ethical passage in the Bible is to place it in its redemptive-historical context.[2] For example, the legal material of Exodus–Deuteronomy was addressed to a specific situation, where the people of God are also a political entity.[3] Doing so will not only help us understand the role of the law in the Old Testament, but will also help us identify how a legal passage now relates to Christians today.

Outside of the patriarchal narratives in Genesis, the two defining acts for Israel as a people are found in the book of Exodus. First, their miraculous deliverance from slavery in Egypt, the most powerful empire in the ancient world at that time (Exodus 1–18); and second, God's constituting them as a people for His name at the foot of Mount Sinai (Exodus 19–Numbers 10:10). It is hard for us even to imagine the enormity of difficulty involved in this second matter. Here were people who knew only Egyptian culture and slavery, and God was now about to reconstitute them into a totally new people. "Not only must [the Israelites] be formed into an army of warriors in order to conquer the land promised to their ancestors (Canaan), but they must also be formed into a community that would be able to live together both during their time in the desert, and eventually in the land itself. At the same time they needed direction as to how they were to be God's people—both in their relationship with each other and in their relationship with God—so that they would shed the ways and culture of Egypt and not adopt the ways and culture of the Canaanites whose land they were about to possess."[4]

This all constitutes the fundamental role the law played in the life of Israel. It was given by God to His people in order "to establish the way they were to live in community with one another, set the boundaries with regard to their relationships with the cultures around them, and, above all, provide for their relationship with and worship of Yahweh, their God."[5] If we are going to read and understand the law well, we must begin with this understanding of its role in Israel's own history. At the same time, we must be aware of its covenantal nature because our understanding not only of the law but of the Prophets and of the New Testament itself as a new covenant depends on it. So, the purpose of this section is to guide you into a good understanding of the nature and function of the law under the Old Testament so that you can better discern the role of these laws for those of us who live under God's new covenant as His people.

What is the Law?

In order to determine the nature and function of the Old Testament law, we need to face at the outset matters brought about by the various usage of "law" found throughout the Bible. We must be cognizant of the fact that the word "law" has more than one connotation in Scripture: it is used (1) in the plural to refer to the 600-plus specific commandments that the Israelites were expected to keep as evidence of their loyalty to God (Exodus 18:20); (2) in the singular to refer to all these laws collectively (Matthew 5:18; Acts 10:28); (3) in the singular to refer to the Pentateuch (Genesis to Deuteronomy) as the "Book of the Law" (Joshua 1:8); (4) in the singular to refer to the entire religious system (the Mosaic covenant) under the Old Testament (1 Corinthians 9:20). Recognizing that the Bible uses the word "law" differently at different times helps the interpreter to appreciate what the many stipulations God gave Israel meant for them, and how we may best read and understand them as Christians.

A second matter that must be considered has to do with what was mentioned with use 4 above: the fact that the law is a covenant. A covenant is a binding contract between two parties, both of whom have obligations specified within the covenant. In Old Testament times, covenants were often given by a powerful suzerain (overlord) to a weaker, dependent vassal (servant). Such a covenant would guarantee that the vassal would receive benefits and protection from the suzerain, who in return was obligated to remain loyal solely to the suzerain. Furthermore, the vassal would show his loyalty by keeping the stipulations (rules of behavior) also specified in the covenant. But when the stipulations were violated, the suzerain was required by the covenant to take action to punish the vassal.

What is important in all of this is for us to realize that in making a covenant with Israel at Sinai, God used this well-known covenant form when He constituted the binding contract between Himself and His vassal, Israel. In return for God's "benefits and protection," Israel was expected to keep the many stipulations contained in the covenantal agreement as recorded in Exodus 20–Deuteronomy 33:

> *Thus you shall say to the house of Jacob, and tell the people of Israel: 'you yourselves have seen what I did to the Egyptians, and how I bore you on eagles' wings and brought you to myself. Now therefore, if you will indeed obey my voice and keep my covenant, you shall be my treasured possession among all peoples, for all the earth is mine; and you shall be to me a kingdom of priests and a holy nation.' These are the words that you shall speak to the people of Israel (Exodus 20:3–6).*

This covenant format had four parts to it: the preamble, the prologue, the stipulations, and the sanctions. The preamble identified the suzerain by his name and title ("I am the Lord your God . . ."[Exodus 20:2a]), while the prologue gave a brief history of the suzerain's dealings with the vassal ("which brought you out of Egypt . . ." [Exodus 20:2b]). The stipulations, as we have noted, are the individual laws themselves—what is required of the vassal, and the sanctions are the blessings and curses that function as incentive for keeping the covenant (e.g., Leviticus 26 and Deuteronomy 28–33). Both the first statement of the law at Sinai (Exodus 20) and the second statement found in Deuteronomy 28–33 (just prior to the conquest) reflects this four-part format.

The importance of properly recognizing the covenantal nature of the law can hardly be overemphasized. It is its covenantal nature that makes the law so important to our understanding of the Old Testament as a whole. Moreover, it is an essential part of Israel's story—God's story—and our own place in the story. As such, it provides the framework for answering what is probably the most difficult question for most Christians with regard to these commandments: How do any of these specific legal mandates apply to us today, or do they? Because this is a crucial matter, we turn next to examine the role of law for the Christian.

Christians and the Old Testament Law

In order to determine how a specific law applies to God's people today, we must first ask how it functioned in its redemptive-historical context. Two types of distinctions emerge from this inquiry. First, a law may be a case law or apodictic law. Second, laws in Israel had to do with government and administration (civil law), ritual practices (ceremonial law), as well as ethics (moral law).

Case Law vs Apodictic Law. Apodictic law expresses general principles. The Ten Commandments in Exodus 20 are an example of apodictic law. "You shall not steal" (v. 15) is a general principle. On the other hand, the Ten Commandments are followed by case law in Exodus 21:22. These laws, which often begin with an *if* or *when* or *whoever* clause, address specific cases. For example, "When a man causes a field or vineyard to be grazed over, or let his beast loose and it feeds in another man's field, he shall make restitution for the beast from his own field or in his own vineyard" (22:5). Case laws are applications of apodictic law, and often express means of identifying and establishing specific violations of an apodictic law within a given context. In the case of Exodus 22:5, quoted above, the moral principle that is being applied, of course, is that of 20:15: "You shall not steal."

It is usually recognized that case laws in the Old Testament are rarely applicable to our present cultural situation, and even if they appear to be relevant, case laws first require the interpreter to extrapolate the moral principle(s) lying behind them (we will expound on this further below).[6]

Civil, Ceremonial, and Moral Law. The second type of distinction that must be made has to do with the categorization of the various laws in to three major groups: civil, ceremonial, and moral. Since there is not an easy way to tell whether a law is in one category or another, some interpreters have doubted whether this distinction is even warranted. There are no typical linguistic forms that mark off one type from another, and the different types are all mixed together. For example, Leviticus 19:18: "You shall love your neighbor as yourself," which Jesus declares to be the second-most important law in the Old Testament, is followed immediately by an injunction not to interbreed cattle, sow a field with two different kinds of grain, or make garments of mixed material (Leviticus 19:19). The only guide to classification, then, is content. Also, the ethical, civil, ceremonial distinction does not originate in the Old Testament itself. Nevertheless, it is useful because it spells out how the relationship of the Old Testament laws to the people of God has changed as their redemptive-historical situation has changed. Each of these types of laws have their meaning and fulfillment in Christ, and each point to our need for Christ, in one way or another.

Ceremonial laws of the Old Testament, laws which functioned primarily as a formal symbol of Christ's redemptive work, have all been fulfilled by Christ and are therefore no longer necessary to perform or observe today. In fact, to require its observance now would negate the purpose of the symbol and would deny the truth that Christ has fulfilled it. Any careful study of the offerings, the sacrifices, the Sabbath days, and many other ceremonial aspects of Old Testament worship will reveal that Christ is their ultimate fulfillment (cf. Colossians 2:16–17; Hebrews 10:1–18). He is the offering, the altar, the high priest, and the temple (Hebrews 9:1–12). He has not only shed his blood as an atonement for sin, He has obviated any need for another (Hebrews 10:14). All the ceremonial laws pointed to and were fulfilled in Him.

The civil laws were those which had respect to the civil order or government and the maintenance of external property among the Jewish people according to the moral commandments. These laws God delivered through Moses for the establishment and preservation of the Jewish commonwealth, binding all the posterity of Abraham, and distinguishing them from the rest of mankind until the coming of the Messiah; and that they might at the same time, by means of preserving proper discipline and order, serve as a paradigm for the order which shall be established in the Kingdom of God. And thus, it too is fulfilled in Christ, who has in fact already reestablished the true Kingdom of God as its sovereign King, although it is not yet fully implemented. The civil aspects of the law do not relate directly to contemporary civil governments, which are not the Kingdom of God (cf. John 18:36).

It is important to note that the precepts of the moral law will find the goal of all other laws. The ceremonial law would not have been necessary, nor would it make sense, if it were not for sins against the moral law. The civil laws applied the principles of the moral law to the specific context of national Israel. Though we are not bound to the particular civil laws themselves, they embody ideals that remain valid to us, though in new ways. An example of this is how Paul applies the principle of "not muzzling the ox" (a civil law found in Deuteronomy 25:4) to the church (i.e., 1 Corinthians 9:9; 1 Timothy 5:18).

Moral law, then, unlike the civil ordinances, abides permanently because it is based on and reflects the moral character of God, which remains the same. He does not change; therefore, His moral laws are not temporarily conditioned. On the other hand, Exodus 25:9, 40; 26:30; and 27:8 show that the laws concerning the tabernacle, its furniture, the offerings, the priesthood, and the like are to be made according to the "pattern" or "copy" in heaven (see Hebrews 9). Of course, when the real tabernacle

(Christ) came, to which these patterns and copies pointed, then there would no longer be any need for the symbolic except to exhibit the principles involved. Therefore, the ceremonial laws had a built-in obsolescence to them, meaning that they were valid as models for only as long as God would say so. Likewise, the civil laws were the application and practice of moral law for the nation of Israel under the Mosaic covenant. Although the moral laws transcend time and are thus eternally binding, the civil laws, as constituted by the Mosaic covenant, were binding so long as the Mosaic covenant was in force.

Moral Law and the New Covenant. In Jeremiah 31:31–34, the prophet states:

> *Behold, the days are coming, says the Lord, when I will make a new covenant with the house of Israel and with the house of Judah--not according to the covenant that I made with their fathers in the day that I took them by the hand to lead them out of the land of Egypt, My covenant which they broke, though I was a husband to them, says the Lord. But this is the covenant that I will make with the house of Israel after those days, says the Lord: I will put My law in their minds, and write it on their hearts; and I will be their God, and they shall be My people. No more shall every man teach his neighbor, and every man his brother, saying, 'Know the Lord,' for they all shall know Me, from the least of them to the greatest of them, says the Lord. For I will forgive their iniquity, and their sin I will remember no more.*

Probably the best-known and certainly one of the most important passages in Jeremiah, this announcement of a new covenant expresses one of the deepest insights in the whole Old Testament. The exact phrase "new covenant" is found nowhere else in the Old Testament, although the ideas associated with it are frequently expressed (e.g., Isaiah 41:18–20; 42:6–13; 43:18–21, 25; 44:3–5, 21–23; 45:14–17; 49:8–13; 51:3–8; 54:9–10; 55:3;

59:21; 60:15–22; 61:1–9; 65:17–25; Jeremiah 54:5; Ezekiel 16:60–63; 34:11–31; 36:8–15, 22–38; 37:11–14, 21–28; Joel 2:18–32).

The text explicitly contrasts a new covenant in relation to the old covenant God made with Israel at Mount Sinai. As already stated above, after producing in Egypt a sizable offspring (Exodus 1–7), God formalized His relationship with them under the Mosaic Covenant (Exodus 19–24), a covenant that specified the right behavior He required and also made provisions for infractions against those regulations. It is quite clear that obedience was expected in order to reap the benefits of such covenant:

> *Now therefore, if you will indeed obey My voice and keep My covenant, then you shall be a special treasure to Me above all people; for all the earth is Mine. And you shall be to Me a kingdom of priests and a holy nation.' These are the words which you shall speak to the children of Israel. (Exodus 19:5–6)*

Disloyalty to the covenant would be signified by such behavior as, idolatry (Exodus 20:1–5; 32:2–35; Deuteronomy 4:23–31), blasphemy (Exodus 20:7; Leviticus 24:15–16), adultery or sexual perversion (Exodus 20:14; Leviticus 18:6–30; Numbers 5:11–31), injustice (Isaiah 1:16–31; 10:1–6), or non-compliance to basic stipulations such as the Sabbath laws (Exodus 20:8–11; Numbers 15:30–36; Deuteronomy 5:12–15) or the tithe (Deuteronomy 14:22–29; 26:12–19; Malachi 3:7–12). These evidences of disloyalty would be judged individually by death or removal from the safety of the covenant community (Deuteronomy 29:18–21), and nationally by the discipline of the covenant curses (Leviticus 26;14–45; Deuteronomy 27:12–26; 28:15–68). It was such disloyalty that the generations of Israel had displayed time after time throughout their history (see Psalm 78; Isaiah 24:5; Nehemiah 9:16–38), disqualifying themselves from the blessing and inviting upon themselves the curses God had promised. It was apparent that although there were certain individuals who had put God's law in their heart, the people as a whole never would (Jeremiah 13:23; 17:1). This was the failure of the Mosaic covenant, caused by the sinful nature of the people ("My covenant which they broke, though I was a husband to them" in verse 32; cf. Exodus 32:9), which led to the promise of a new covenant ("not according to the covenant that I made with their fathers . . .,) to supersede it (cf. Hebrews 7:18–22; 8:6–13; 9:10).

Under this new covenant, God promises three things that clearly contrast against the Mosaic covenant: (1) "I will put My law in their minds, and write it on their hearts;" (2) "no more shall every man teach his neighbor, and every man his brother, saying, 'Know the Lord,' for they all shall know Me, from the least of them to the greatest of them;" (3) "I will forgive their iniquity, and their sin I will remember no more."

In Matthew 26:26–29, Jesus redefines the Jewish Passover meal as a drama portraying His atoning death on the cross. This drama then interprets His crucifixion as a new Exodus that brings about forgiveness and reconciliation on the basis of the sacrifice of Himself as a "Passover lamb." In this drama, the cup represents the "blood of the new covenant, which is shed for many for the remission of sins." Just as the old covenant was inaugurated by the shedding of blood, so too was the new covenant (Hebrews 9:18–28). But unlike the old covenant, the blood of the new covenant would permanently forgive the sins of many through the atoning work of Jesus (Hebrews 10:14). Once the connection between the Lord's Supper and Jeremiah 31:31–34 is made, it answers two important questions: (1) When will the new covenant be put into force? In Jeremiah, the timing is not clearly defined, simply stating, "Behold, the days are coming, says the Lord, when I will make a new covenant. . ." But in Matthew, it is clear that the new covenant is ratified at the cross, with the death of Jesus. This was certainly apparent to the writer of Hebrews when he stated,

> But now He has obtained a more excellent ministry, inasmuch as He is also Mediator of a better covenant, which was established on better promises. For if that first covenant had been faultless, then no place would have been sought for a second. Because finding

fault with them, He says: "Behold, the days are coming, says the Lord, when I will make a new covenant with the house of Israel and with the house of Judah--not according to the covenant that I made with their fathers in the day when I took them by the hand to lead them out of the land of Egypt; because they did not continue in My covenant, and I disregarded them, says the Lord. For this is the covenant that I will make with the house of Israel after those days, says the Lord: I will put My laws in their mind and write them on their hearts; and I will be their God, and they shall be My people. None of them shall teach his neighbor, and none his brother, saying, 'Know the Lord,' for all shall know Me, from the least of them to the greatest of them. For I will be merciful to their unrighteousness, and their sins and their lawless deeds I will remember no more." In that He says, "A new covenant," He has made the first obsolete. Now what is becoming obsolete and growing old is ready to vanish away. (Hebrews 8:6–13)

(2) Who is the covenant for? In our text in Jeremiah only two parties are mentioned: God and Israel. Yet the New Testament makes clear that the covenant was intended for a wider audience. If the new covenant affords the forgiveness of sins for those who are under it, it is clear from the New Testament that all who repent and believe the gospel are made part of the new covenant (John 1:29; 3:16). Otherwise, it would be difficult to understand the writer of Hebrews when he says, "And for this reason He [Jesus] is the Mediator of the new covenant, by means of death, for the redemption of the transgressions under the first covenant, that those who are called may receive the promise of the eternal inheritance" (Hebrews 9:15). Thus there is only one new covenant people of God. "There is neither Jew nor Greek, there is neither slave nor free, there is neither male nor female; for you are all one in Christ Jesus" (Galatians 3:28). In the new covenant community there is no black, no white, no brown. There is no rich, no poor. There is only one new covenant people in Christ.

Writing to Gentile Christians, Paul emphasizes the unity of covenant community in Ephesians 2:

> *Therefore remember that you, once Gentiles in the flesh—who are called Uncircumcision by what is called the Circumcision made in the flesh by hands—that at that time you were without Christ, being aliens from the commonwealth of Israel and strangers from the covenants of promise, having no hope and without God in the world. But now in Christ Jesus you who once were far off have been brought near by the blood of Christ. For He Himself is our peace, who has made both one, and has broken down the middle wall of separation, having abolished in His flesh the enmity, that is, the law of commandments contained in ordinances, so as to create in Himself one new man from the two, thus making peace, and that He might reconcile them both to God in one body through the cross, thereby putting to death the enmity. And He came and preached peace to you who were afar off and to those who were near. For through Him we both have access by one Spirit to the Father. Now, therefore, you are no longer strangers and foreigners, but fellow citizens with the saints and members of the household of God, having been built on the foundation of the apostles and prophets, Jesus Christ Himself being the chief cornerstone, in whom the whole building, being joined together, grows into a holy temple in the Lord, in whom you also are being built together for a dwelling place of God in the Spirit. (Ephesians 2:11–22)*

Paul clearly states that Gentile believers—members of nations and peoples in the earth outside the nation of Israel—are no longer "aliens from the commonwealth of Israel" or "strangers from the covenants of promise." But rather, "fellow citizens with the saints and members of the house of God." Moreover, in Christ, Gentile believers have been forged together with believers from Israel into "one new man." This "one new man" or "one body" is the church, "built on the foundation of the apostles and prophets, Jesus Christ being the chief cornerstone . . ."

A second promise given in the new covenant is, "No more shall every man teach his neighbor, and every man his brother, saying, 'Know the Lord,' for they all shall know Me, from the least of them to the greatest of them." This promise is given as the result of the other two promises, which is, the universal knowledge of God. This then will be the climax of the new covenant. The Bible often commands believers to teach one another to "know the Lord" (Deuteronomy 6:19; Colossians 3:16). But Jeremiah promised a day when such teaching would no longer be necessary because everyone—from the youngest babe to the oldest saint—would know God. Here the word "know" carries its most profound connotation, the intimate personal knowledge which arises between two persons who share a relationship that touches their most inner being. The promise of the end of evangelization is especially for the new heaven and new earth. There will be no revival meetings in the age to come. No one will stand on the corner and pass out tracks. No one will knock on your door and ask, "If you were to die tonight, what would you say to God when He asks, 'Why should I let you into My heaven?'" There will be no evangelism because there will be no need. One day, with Christ ruling the nations (Psalm 2), everyone will know God, "from the least to the greatest."

The third and final promise, and one that is crucial for this study, is, "I will put My law in their minds, and write it on their hearts." The prophet Ezekiel foresaw a day that God would do a supernatural work in the hearts of His people:

> *I will sprinkle clean water on you, and you shall be clean from all your uncleanness, and from all your Idols I will cleanse you. And I will give you a new heart, and a new spirit will I put within you. And I will remove the heart of stone from your flesh and give you a heart of flesh. And I will put my Spirit within you, and cause you*

to walk in my statutes and be careful to obey my rules. (Ezekiel 36:25–27)

Israel's hardness of heart had caused a great chasm between them and God (Isaiah 59:2; Jeremiah 6:8; Ezekiel 14:4–7). Their carnal nature had made it impossible for them to walk in obedience to God's will. But God would intervene with what was necessary to enable them to "walk in My statutes and be careful to obey My rules." Namely, God would remove their "heart of stone" and replace it with a "heart of flesh."

It is this new heart that is being referred to in Jeremiah 31 when God promises to write His law "on their hearts." Under the old covenant God demanded obedience, but never offered any help to those who were under it. Under the new covenant, however, God would enable believers to do what they otherwise could not do: obey the moral law. God would give us His Spirit to radically transform us into the image of Christ. In other words, He would empower us to be like Jesus. Notice how Paul contrasts the old covenant with that of the new covenant in 2 Corinthians 3. (1) He states the letter (old covenant) kills, but the Spirit (under the new covenant) gives life (v. 6). (2) He calls the old covenant the "ministry of condemnation," whereas the new covenant is called the "ministry of righteousness." (3) The ministry of the old covenant is said to be "passing away," but the ministry of the new covenant "remains" (v. 11). (4) The glory of God under the old covenant was concealed and could not be approached (v. 7). But under the new covenant, not only is God's glory being revealed, we as believers are being transformed into the same image of glory (vv. 12–18), which is the image of Christ (cf. John 1:14; Hebrews 1:3; see also Romans 8:28–30). So then, even though the Mosaic covenant is no longer in force, God's moral law "remains." And the Holy Spirit is at work in the lives of all believers to produce in us obedience to His will.

To summarize, Jesus did not come to exempt us from obedience to God's moral law, but rather to restore in us a "new heart" so that we would obey it. Not under bondage, but in liberty. Not only as a mandate, but out of a true desire of the heart to do the will of God. This He did, first, by taking upon Himself the condemnation of all who have broken God's law (Romans 8:3). Jesus's perfect life and death on the cross satisfied the laws' demand and the legal repercussion for our disobedience. He, the innocent, was condemned so we, the guilty, could go free (2 Corinthians 5:21). Secondly, Jesus sent His Spirit to enable us to "walk in newness of life" (Romans 8:4; cf. Romans 6:1–14). To remove in us the "old man" that we may "put on the new man" (Ephesians 4:22–24). Thus, Jesus's words ring true, "I did not come to destroy [the law], but to fulfill [the law]." The law under the old covenant was designed to drive us to Jesus (Galatians 3:24) so that Jesus, through the work of the Spirit in our heart, could enable us to fulfill the mandates of God's holy law. Thus, God's grace, said so eloquently by the great apostle, does not make void the law of God, but rather "establishes it" (Romans 3:31).

In conclusion, two hermeneutical methods pertaining to the roll of the Old Testament law for the believer that are most commonly proposed are: (1) all the Old Testament laws apply except what the New Testament repeals (Covenant Theology), and (2) none of the Old Testament laws apply except what the New Testament repeats (Classical Dispensationalism). The former, however, would logically lead to prohibitions against most modern farming practices and clothing fashions (Deuteronomy 22:9–12), while the latter would logically lead to the acceptance of sorcerers and mediums (despite Deuteronomy 18:9–13). For in neither case does the New Testament say anything one way or the other about these specific practices. Instead, we suggest that a clear distinction be made between that of the law enforced by the Mosaic covenant, which is made "obsolete" (Hebrews 8:13), and the moral law which is found both in and outside of the Mosaic covenant, and which is eternally binding. It is the moral law that all other laws find their goal; and it is the moral law that has as its aim, and is precisely fulfilled, in loving God and loving one another (Matthew 22:36–40; Romans 13:8).

8

POETRY

After narratives, poetry is the most common literary form in our Bible. Virtually every biblical book, even those not typically called "poetical," contains some form of poetry. While poetry is usually listed along with the other major genres of Scripture, to be technical, poetry is not actually a genre, but a literary form—the alternative to prose. To know the difference, literary form has to do with the structure of any writing—how it is constructed and organized. A "genre," on the other hand, represents a specific style or category of artistic composition. Genres make use of the various literary forms as a foundation from which to build its meaning through artistic expression. So in order to study biblical poetry, we will have to survey the major literary types (or genres) of poetry that are used throughout the Old Testament (and sometimes the New Testament).

Unlike the Western poetry with which we are most familiar, poetry in the Old Testament rarely makes use of rhyme, alliteration, or meter (although these do occur from time to time—for example, all four lines of Isaiah 33:22 end with the same sound in Hebrew), but more commonly uses what is called parallelism. Parallelism occurs where two or more symmetrical lines of similar grammatical structure deal with the same subject matter. The second line usually provides more detail or an alternative depiction than the first line, either by addition, contrast, or specification. So then, when interpreting an Old Testament poetic text, it is often useful to consider how the second (or third) line adds to or advances the first. The fact that lines are at least partly reiterative often helps the reader clarify the meaning of cryptic lines. As an example, the meaning of "But I am like a green olive tree in the house of God . . ." (Psalm 52:8) can be understood as God's loving care and protection for David at least in some way, because the next line is parallel: "I trust in the steadfast love of God forever and ever." Fortunately, identifying poetry in the Bible has become much easier with the help of most modern translations, which set out poetic sections in strophic format so readers can easily see the poetic lines.

Although parallelism is the chief characteristic of biblical poetry, it has other features that distinguish it from the typical prose or narrative we find in the rest of Scripture. First, there is a relatively greater conciseness or terseness of form, and second, there is a greater use of certain types of rhetorical devices such as imagery and figures of speech. Some of these are as follows:

1. **Simile**: This is the simplest of all the figures of speech. A simile is a direct comparison (using the key terms "like" or "as") between two things that resemble each other in some way (cf. Psalm 1:3–4; 5:12; 17:8; 131:2; Hosea 13:7–8).

2. **Metaphor**: This is a comparison in which one thing is likened to another without the use of comparison terms "like" or "as." In Psalm 23:1, David says, "The Lord is my Shepherd"; that is, He is to me like a shepherd is to his sheep (see also 84:11; 91:4).

3. **Implication**: This occurs when there is only an implied comparison between two things in which the name of one thing is used in place of the other (cf. Psalm 22:16; Jeremiah 4:7).

4. **Hyperbole**: Probably the figure of speech that is most frequently overlooked, hyperbole is the use of exaggeration or overstatement to stress a point (Psalm 6:6; 78:27; 107:26; Job 37:1).

5. **Idiom**: This is an expression whose meaning is not predictable from the usual meanings of its constituent elements. An example of this is the phrase "drop from a bucket" in Isaiah 40:15, which, of course, is a figure of speech that implies insignificance.

6. **Paronomasia**: This refers to the use or repetition of words that are similar in sound, but not necessarily in meaning, in order to achieve a certain effect. This can only be observed by those who can read the original Hebrew text. Psalm 96:5 reads, "For all the gods (*elohim*) of the nations are idols (*elilim*). This latter word means nothings, or things of naught; so that we might render it, "The gods of the nations are imaginations" (see also Psalm 22:16; Proverbs 6:23).

7. **Pleonasm**: This involves the use of redundancy for the sake of emphasis. This may occur with the use of words or sentences. In Psalm 8:4 David asks, "What is man that You are mindful of him, and the son of man that You visit him?" Here the second line appears to be redundant, stating essentially the same meaning in the second clause as the first.

8. **Rhetorical Question**: The use of a question to confirm or deny a fact (Psalm 35:10; 56:8; 106:2).

9. **Metonymy**: This occurs where one noun is used in place of another because of some relationship or type of resemblance that different objects might bear to one another (Psalms 5:9; 18:2; 57:9; 73:9)

10. **Anthropomorphism**: The assigning of some part of the human anatomy (eyes, ears, etc.) to God's Person in order to describe some characteristic of God in human terms (cf. Psalms 10:11, 14; 11:4; 18:15; 31:2).

11. **Zoomorphism**: The assigning of some part of an animal to God's Person to convey certain attributes or truths about God (cf. Psalms 17:8; 91:4).

Biblical poetry can be placed into three major genres: (1) lyric poetry, which was originally accompanied by music (most recognizably the Psalms); (2) didactic poetry, which, using maxims, was designed to communicate basic principles for life (i.e., Proverbs, Ecclesiastes); and (3) dramatic poetry, which used dialogue to communicate its message (i.e., Job, Song of Solomon). While biblical poetry occurs in some of the historical material (e.g., Exodus 15; Judges 5), as well as the prophetic books (which is mostly poetry), it is more commonly and consistently represented by the worship (the Psalms) and wisdom literature (Proverbs, Ecclesiastes, Song of Solomon, and Job) of Scripture. For the purpose of this study, we will divide biblical poetry into these two types (worship and wisdom literature), and offer helpful suggestions for their interpretation.

Worship Literature

The book of Psalms was the hymnal of ancient Israel. Psalms were sung, and singing was intrinsic to worship (note how the heading of many of the Psalms will specify the tune that was used: *Maschil*, *Neginoth*, etc.). There are several different types of psalms, which have typically been categorized as follows: laments, thanksgiving psalms, psalms of praise, royal psalms, wisdom psalms, and psalms of trust. Though these categories may overlap somewhat or have subcategories, they serve well to classify the psalms and thus to guide the reader toward making good use of them.

Laments. Laments constitute the largest group of psalms in the Psalter. There are more than sixty (the actual number is debated among scholars since a few of these psalms fit equally in other categories), including individual laments (3–7; 10; 12; 13; 22; 28; 31; 35; 39; 42; 57; 64; 71; 88; 102; 108; 120; 140–143) and corporate laments (44; 60; 74; 79; 80; 85; 90; 94; 137). Both types of laments (individual and corporate), while explicitly expressing or presupposing deep trust in Jehovah-God, express struggles, suffering, or disappointment to the Lord. The defining elements that these psalms share in common are the following: (1) There is a solicitous complaint: the psalmist pours out an urgent and pressing complaint unto the Lord, identifying the trouble he is in (or they are in), and why the Lord's help is being sought. (2) There is a declaration of trust: the psalmist, sometimes before and sometimes after the complaint, expresses his trust in God. (This declaration serves as the presuppositional basis for his complaint, for what need is there to voice a complaint to God if you do not trust Him?) (3) There is a cry for help: the psalmist cries out to God for deliverance from the situation described in the complaint. (4) There is an affirmation of assurance: the psalmist expresses the assurance that God will hear his/ their cry and deliver him/them.

The importance of these psalms is twofold: First, they reveal to us, in very raw terms, the reality of a world that is filled with chaos and trouble. Why is this important? It serves as a model for our own particular struggles so that when we hurt, when we feel abandoned or discouraged in some way, we are given permission to come before the Lord with these thoughts and feelings and petition God for help. And these psalms help us voice our struggles through the carefully voiced and inspired complaints of the psalmists. Secondly, they give the reader confidence that God hears His people when they cry out to Him, and that we, as did the psalmists, have every reason to trust Him in times of difficulty.

The fact that some of the lament psalms direct curses toward those who wished the psalmist harm (sometimes categorized as imprecatory psalms) creates a tension for the modern reader. It is necessary, therefore, to offer a few words of clarification on this issue. There are about eighteen psalms with such curses, including 5; 10; 27; 31; 40; 83; 88; 137; and 140. But the three psalms that have the curses in their strongest form are Psalms 3; 69 and 109. At first glance it looks as if these imprecations reflect the psalmist's personal vengeance. One would then have to conclude that the Bible is recording what they said but not holding that up as a model for praying, since vengeance is elsewhere condemned in Scripture (Leviticus 19:18; Matthew 4:43–44). Furthermore, Paul, in Romans 12:19, forbade this very sin of a revengeful spirit by means of two quotations from the Old Testament (Deuteronomy 32:35 and Proverbs 25:21–22). The psalmist surely knew of such teachings. In fact, in some of the psalms with imprecations, the writer protests the kind feelings he had for those who were persecuting him (cf. 109:4, 5).

When reading these psalms, then, the first thing to be kept in mind is that these prayers to God are written in lyrical poetry, and thus figures of speech, such as hyperbole, are frequently used in the psalms. In the mentality of the psalmists, especially when suffering, feelings were often expressed extravagantly. Secondly, these imprecations are the expression of the longing of the Old Testament believer for the vindication of God's righteousness. Their faith in God's goodness and righteousness was put to the test by malicious wickedness, and so they were left longing for vindication. Moreover, the imprecations made it clear that the wicked deserved their curse. Even in the New Testament we have the cry of the Lord to avenge the blood of His people (Revelation 6:10).

Finally, these imprecations form prophetic teachings about God's future dealing with sin and impenitent and persistent sinners. Of all the psalms that Jesus applied to Himself, Psalms 69 and 109 appear frequently. David was a prophet; the psalms were inspired. And so there is nothing in these imprecations that is out of harmony with God's intent for the wicked. They are not, then, simply statements of that which the psalmists wish God to do, but of that which God has done or certainly will do. There are no imprecations that lay upon the wicked anything more terrible than that which is laid up for them if they persist in wickedness and rebellion. In short, imprecations address the age-old conflict of good and evil that will end in the triumph of righteousness. And living in an evil and cursed world, the psalmists wanted to make it absolutely clear where their loyalties lay.

Thanksgiving Psalms. These psalms, as the name suggests, conveyed circumstances very opposite from that of the laments. Such psalms expressed thankfulness to the Lord because times were good, or because something good had happened and the psalmist, therefore, had reason to render thanks to God for His faithfulness, protection, and/or blessings. Furthermore, these psalms often expressed appreciation for past mercies and gratitude for what God had already done. The thanksgiving psalms remind the reader of his own need to express thoughts and feelings of gratitude to God for the many blessings in his own life, and thus they serve as powerful aids for our own individual, as well as corporate, worship. In all, there are six community psalms of thanksgiving (65; 67; 75; 107; 124; 136) and ten individual psalms of thanksgiving (18; 30; 32; 34; 40; 66; 92; 116; 118; 138) in the Psalter.

Psalms of Praise. These psalms center on the praise of God for who He is (unlike the thanksgiving psalms that focused more particularly on something God had done) and for His greatness and His beneficence toward His own people, as well as the whole earth. God may be praised as creator of the universe (as in Psalms 8; 19; 104; and 148), as the Lord of history (as in Psalms 33; 103; 113; 117; and 145–147), or as the protector and benefactor of Israel (as in Psalms 66; 100; 111; 114; and 149). These psalms magnify God as the One who alone deserves our praise. In either individual or group worship, they help us "sing praises to our God," something that is truly "good," "pleasant," and "beautiful" (Psalm 147:1).

Royal Psalms. A number of psalms focus on the Davidic king who rules the nation of Israel as God's appointed ruler (2; 18; 20; 21; 45; 72; 89; 101; 110; 144). Scholars designate these psalms as royal psalms. Royal psalms remember and reflect on God's covenant promises to David (see 2 Samuel 7:12–16). In these psalms, the Davidic king is referred to as "the anointed one" (Hebrew *mashiach*; see 2:2), which is a clue to the proper identification of these types of psalms. The language of the royal psalms helps us to determine the original use of most of these psalms. For example, some of these psalms were used during the time of coronation (such as 2, 21, 72, 101, and 110). Psalm 72 contains the prayer of the nation on behalf of the king on the day of coronation. Psalm 101 is an oath taken by the king on the day of his coronation to faithfully carry out the duties as God's appointed ruler over His people. Psalm 110 is for the most part in the form of God's speech to the king on the day of coronation. The early Christian church interpreted the royal psalms in light of the kingly ministry and lordship of Jesus (see Matthew 22:44; Acts 2:34; 1 Corinthians 15:25; Ephesians 1:20; Hebrews 1:5, 8, 13; 5:5). These psalms have thus become for the church "messianic psalms" because the church found in these psalms the Old Testament portrait of Jesus the Messiah.

Wisdom Psalms. These psalms, nine in total (1; 36; 37; 49; 73; 112; 127; 128; 133), like the Proverbs, have a didactic nature and emphasize the Torah as fundamental for blessing. According to Ross, wisdom psalms consistently include four major motifs:[1]

1. *The fear of the LORD and the veneration of Torah.* The wise knew that the fear of the Lord was the beginning of knowledge, and that fear was gained from the Torah. Thus, wisdom psalms (as with all wisdom literature) place a heavy emphasis on the Torah and the subordination of the wise to the divine will.

2. *The contrasting lifestyles of the righteous and the wicked.* The righteous and the wicked figure predominantly in the Bible. The wicked live a godless life of self-indulgence; this is the fool and the sinner. The righteous live untarnished, prosperous lives in compliance with the fear of the Lord. Wisdom psalms often contrast features of these two lifestyles; see Psalm 1 for the clearest example, but also Psalm 37.

3. *The reality and inevitability of retribution.* The problem that all wisdom literature grapples with is that of injustice in this life. How is it that the righteous one who lives in the fear and obedience of the Lord often suffers while the wicked prosper? Wisdom finds

a solution for this tension with an understanding of retribution (cf. Psalm 73) either in this life or beyond. The contrasting fate of the pious and impious appears clearly in wisdom psalms such as Psalm 49 and Psalm 1. The presence of it in Psalm 73 has caused many to classify that psalm as wisdom as well.

4. *Miscellaneous counsels pertaining to everyday conduct.* Wisdom text give basic, practical advice: use gracious and honest speech (Psalm 36:3), cease from anger (Psalm 37:8); be mindful of the company kept (Psalm 1); live in harmony (Psalm 133), integrity (Psalm 112), and generosity (Psalm 112); trust in the Lord and not your own understanding (Psalm 112); shun evil and do good (Psalm 1).

Due to the distinctive features of psalmic wisdom, these psalms may be read profitably along with the book of Proverbs. In fact, Proverbs 8 is itself a psalm, praising, as these psalms do, the merits of wisdom and the wise life.[2]

Psalms of Trust. Psalms of trust (11; 16; 23; 27; 62; 63; 91; 121; 125; 131) center their attention on the fact that God can be trusted and that, even in times of despair, His goodness and care for His people ought to be expressed. God delights in knowing that His people trust Him with their lives, and to provide for them what He has promised. These psalms help us express our trust in God, no matter our circumstances.

These categories represent the major genres that characterize the Psalms. It should be noted, however, that not all agree as to the classification of every individual psalm, and some lists will include other categories (such as liturgical psalms, enthronement psalms, and Zion or pilgrim psalms) while other lists will appear much shorter. For those who wish to further explore the different categories of the psalms and to understand the characteristics that determine how psalms are categorized, we recommend Alan P. Ross, *A Commentary on the Psalms* (three volumes). Along with providing exegetical commentary on all 150 psalms, these books contain additional information of how the psalms functioned in ancient Israel, and also make further suggestions for the way they might function in the lives of believers today.

Basic Benefits of the Psalms. By recognizing how the Psalms were used by ancient Israel (as well as the New Testament church), we discover at least three important ways in which Christians should make use of them today. First, the Psalms, as worship literature, serve as both aids and guidelines for our own worship. By this we mean that the worshipper who seeks to praise and honor God can use the Psalms as a formal means for expressing their own desire to magnify and glorify Him, or for voicing thanksgiving to the Lord for His love and protection in their own individual lives. "A psalm is a carefully composed literary preservation of words designed to be spoken."[3] Psalms that express praise and thanksgiving to the Lord help us to express the same in spite of our own inability at times to find the words that are most fitting.

Secondly, the Psalms help us, by example, to be honest and open before God in expressing disappointment, anger, or other emotions. In expressing these types of emotion, the reader is encouraged that God concerns Himself with and makes provision for our help. Third, the Psalms demonstrate the importance of reflection and meditation on the things that God has done, and is doing, for us. They invite us to prayer and to center our thinking on God's Word (which is what meditation is). Such things help shape in us a life of obedience and charity. "The Psalms, like no other literature, lift us to a position where we can communicate with God, capturing a sense of the greatness of His Kingdom and a sense of what living with Him for eternity will be like. Even in our darkest moments, when life has become so painful as to seem unfair and unendurable, God is with us. 'Out of the depths' (Psalm 130:1), we wait and watch for the Lord's deliverance, knowing we can trust Him in spite of our feelings. To cry to God for help is not a judgement on His faithfulness, but an affirmation of it."[4]

Principles for Interpreting the Psalms. From this general overview of the Psalms, we can suggest the following interpretative principles:

1. Psalms should be read as lyric poetry—skillfully crafted with words that are meant to incite images in our mind and are often intended to evoke an emotive response. Thus, we should be mindful of their frequent use of figurative speech and interpret verses such as Psalm 6:6 ("I am weary with my groaning; All night I make my bed swim; I drench my couch with my tears") as hyperbole (language exaggerated for effect) rather than literally.

2. Psalms originated as complete units, and thus the student should interpret them in their entirety rather than as isolated verses. Furthermore, psalms originated independent of each other, and thus each psalm serves as its own literary context for its interpretation. On the other hand, we may use psalms of the same genre as a means of comparison since they share a common literary form and purpose. But in so doing we must treat them as representatives of a common literary type with a shared background, not as literature composed by the same person or with the same set of circumstances in mind.

3. If a psalm implies the presence of several speakers (notice the use of pronouns: "I," "we," "you," etc.), our interpretation must incorporate that fact together with knowledge of its underlying setting. In other words, we must interpret communal psalms as the petitions or praises of Israel as a nation, not those of an individual Israelite.

4. Application must conform to the situation behind each genre. In other words, apply corporate texts to Christian community and individual texts to the Christian individual. Corporate psalms of praise, then, are best used in corporate worship. Of course, it is permissible to appropriate principles and lessons that may generally

apply to either one, but we must never lose sight of the distinctive purpose for the psalm.

5. The New Testament lays the foundation for the Christian belief that Christ is the new David who fulfills the latter's kingship. Thus, we may rightfully apply the royal psalms typologically to the kingly role that the New Testament gives to Jesus as Lord. The Old Testament kings pictured and anticipated the reign of their greatest descendant. However, we must be careful not to apply principles of leadership from the royal psalms inappropriately to church leaders today. While certain principles may overlap, it is crucial that principles of pastoral leadership be developed by the texts that relate specifically to the church, not a kingdom.

Wisdom Literature

Our previous discussion of the wisdom psalms introduced the interpreter to several components of wisdom literature. Here we survey the major genres of the Old Testament wisdom literature, the larger categories that include the books of Proverbs, Ecclesiastes, Job, and Song of Solomon. Not everything in these books, except for the book of Proverbs, is, strictly speaking, concerned with wisdom. But in general, they contain the type of material that is most consistent with that which bears the wisdom label. Old Testament wisdom offers sharply different perspectives on life—for example, the author of Ecclesiastes believes that everything under the sun that can be known is fruitless, whereas the authors of Proverbs stress the importance of wisdom as a path for the straight and narrow, looking to the commandments as guideposts for people's lives—and one glimpses the full spectrum of biblical wisdom only by reckoning with its several perspectives. Finally, its literary nature also requires readers to apply principles for interpreting both poetry and narratives (treated earlier; i.e., Job). To understand it one must carefully capture the dynamics of its parallelism, the meaning of its metaphors, and its subtle use of drama, characterization,

and plot. As Altar rightly warns, the subtle literary craft of wisdom literature ensures that "if we are not good readers, we will not get the point of
the sayings of the wise."[5]

Proverbs. Probably the best-known form of wisdom literature is the
proverb: a short, pithy statement of truth learned over extended human
experience.[6] Imagine, for example, all the many occasions, over many years,
that produced this proverb: "A man of quick temper acts foolishly, and a
man of evil devices is hated" (Proverbs 14:17). Grammatically, a proverb
occurs in the indicative mood and thus makes a simple declaration about
life as it is.

Among the Proverbs, interpreters will find great variety in form and
content. There are *descriptive proverbs*, for example, which state a simple
observation about life without any notion of expectation or further applications: "One gives freely, yet grows all the richer; another withholds what
he should give, and only suffers want" (Proverbs 11:24). On the other hand,
a *perspective proverb* does more than observe something significant about
life. It states its truth with a specific aim to influence human behavior. For
example, Proverbs 14:31 is clearly intended to incite a certain response of
obedience when it says, "Whoever oppresses a poor man insults his Maker,
but he who is generous to the needy honors Him." Furthermore, a specific promise of benefit, often by God's intervention, is frequently a component of perspective proverbs, as in, "Whoever is generous to the poor
lends to the Lord, and He will repay him for his deed" (Proverbs 19:17).
It is the promise that is being extended that subtly appeals for the readers' obedience, and that, likewise, distinguishes perspective proverbs from
their descriptive counterpart (cf. Proverbs 19:17). Some proverbs make
their point by using comparisons (commonly called *antithetical proverbs*):
"Better is a dinner of herbs where love is than a fatted ox and hatred with
it" (Proverbs 15:17). Such comparisons seek to underscore the superiority
of certain character traits of personal conduct over others (in the example
above, love in the home is being presented as far more important than that
of material wealth). It is this type of proverb that dominates the section of

proverbs found in chapters 10–15. Since antithesis is the key to this form, proper interpretation requires the reader to focus on the contrast that is being presented. One must isolate the two traits or types of people that the proverb sets side by side and then decide which of the two opposites is the proverb commending and why. For instance, note the following examples:

Whoever guards his mouth preserves his life; he who opens wide his lips comes to ruin. (Proverbs 13:3)

The simple believes everything, but the prudent gives thought to his steps. (Proverbs 14:15)

A hot-tempered man stirs up strife, but he who is slow to anger quiets contention. (Proverbs 15:18)

The first example compares those who practice constraint with their choice of words with those who use unfiltered speech. The emphasis here, of course, is that the one who holds his tongue retains his life. The tongue's powerful potential for self-inflicted ruin is a frequent part of these proverbs. The second example contrasts the naivete of the simpleton (one who is easily persuaded) against the prudent person who wisely considers his choices; and the third example, the quick-tempered man with the patient one. The meaning of this last proverb is fairly simple: ill-tempered people cause dissension, while patient people bring calmness.

Other proverbs, however, use a numbering formula—"there are x amount and one more"—to drive home its point. For example,

Three things that are too wonderful for me; four I do not understand: the way of an eagle in the sky, the way of a serpent on a rock, the way of a ship on the high seas, and the way of a man with a virgin. (Proverbs 30:18–19)

In this case, "X" is three and the "one more" is four. The first clause introduces the subject—things too wonderful to understand—while the subsequent list enumerates four examples. The greatest emphasis, however—the truly amazing thing—falls on the last item ("the way of a man with a virgin"). The previous ones merely serve to heighten the wonder, and in some proverbs, the disgust of the final point. In such cases, proper interpretation should focus not on the list as a whole but on the final element of how it differs from or even surpasses the others.

Proverbs also provide general instruction. *Instruction proverbs* are usually a brief exhortation presented in the form of a prohibition ("do not"), as in Proverbs 3:30: "Do not contend with a man for no reason, when he has done you no harm." Sometimes these prohibitions are supported by a motive clause ("for" or "because"): "Do not rob the poor, because he is poor, or crush the afflicted at the gate, for the Lord will plead their cause and rob of life those who rob them" (Proverbs 22:22–23, directly prohibiting what 14:31 implies; cf. 16:3 and 20). As this example illustrates, the purpose of instruction proverbs is to persuade the hearer to adopt or abandon a certain conduct or attitude. The frequent motive clauses (e.g., "for the Lord will plead their cause") give the reasons for compliance, making the teaching all the more persuasive.

On the other hand, instruction proverbs may be connected together to form longer units. For example, at the heart of Proverbs is the series of lengthy instructions in which the wisdom teacher urges his child(ren) to follow the way of wisdom (e.g., 1:8; 2:1; 4:1; 7:1; etc.). Another example of the longer form of instruction proverbs is found in the lengthy sections that personify wisdom as a woman who openly proclaims her message in the streets, the marketplace, and the public square as an invitation for all to know her (1:20-33; 9:1-6; cf. 13–17).

Finally, proverbs often use *synonymous parallelism*. Again, the dominant characteristic of poetry in the Old Testament is Hebrew parallelism in which one line corresponds with the other in some way. In synonymous parallelism, the second line of the proverb repeats the idea of the first line without making any significant addition or subtraction. An example is

Proverbs 11:25: "Whoever brings blessing will be enriched, and one who waters will himself be watered." The idea being conveyed in both lines are the same, only put in different terms: to him who gives, it will be given. As Osborne notes, "The interpreter in some instances should not read too much into the semantic variation between the two lines, for that could be intended more as a stylistic change for effect."[7] In other words, the student of Proverbs should guard against the common error of seeing anything more than a subtle difference in meaning between two lines being used synonymously. In addition, when the interpreter encounters synonymous parallelism and comes to an obscure Hebrew word whose definition is unclear, comparing it to its synonymous counterpart will usually shed light on its meaning.

Principles for Interpreting Proverbs. Here we encapsulate summary guidelines for interpreting and applying the Proverbs properly:

1. *Proverbs teach probable truth, not absolute truth.* Proverbs point out patterns of conduct that, if followed, give us the best chance for certain outcomes—they do not guarantee a certain outcome. In other words, they offer general principles for successful living rather than legal guarantees for a successful life. Consider these two examples:

   Be not one of those who give pledges, who put up security for debts. If you have nothing with which to pay, why should your bed be taken from under you? (Proverbs 22:26–27)

   Train up a child in the way he should go; even when he is old he will not depart from it. (Proverbs 22:6)

   . If you were to take the extreme approach in considering the first of these two proverbs as an all-encompassing command from the Lord, you might not buy a house in order to avoid incurring a mortgage (a secured debt). Or you might take this proverb as a guarantee that if you default on any payment due (such as a credit card), you will eventually lose all your possessions—even your bed. Such a literalistic interpretation misses the point of the proverb, however, which states in poetical and figurative language that debts should been taken on with extreme caution, because they, if not settled, may result in painful and serious consequences. The second example, to the dismay of many Christian parents, does not guarantee that if we raise our children as godly parents (training our children with biblical principles), they will themselves behave godly. In fact, personal examples abound that seem to contradict an interpretation that views this proverb as a promise or guarantee. This is because the ancient proverb was never designed to be an absolute guarantee of what will always be true, in every case, without exception, but rather an accurate observation of the basic principles for a secure and calm life.

2. *Proverbs are worded to be memorable, not to be theoretically accurate.* No proverb is worded so perfectly that it could stand up to the unreasonable expectation that it apply in every situation at all times.[8] Rather, the primary goal of proverbs is to state an important, simple truth about life in an easy-to-remember way. Consider this example: "In all toil there is profit, but mere talk tends only to poverty" (Proverbs 14:23). This proverb teaches that success always hinges on hard work, not on idle chatter. But this general principle does not intend to take into consideration other factors that might hinder success (economic recession, personal tragedies, or any other unfortunate circumstances) despite one's best effort. Thus, to interpret proverbs properly, we must consider that proverbs try to impart general principles that can be retained, not to give statements of truth that will apply to every individual case.

3. *Proverbs must be read in balance with other proverbs, and with the rest of Scripture.* An individual proverb, if read in isolation, may lead you to adopt attitudes and behaviors that would otherwise

be tempered if you read proverbs as a whole. The overall structure of Proverbs reflects that it is a collection of collections of wisdom material. There are seven sections in Proverbs that have their own unique introduction. These introductory headings are found at 1:1; 10:1; 22:17; 24:23; 25:1; 30:1; and 31:1. These various headings reflect that there were initially seven different collections of proverbial material that was eventually collected into one book (the book of Proverbs). In light of this structural arrangement, it would appear that each individual passage or proverb should be interpreted in light of the section in which it is found. After this, we would then want to consider how the passage fits into the book of Proverbs as a whole. For this purpose, it is best to study proverbs either topically (e.g., family relations, business dealings, caring for the poor, etc.) or by character studies (e.g., the fool, the prudent, the scoffer, etc.). Moreover, we must guard against overly emphasizing the practical matters for accumulating wealth, frequently discussed throughout Proverbs, over the warnings of materialism and worldliness found throughout the rest of Scripture. By failing to balance proverbs against one another and with the rest of Scripture, many interpreters, sometimes with good intention, have done for themselves and others much injustice.

4. *Proverbs must be interpreted according to their historical backdrop.* In order to understand many of the proverbs, we must interpret and apply them in light of their historical meaning and significance. While many proverbs are straightforward, others will express their truths in accordance with practices and institutions that no longer exist, although they were common to the Old Testament Israelites. Unless we think of them in terms of their modern equivalents (practices and institutions that exist today), their meaning may seem irrelevant, or lost altogether. Consider Proverbs 25:24: "It is better to live in a corner of the housetop than in a house shared with a quarrelsome wife." Many readers of this proverb

unfortunately view our modern pitched-roof houses when trying to understand this proverb. Yet the writer had a very different rooftop in mind (a flat-rooftop), where lodging was not only possible but common (cf. Matthew 24:17). Its meaning is not too difficult to discern if we make the necessary "translation" from that culture to ours. We could even reword it this way: "It is better to live in the tiny basement of a house than in a spacious home with a cantankerous wife." The proverb is not intended to teach where one should dwell during marriage difficulties. It is intended to advise the reader toward carefully selecting their lifelong spouse.

Reflection. At the polar opposite of the practical wisdom of Proverbs sits the speculative, reflective wisdom of Ecclesiastes. In a reflection, a somewhat autobiographical genre, a writer reports personal musings and conclusions about a truth, often citing firsthand observations, example stories, and lengthy thoughts. Though often loosely organized, reflections have the following structural features: (1) opening statements such as "I saw and considered" or "I passed by"; (2) the quotation of a proverb, use of rhetorical questions, or the use of an example story; and (3) a concluding moral. Proverbs 24:30–34, in a less cynical tone than its Ecclesiastes counterpart, represent the reflective genre quite well:

Opening:	I went by the field of the lazy man, and by the vineyard of the man devoid of under-standing; and there it was, all overgrown with thorns; its surface was covered with nettles; its stone wall was broken down.
Example Story:	When I saw it, I considered it well; I looked on it and received instruction: A little sleep, a little slumber, a little folding of the hands to rest; so shall your poverty
The Moral:	come like a prowler, and your need like an armed man.

The reflection genre dominates the book of Ecclesiastes, though with less obvious structure than the above example. Section after section begins with the formal statement "I saw," or "I have seen" (e.g., 1:14; 3:16; 4:1; 5:13; 6:1). Then, through a mixture of poetic musings, example stories, and proverbial quotations, the writer wrestles with the futility of life. Finally, at intervals, the writer (who refers to himself as *Qohelet*, traditionally taken to be a nickname for Solomon) draws the morals from his observations (e.g., 2:24–25; 3:22; 5:18–20). The book's literary tone is sobering and vulnerably honest—a tone that readily draws readers into its world of raw emotion and candid commentary—relatable to all generations. Yet, at the same time, its despairing undertone has puzzled many would-be interpreters, especially those who have read it with a careful eye. There is good reason for this, because Ecclesiastes is a very difficult book to understand, with several passages that seem self-contradictory and others that seem to contradict Scripture as a whole. This confusion has led to polar-opposite interpreta-tions, along with various interpretations that fall somewhere in between. It is important for Bible students, therefore, in approaching Ecclesiastes to have an overall strategy for reading it. And whatever else, it is import-ant here—as with Proverbs—that you not take phrases and passages out of their context and give them a meaning that goes beyond the author's purpose. Furthermore, we should be mindful of the nature of speculative wisdom, which is not so much trying to provide answers as it is to remind its readers of the hard questions—one that ultimately points us to a hope outside of what this world can offer!

Principles for Interpreting Reflection. The key to interpreting reflection is to determine how each structural component supports the concluding moral. For example, the reflection found in Ecclesiastes 4:7–12 extols the value of human companionship. The example story of a rich but lonely single person (v. 8) poses the problem—how miserable it is to be alone. The following discourse (vv. 9–12) illustrates the moral—that life is better when two people share it than when one lives alone. The concluding moral merits careful attention because it expresses the writer's main point. So Ecclesiastes 4 challenges believers to cultivate intimate friendships in order to make life less miserable. For Christians, a local church provides one good opportunity for this. Ultimately, in reading reflection students should, on the one hand, fully appreciate its unique literary style and grapple with its realistic perspective and, on the other, interpret its moral conclusions in light of other biblical revelation.

Poetic Dialogue. The final two books that make up what many have deemed as the wisdom literature, namely the Song of Solomon and Job, have caused significant difficulty for those who have tried to place them into one overarching literary genre. This is especially true of Job, a magnificent work of literature that incorporates narrative, legal speech, lament, and disputation speech, all masterfully woven together in a complex literary tapestry. What is consistent in these two books is their use of dialogue, a prominent feature of Hebrew literature. In the case of Job, the dialogue is argumentative in nature, what is more commonly categorized as *disputation speech*. In a disputation a speaker seeks to persuade the audience of some perceived truth. In contrast to the many biblical examples that report only one side (i.e., most of the prophets), Job reports the arguments of both Job and his friends. These disputations specifically circulate around the suffering of Job, in which each person debates their perspective for the cause of such suffering. In the end, however, "the Lord's dramatic, irrefutable speeches (chapters 38–39; 40–41) reduce Job [and his friends] to humble acquiescence (42:1–6)."[9]

This dialogue plays an important role in challenging the mistaken assumption that personal sin is always the cause of suffering. Job's friends, holding to a rigid view of retribution, reasoned that if wisdom leads to blessing and life, and folly leads to suffering and death, then every case of suffering presupposes some prior act of personal sin. While Job rejected their assessment of his guilt, he nevertheless agreed with their premise of logic. Both the prologue (chapters 1–2) and the epilogue (42:7–17) make it clear, however, that both Job and his friends have accepted a premise that, although true in general terms, is too limited to account for all of life's many peculiarities. God's rule is far too complex to be reduced to the tidy formula of a rigid retribution. So then, Job sets forth our human limitations by probing the issues of social justice. One of the key features of the book is that the drama of the story is being presented on two stages. On one stage, Job is living on earth, first in blissful prosperity and then in devastating agony, unaware of the parallel events that are transpiring in heaven. On second stage is the unfolding of God's secret initiative for exposing the falsehood of the Accuser and proving the validity of Job's faith. Job wrestles intellectually and theologically with God's divine justice, and then he finally places his cause in the hands of God (31:35)—a clear admission that its resolution lies outside the limits of human understanding. What is more, the book reveals that God, as the sovereign ruler of the universe, is free and beyond human comprehension. In other words, the sovereign God is not a captive to a rigid law of retribution. While the practical wisdom theology of retribution accurately summarizes in general terms how God orders the world, the book of Job demonstrates that God's ways may at times transcend His normal pattern of operation; and thus we should not be so eager to place God in a box of absolutes that are not first mandated by His own revelation. This fact opens up the prospect of grace, in which God favors those who are undeserving of anything but His judgment.

Principles for Interpreting the Genre of the Book of Job:

1. Since disputation speeches dominate the book, the student should determine what "truths" are motivating each speaker's attempt at persuasion. Remember, these speeches will often mix what is fundamentally true with that which is only perceived to be true. The purpose of these dialogues is not to establish theology; it is to prepare the reader for the major themes and purpose of the book itself and to project forward the book's plot, like scenes of a narrative, to its literary climax and resolution in the ending chapters.

2. Job's avowal of innocence (chapter 31) plays a crucial role for interpreting the book. By forcibly affirming his innocence, Job denies that his own guilt has caused his suffering. Chapters 1–2 seem to confirm this claim by portraying Job's righteousness and God's recognition of it. Moreover, central to Job's argument is his plea to receive legal vindication from God. In the end God sides with Job against his accusers (42:7–9) and restores twice as much of all that he had lost (42:10–17). Thus, the student should pay careful attention to Job's self-defense and beware that the seemingly good advice of his "comforters" often reflects a position that is diametrically opposite from God's.

3. In light of the above, the student must decide from careful consideration of God's long, poetic deliberation, what His main point is and to what degree it answers Job's disputation. From Job's response (chapters 42:1–6), one must ponder whether Job is truly innocent and what the book teaches about the cause and purpose of his (and our) suffering. Consequently, we suggest that the book's lesson is that the ultimate root of some (not all) human suffering lies in the mysterious, hidden purpose of God.

4. The book's ending provides a crucial clue to the interpretation of the whole book. While God vindicates and rewards Job and

criticizes the arrogance of his friends, He otherwise addresses Job's call for God to answer him (31:35) by hurling at him a slew of rhetorical, unanswerable questions (38–39). In a sense God was saying, "I will answer you, if you can answer Me!" Instead of arguing against Yahweh, Job found his place in humble silence before His Majesty (40:1–5). Overall, the book of Job encourages believers to trust God for similar, ultimate vindication from unjust suffering, whether it comes in this life or the life that is to come.

5. As with Ecclesiastes and Proverbs, whatever main themes one concludes from Job must be understood alongside the perspectives of the other wisdom books and in light of other revelation.

As for the Song of Solomon, it features a dialogue between lovers, written in the style of an ancient Near Eastern love song (cf. Ezekiel 33:32). The book is similar to Ecclesiastes in that no divine revelation is assumed. In fact, God is not even spoken of in the third person. In content and thrust, the Song also resembles Ecclesiastes in that its interest lies in pleasure, not ethics. What is noticeably different, however, is that it reaches this point via a positive rather than a negative outlook.

One might wonder, however, how does a love song fit the category of wisdom, and why is such love poetry in the Bible at all? The answer, according to Dr. Fee and Dr. Stuart, is twofold: "First, it was associated with Solomon (1:1; 3:6–11; 8:11–12), whose name in Israel was synonymous with wisdom. But at a deeper level, it deals explicitly with a category of wisdom found in the Proverbs: the wise choice of marital and sexual fidelity."[10] God has wired our brains and designed our bodies for love and sex— a part of our humanity that God has declared "good" (Genesis 1:31). But sin, unfortunately, as with everything else, has corrupted this aspect of our lives. What was intended to be a source of joy and blessing, within the confines of a monogamous marriage, has more often than not been reduced to a means of selfish gratification and exploitation, motivated by all sorts of lusts and evil desires. But, in keeping with God's design, true intimacy and romance can be celebrated to the glory of God; and this is what Song of Songs (Solomon) seeks to accomplish.

Throughout the years the Song has been subjected to many odd interpretations. At the heart of this lay the forthright, explicit exaltation of human sexual love that is graphically presented throughout its text, causing many readers much uneasiness. Some early interpreters (both Jews and Christians alike), in order to avoid the obvious, had chosen to view its message as an allegory—either as God's "love" for Israel (a Jewish interpretation), or of Christ's "love" for the church (the Christian interpretation). In fact, an early church council (in AD 550) forbade any other interpretation, leaving a precedent that has prevailed until recent times.[11] But even a casual reading of the book makes it obvious that the Song is far from allegorical. Rather, its focus is on human love—love between a man and a woman, celebrating both this love itself and the physical attraction and desire that is shared for one another. Beyond this, the Song also presents advice and challenges from observers of the romance (1:8; 5:9), the importance of resisting the temptation to be unfaithfully attracted to anyone else (6:8–9), and the need for continually affirming their vow of faithfulness to one another, so as to reassure any insecurities (8:6–7).

Principles for Interpreting the Genre of the Song of Solomon.

Along with an appreciation and proper use of its figurative language, the key to interpreting the Song of Solomon (a work of lyric wisdom) is to appreciate its overall ethical context. Monogamous, heterosexual marriage was the proper context for sexual activity according to God's revelation in the Old Testament. The Song, therefore, extols the beauty and blessing of such a relationship under the confines of holy matrimony. Furthermore, the attitude and thrust of the Song is the very antithesis of unfaithfulness, either before or after marriage. Marriage consummates and continues love between a man and a woman. This is what the Song points toward. Furthermore, we must be aware that the Song focuses on very different values from those of our modern culture. As Dr. Gordon Fee and

Dr. Douglas Stuart have well stated, "Today's 'experts' talk about sex techniques but almost never about virtuous romance, the attraction of a man and a woman to each other that leads to lifelong marriage. Some 'experts' advocate self-indulgence; the Song emphasizes just the opposite. Our culture encourages people to fulfill themselves, whatever their sexual tastes, whereas the Song is concerned with how one person can respond faithfully to the attractiveness of another and fulfill the needs of this person. In most of the modern world, romance is thought of as something that precedes marriage. In the song, romance is something that actually characterizes marriage. Let it be so."[12]

9

PROPHECY

For many Bible readers the word "prophecy" strikes fear and trepidation. This is not only due to the highly complex and difficult nature of the genre, but also due to the endless parade of doomsday predictions concerning Jesus's return and the coming apocalypse. While many of these so called "interpretations" are unfounded (even some that are very popular), the Scriptures nevertheless point to a coming day that is categorized as worldwide calamity and martyrdom; and, as a result, many simply try to avoid the subject altogether. But like all Scripture, prophecy is "given by inspiration of God, and is profitable for doctrine, for reproof, for correction, for instruction in righteousness" (2 Timothy 3:16). Prophecy not only informs the reader of who God is (His sovereignty, power, holiness, mercy, etc.), but, in both general and specific terms, what God is doing (His predestined plan for humanity). They encourage believers regarding the future, not because they give us perfect insight into all future events, but by pointing us to our coming King and His impending victory over all the earth. Furthermore, it reminds us of our obligations and obedience to God, the consequences of our disobedience, and our immediate need for repentance. Thus, they serve an important role in biblical interpretation.

On the flip side, many Bible students have taken an overzealous, and at times obsessive, approach to biblical prophecy: a tendency to focus on prophetic fulfillment at the expense of all other Scripture. Every student must strive for a whole-Bible-concept, and this means we must study Bible prophecy with a strategic and well-balanced approach: an approach that refrains from reading into passages what is not there, that seeks to understand clearly what each prophet said or wrote and why they said or wrote what they did, and, finally, that seeks to correctly apply their messages to both contemporaneous and future times. In this introductory study we cannot hope to cover every aspect of this complex genre, but we shall endeavor to cover the basics— namely, the role of the prophets, the nature of prophecy, and the rules and methods for deciphering and applying prophetic messages.

The majority of our Old Testament books fall under the prophecy genre—divided into major (Isaiah, Jeremiah, Lamentations, Ezekiel, Daniel) and minor prophets (the final twelve books of the Old Testament)— which were written in ancient Israel between 850 BC and 430 BC. The terms "major" and "minor," a bit of a misnomer, refer to the length of the books and have nothing to do with the importance of the content inside the books. For example, if we add together all the chapters of every book in the minor prophets (67), it will equal to just one more chapter than the entire book of Isaiah (66). Perhaps, it would be best to divide these books by chronology: ninth century (Obadiah, Joel), eighth century (Hosea, Amos, Jonah, Isaiah, Micah), seventh century (Nahum, Zephaniah, Habakkuk, Jeremiah/Lamentations), exilic prophets (Daniel, Ezekiel), and post-exilic prophets (Haggai, Zechariah, Malachi). These books represent the "writing prophets," prophets whose prophetic utterance(s) had been written down and therefore became the subject matter of an entire book. Yet, prophets can be found as far back as the time of Moses, who, like Abraham, was called a prophet, but who, unlike Abraham, also spoke prophetically in Scripture (Deuteronomy 34:10). More notable are the prophets during the post-monarchical era—particularly Elijah and Elisha. In fact, it was during this era that the prophetic ministry was at its peak. The two primary reasons for this are as follows: (1) the political, military, economic, and social spheres of Israel were at this time in a terrible crisis; and (2) there was great religious upheaval, as the divided kingdom progressively turned from Yahweh and His covenant to serve other gods. "Therefore, the divine message was needed anew, and God chose the prophetic medium to force Israel to realize that He was speaking."[1]

This latter category of prophets is called the "speaking prophets"—prophets who, though important, have no official book bearing their name. So then, to understand the nature and role of the prophetic ministry, we will have to reckon both with the "writing prophets" and with the "speaking prophets" (the nature of their calling, their role as prophets, and the content and characteristics of their message, all within their historical context).

The Ministry of the Prophet

Before interpreting any prophetic passage, we must first understand how and why prophets functioned as they did. Each prophetic message is intrinsically connected to the call and role of the prophet and develops out of the social environment of his or her day. Virtually all scholars are in agreement that the prophets were primarily "forthtellers," and secondarily "foretellers." As Stein notes, "This aspect of prophecy is evident from the fact that within the Hebrew Old Testament canon, the books of Joshua through 2 Kings, which consist primarily of narrative, are called the Former Prophets. This reveals that a prophet was understood as a forthteller of the divine message, not just a foreteller of future events."[2]

For many people, the terms "prophecy" and "prediction" are understood and often used synonymously. However, "telling the future" is only one aspect of biblical prophecy. In fact, the greater part of prophetic literature has little or nothing to do with the predicting of future events (foretelling); and, more so than not, foretelling was used primarily to assist and strengthen the larger prophetic message (forthtelling). So then, the Old

Testament prophets are best understood as forthtellers, that is, as spokesmen for God who "spoke forth" God's Word as they were directed by Him to do so. Normally their messages centered around God's covenant with Israel—either to inform its strict observance (cf. Jeremiah 11:6–8) and to encourage obedience through the promise of future blessings and prosperity (cf. Amos 9:11–15), or to deliver warnings of judgment to those who had broken it (cf. Hoses 6:7; 8:1–10). "In many instances, the words of the prophets did not bring new revelation; rather, they called the people to remember and abide by the covenant God had made with them. Within the Covenant, God's people were to love and serve Him and were to express their love and service through obedience to His moral, civil, and ceremonial laws. Such obedience honored God, respected His holiness, and displayed His character to the surrounding nations."[3]

Unlike priests and kings, prophets never took their office through hereditary succession or by inheritance, but rather by divine calling. This call may come directly via a supernatural revelation, as in the case of Isaiah (6:1–13) or Jeremiah (1:2–10); it may also occur indirectly through mediation, as when Elijah passed his mantle to Elisha (2 Kings 2:11–14; see 1 Kings 19:16), signifying the transfer of his prophetic authority and power.

Often as a way of introducing their prophetic utterances, the prophets would openly declare their own awareness of God's summoning and sustaining them to deliver His message. Amos, the herdsman from Tekoa, declared that he prophesied not out of personal choice, but because God took him from the sheepfolds and inducted him into the prophetic ministry (Amos 7:14–15). Hosea, out of his tragic domestic experience, was constrained by God to proclaim the suffering love of Israel's Maker (Hosea 3:1–4). Isaiah, in a vision, heard the voice of the divine Sovereign calling for a messenger and knew that the call was meant for him (Isaiah 6). Micah's call for justice was motivated by an awareness of God's will and power over his life (Micah 1:1; 3:8). Jeremiah, a shy youth from the small Benjamite village of Anathoth, reluctantly was thrust into his role as the "weeping prophet" (Jeremiah 1:6). Ezekiel, a captive of Judah, was set as a watchman over Israel in order that he might warn them to turn from their wicked ways (Ezekiel 1–3). These men, therefore, reveal the fount of their inspiration in the accounts of how they were divinely led into the prophetic ministry. They lived constantly under the lengthened shadow of this initial experience with God.

The Nature of the Prophetic Message

Just as the whole Bible is composed of many different kinds of literary forms, so also the prophets employed a variety of literary genres in the delivery of their divinely appointed messages. Some of the more common prophetic genres are as follows:

1. *Prophetic narratives,* where a prophet reports some historical event. Usually prophetic narratives recount the prophet's personal experience of being called and commissioned as a prophet.

2. *Woe oracles,* where a prophet would pronounce imminent doom through the use of the very familiar condemnatory formula "Woe to you," followed with descriptive details of the evil practices of those who are being addressed (e.g., Isaiah 28–31).

3. *Lawsuit speech,* where a prophet speaks as if Israel is on trial. Israel is summoned to stand before God, who assumes the imaginary roles of the plaintiff, prosecuting attorney, and Judge (e.g., Amos 3–4; Jeremiah 2–3).

4. *Enactment prophecy,* where a prophet would make their point through the use of visual aids (e.g., Isaiah 20 describes how God instructed Isaiah to "walk naked and barefooted").

5. *Poetic speech,* where a prophet would deliver their message through the use of poetic devices, such as imagery, personification, hyperbole, parallelism, disputation, a hymn, and others.

6. *Prophetic dirge,* or a funeral lament, where a prophet addresses Israel as if they were a corpse ready for burial (e.g., Amos 5:1–2; Jeremiah 7:28–34).

7. *Prophetic vision report,* where a prophet reports God's message by conveying what he had seen and heard in a vision (i.e., Isaiah 6, and Ezekiel 1–3).

By making use of these literary genres (and more), the prophets faithfully, and oftentimes painfully, proclaimed, "Thus says the Lord." Sometimes their messages were positive, announcing restoration and blessing for individuals and nations. More often, however, their messages were unwelcomed, predicting disaster and judgment. Prophetic judgment, along with its positive counterpart (prophetic blessing), has essential guidelines that are necessary for properly interpreting them. First, and what is probably foremost, historical distance makes interpretation difficult, for the prophetic books use analogies and language that stem from their contemporary periods. We often fail to interpret prophecies correctly because we have not first attempted to recreate the historical background behind them. Unfortunately, prophetic books such as Obadiah, Joel, and Jonah provide no historical reference and thus a certain subjectivity becomes unavoidable in our search for background information. Nevertheless, it helps to know that the invasion of Jerusalem and involvement of the Edomites, central to Obadiah's message, could have occurred during the reign of Jehoram (853–841 BC) when the Philistines and Arabians carried away the king's son and possessions from his household (2 Chronicles 21:16–17), during the reign of Ahaz (743–715 BC) when Edom took part in a Philistine invasion (2 Chronicles 28:16–18), or during the fall of Jerusalem under Nebuchadnezzar in 586 BC (2 Chronicles 25:1–21). The first is the only one to combine an invasion of Jerusalem with Edomite involvement and therefore is more likely. While we can catch the basic sense of the text without this data, it aids our understanding greatly. The prophets addressed issues relative to their time, and their message is set against the backdrop of these historical problems.

Second, judgment prophecies, unless it can be reasonably shown otherwise, apply only to the people and time they were given. It is not permissible, therefore, to apply these same prophecies to nations today. We have no basis for expecting God to intervene in the course of human history in the same way He had done in the past. While it is true that one day God will judge all nations, this judgment is specifically reserved for the end of the age (Matthew 25:31–46). This does not mean, however, that prophecy does not speak to us today. Take, for example, 2 Chronicles 7:14, which says, "If my people, who are called by my name, will humble themselves and pray and seek my face and turn from their wicked ways, then I will hear from heaven and forgive their sin and heal their land." The phrase "called by my name" would certainly include believing Gentiles, and the promise would therefore apply to the church today. Indeed, a careful reading of the characteristics of prophecy shows the applicability of these analogous situations and themes to believers today. As Osborne rightfully states, "The necessity of dwelling within God's New Covenant, the judgement warnings and salvation promises speak to the modern Christian with the same clarion voice they held for the Israelites. The condemnation of social justice and morality are as needed today as then."[4]

Third, both judgment and blessing prophecies were almost always conditional. For example, in Jeremiah 18:7–10, God declared:

> *If at any time I declare concerning a nation or a kingdom, that I will pluck up and break down and destroy it, and if that nation, concerning which I have spoken, turns from its evil, I will relent of the disaster that I intended to do to it. And if at any time I declare concerning a nation or a kingdom that I will build and plant it, and if it does evil in my sight, not listening to my voice, then I will relent of the good that I had intended to do to it.*

This principle is important because not all conditional prophecies are prefaced with a conditional clause (such as the *if* clause in the verse above). However, a close evaluation of Scripture will show that most prophecies (whether they indicate conditionality or not) were generally understood to be conditionally based upon the response of the intended recipients. For instance, Jonah went throughout the city of Nineveh proclaiming the message of the Lord: "Yet forty days, and Nineveh shall be overthrown!" (Jonah 3:4). Yet, when the people heard the message, "from the greatest of them to the least of them," they put on sackcloth and began fasting as a sign of remorse and repentance (v. 5). Consequently, we read in verse 10, "When God saw what they did, how they turned from their evil way, God relented of the disaster that he had said he would do to them, and he did not do it." So then, Jonah's initial warning to Nineveh was understood by the people as a conditional warning. If unmoved toward repentance, the people would have perished. However, since they repented, God withheld His judgment. Another example is found in Micah 3:12 where the Judean prophet states, "Therefore because of you [Judah] Zion shall be plowed as a field; Jerusalem shall become a heap of ruins, and the mountain of the house a wooded height." Interestingly, this same prophecy is quoted in Jeremiah 26:18–19, where it is noted that because King Hezekiah feared and besought the Lord, the prophecy never came to pass. An important rule, then, involving judgment prophecies, understood by both the prophets and their hearers, is that interpreters should expect, unless demonstrated otherwise, these prophecies to be contingent on the behavior of those they are directed toward.

Before concluding this point, a word of caution is in order. While we believe that a proper study of Scripture will show that an overwhelming majority of prophecy is conditional in nature, clearly others were meant to be understood as unconditional promises. Most recognizable are the unconditional prophecies that promise messianic fulfillment. God's promises of a Deliverer (Genesis 3:15), a King and Kingdom (2 Samuel 7:8–16;

Isaiah 9:7), and a new heaven and a new earth (Isaiah 65:17) are a few examples of prophecies with unconditional fulfillments.

Finally, when it comes to predictive prophecies, the present and future will at times interact. A good example to note is found in 2 Samuel 7, where the prophet Nathan informs King David that his "seed" will "build a house for My [God's] name." Unquestionably, this is predicting the day that Solomon (David's future son) would build the temple (966 BC). However, the prophecy continues to say, "and I will establish His kingdom forever." Of course, Solomon did not retain the throne of David "forever," nor could he have. This prophecy goes well beyond Solomon to a much farther descendent, namely Jesus (see Luke 1:32). Yet, the prophecy makes no distinction between the two, and, if not careful, one could easily assume that this prophecy pointed to one person and one event (as another example, see Joel 2:28–31; cf. Acts 2:16–17; Revelation 6:12). Furthermore, the same prophetic utterance will at times point to two or more different events. For example, the book of Daniel speaks of the desecration of the temple, known as the "abomination of desolation" (9:27; 11:31; 12:11). Few would argue against this prophecy being originally fulfilled by Antiochus Epiphanes (ruler of the Seleucid Empire), who had an altar of Zeus Olympios erected inside the holy of holies and forced Jews to sacrifice pigs on it in his honor. However, it was fulfilled again in the destruction of Jerusalem in AD 70 by Titus (the Roman general), and will be fulfilled a final time in the end-time events by the future Antichrist (Matthew 24:15; cf. 2 Thessalonians 2:4).

This prophetic phenomenon has resulted in significant hermeneutical debate. The issue is whether prophecies should be seen as having single or multiple meaning. Advocates for the multiple-meaning position use a variety of terms to describe their position, such as "double meaning," "dual reference," "manifold fulfillment," or "multiple sense." Biblical scholar, J. Dwight Pentecost, defends this position as follows: "Two events, widely separated as to the time of their fulfillment, may be brought together into the scope of one prophecy. This was done because the prophet had a message for his own day as well as for a future time . . . It was the purpose of

God to give the near and far view so that the fulfillment of the one should be the assurance of the fulfillment of the other."[5] Others, such as J. Barton Payne, would argue that the notion of a "double meaning" prophecy would ultimately lead to something other than an "author-centered-meaning," which is fundamental to biblical hermeneutics. They rather would argue that prophecy, as with all Scripture, has a single meaning, yet may have a variety of applications in different situations. As Payne illustrates,

> The NT epistles thus repeatedly quotes OT prophecies, though not in reference to their actual fulfillments; for example, 2 Corinthians 6:16 cites Leviticus 26:11 (on God's presence with His people in the yet future testament of peace), 6:17 cites Isaiah 52:11 (on Israel's departure from unclean Babylon), and 6:18 freely renders Hosea 1:10 (on the inclusion of Gentiles in the family of God), all to illustrate that Christians' present enjoyment of the presence of God and our need to maintain separation from the uncleanness of the world, though only the last, Hosea 1:10, had this originally in mind. [Milton S. Terry] therefore makes it clear that, "We may readily admit that the Scriptures are capable of manifold practical applications; otherwise they would not be so useful for doctrine, correction, and instruction in righteousness (2 Timothy 3:16)," though he remains firm in his insistence upon single fulfillment for biblical prophecy.[6]

For many scholars, the key is to view prophecy analogous to how one would view a mountain range. At a distance, the peaks of each mountain appear to be quite near to one another. However, up close it becomes evident that each mountain is separated by wide valleys for several miles. When prophets looked toward the future, they also saw things that appeared to them to be side by side, yet as time moved closer to fulfillment, significant gaps became more and more obvious. This concept, referred to as *prophetic telescoping*, is further demonstrated by the messianic prophecies that seem to blend the first and second advents of Christ (i.e., Isaiah 61:1–3). It serves well in explaining prophecies such as the one observed in Joel 2:28–31, which points to the Day of Pentecost (Acts 2:14–21) as well as the Day of the Lord (Revelation 6:12–17), though they are separated by a sizable time gap (cf. 2 Thessalonians 2:1–4).

Perhaps, it is best if we simply view predictive prophecies with supposed "double fulfillment" typologically: as preliminary and complete, or typical (shadow) and antitypical (reality) fulfillment. In other words, the earlier fulfillment is itself prophetic of the later fulfillment. Again, as an example, 2 Samuel 7:14 had a preliminary, but incomplete fulfillment in Solomon, and an extensive and complete fulfillment in Christ (Hebrews 1:5). The preliminary fulfillment acts as a down payment on the final and ultimate fulfillment. Another important example of this is found in the New Testament. During His Olivet discourse, Jesus makes important references to a future temple destruction (Mathew 24; Mark 13; Luke 21). Here there are clear references to events that happened in AD 70: the temple was left with not one stone on another, when Jerusalem was besieged by Roman authority. But there are other elements that seem to go beyond what happened in the Jewish War—the gospel being preached throughout the world before the end (Matthew 24:14), the sign of the Son of Man appearing in the heavens, and the angels gathering the elect from all over the earth (vv. 30–31). This has led some interpreters to see the entire discourse as somehow symbolically fulfilled in AD 70, and others to see the entire discourse as an event that is completely fulfilled at the end of history (although most who interpret this way would acknowledge various parallels in the text that did occur in AD 70). And various attempts have been made to assign one paragraph to AD 70, and another to the end. But it might be simpler to take the whole as immediately, but partially or typically fulfilled in the Jewish War, but also to recognize that the events of the war point forward to the end of history (it's more important and climactic fulfillment).

Moreover, it is essential that we recognize the progressive nature of prophecy. Particularly how prophetic passages, although having a single intended fulfillment, will often exhibit a pattern of chronological progress toward its fulfillment (this is often referred to as *subsequently fulfilled prophecy* or *progressive prophetic development*). An example is the Genesis 3:15 prophecy, which speaks in obscure terms of the bruising of Satan's head. The progressive stages in the fulfillment of this prophecy began with Christ's death, resurrection, and ascension (John 12:31–32; Hebrews 2:14–15; 1 John 3:8; Colossians 2:14–15), continues in the church (Ephesians 6:11–13; Revelation 12:11; Romans 16:20), and will end with Satan's imprisonment in the abyss (Revelation 20:3) and the lake of fire (Revelation 20:10). The importance of identifying the progressive nature of prophecy cannot be overstated. This is especially true for prophecies pertaining to the unfolding drama of redemptive history. Many of these prophecies grow, at each stage of their witness, from the lessor to the greater revelation (as with the Genesis 3:15 prophecy above), and thus their fulfillment is progressively realized.

Principles for Interpreting Prophecy:

1. It is necessary first to reiterate a general, fundamental rule of interpretation: *prophecy must be allowed its ordinary, or common sense meaning.* The historical-grammatical interpretation of a prophecy is the only basis of objectivity. Without it, any interpreter with his own system can make any prophecy mean anything. However, this principle is not as easy as simply adopting a strict literal interpretation; for even the strictest literalist takes some things symbolically. Conversely, even the most thoroughgoing symbolist interprets some things literally. Thus, the difference between literalists and symbolists is relative rather than absolute, involving questions of how much and which parts of prophecy should be interpreted symbolically rather than literally. Unfortunately, whether a word or phrase should be interpreted literally or symbolically sometimes has no easy answer. As a helpful aid, G. B. Card offers six noteworthy indicators for identifying when an author does not intend for his words to be taken literally: (1) the author makes an

explicit statement to that end, (2) a literal interpretation is impossible, (3) a low degree of correspondence exists, (4) the imaginary is highly developed, (5) the author piles up multiple images, and (6) the author uses original imagery.[7] The context and the historical use of the words are the best general guides in making decisions concerning their use within a specific passage.

2. *Distinguish between conditional and unconditional prophecy.* Conditional prophecy presents a scenario that may or may not ensue depending on the response of the people, while unconditional prophecy looks only to the faithful character of God as the basis for its realization. Walter Kaiser Jr. comments, "The actual list of unconditional prophecies is not long, but they occupy the most pivotal spot in the history of redemption."[8] He continues to identify the most common unconditional prophecies as those relating to the New Covenant promises.

3. *Study prophecy chronologically throughout the Scriptures.* Prophecy is interwoven with redemptive history and is therefore largely developed progressively. Thus, we must begin at the beginning and work onward, not at the ends to work backward. The great prophecies of Moses in Leviticus 26 and Deuteronomy 28 are fundamental to an understanding of Jeremiah 25:11–12 and Daniel 9; and Daniel 9:20–27 is essential for understanding Matthew 24. Parallel prophecies must be searched out and compared, as for example, those prophecies that point to the coming "Day of the Lord" (Joel 2:1–2; 10–11; 30–31; Amos 5:8–20; Isaiah 2:10–21; 13:6–13; 24:21–23; Zephaniah 1:14-18; cf. Matthew 24:29–31; 22:1–4; Revelation 6:12–17).

4. *Distinguish between the message of the prophet and the fulfillment.* As a matter of procedure, the meaning of the prophetic text should be determined first. Only after this should the question of fulfillment be considered. It is true that certain passages which remain

obscure or ambiguous may find clarification by consulting later revelation. Nevertheless, the interpreter must resist the temptation to wrongly identify the prophecy with a particular fulfillment in order to impose their theological system on a text.

5. *It is necessary to recognize the complete fulfillment of a prophecy as the true fulfillment.* Whether we view prophecies telescopically or typologically, it is important that we recognize that the complete fulfillment is the true fulfillment. Predictive prophecies will often use language that points to an initial, preliminary fulfillment as well as a complete and final fulfillment. 2 Samuel 7:14, as we observed above, had a preliminary, but incomplete fulfillment in Solomon, and an extensive and complete fulfillment in Christ. Yet it is the completed fulfillment, Christ's ascension to the throne of David (cf. Acts 2:30–31; Ephesians 1:19–23), which is its main focus and therefore the true fulfillment.

6. *The question of fulfillment presupposes that the student of prophecy must also be a student of history.* One cannot discover the fulfillment of Daniel 11 without learning in some detail about the wars between the Seleucids and the Ptolemies in the third and second centuries BC, and neither can he know the significance of the many other prophecies that relate to a particular historical event without first understanding the historical significance of the event itself. Careful historical analysis also remains the only way of determining whether a prophecy has already been fulfilled.

10

APOCALYPTIC LITERATURE

While an apocalypse should be considered a form of prophecy, it features unique characteristics that distinguish the literary style significantly from most of the prophecy genre and thus deserves its own consideration. The term "apocalypse" was not used as an official genre for any portion of the Bible until it appeared in Revelation 1:1, and it was not until the second century that the term regularly appeared for this genre.[1] The Greek term (*apokalypsis*) conveys the idea of uncovering or revealing something that had been previously hidden or unknown. Thus, the genre classifies those books whose focus is primarily on the revelation of what has been "hidden," particularly with regard to the end-times (i.e., Ezekiel, Daniel, Zechariah, Revelation, and parts of Isaiah and Joel).

Apocalyptic literature shares a number of similarities with biblical prophecy, and scholars even treat it as a subgenre of prophecy. Both are concerned with the future, and both frequently use figurative and symbolic language to convey its message. However, as was previously said, it also presents a number of differences. While scholars have vigorously debated the formal features of the genre, the following characteristics are those that are most agreed upon as being unique to apocalyptic literature:

1. The initial prophetic message was usually spoken first and later written down, whereas apocalyptic literature was almost always written first.

2. Prophecies were usually presented as separate, brief oracles, while apocalyptic literature is often longer, continuous materiel (cycles of material are often repeated a second or third time in parallel form).

3. While both prophecy and apocalyptic literature use symbolism, prophecy more commonly draws its symbols from the practical realities of our human experiences, such as salt, lamps, water, and fire. The apocalyptists, on the other hand, along with those things, would use many symbols from the world of fantasy or the imaginary, such as seven-headed beasts and locusts with women's hair and the tails of scorpions.

4. Apocalyptic literature places a greater emphasis on a moral dualism (God/Messiah and His angels vs Satan, the Antichrist, and their supporters) than does prophecy. Ultimately, apocalyptic literature encourages the faithful reader through revelation concerning the victory of Messiah and the Kingdom of God, the consequential and impending doom of the Adversary, and the final restoration of heaven and earth.

5. Apocalyptic literature is generally pessimistic toward the effectiveness of human intervention. While biblical prophecy in general argued for the repentance of Israel and promised if they would return to God the prophecy of doom would be avoided, the apocalyptist could offer no such optimism but could only comfort the reader that God in the future would bring this age to its end and vindicate His people.

In closing, it is important to note that these distinctions are a matter of emphasis rather than absolute differences. Exceptions can be cited for each of them; however, most conservative Bible scholars would agree with these distinctive characteristics.

Principles for Interpreting Apocalyptic Literature:

1. *Note the type of literature.* None of the books of the Bible are purely apocalyptic. For instance, Zechariah 1–6 is primarily apocalyptic, but Zechariah 7–14 is primarily prophetic. Likewise, Daniel is an obvious blend of the two genres, and the book of Revelation is a composite of apocalyptic, prophetic, and epistolary forms. Thus, the interpreter must work carefully in determining the literary type of each passage under study, so as to ensure the proper use of interpretive methods for the respective genres.

2. *Note the structure and perspective of the passage or book.* While the first point centers on the formal features of the work, this concerns more the aspects that are emphasized and particularly the pattern by which they developed. For instance, Daniel 2–12 follows a nested parallel structure, otherwise called a chiasm, in a thematic order of A, B, C, C, B, A. Chapter 2 (A) focuses on the overthrow of pagan nations; chapter 3 (B), the fiery furnace; chapter 4 (C), the judgment of a king (Nebuchadnezzar); chapter 5 (C), the judgment of a king (Darius); chapter 6 (B), the lion's den; chapters 7–12 (A), the overthrow of pagan nations. The perspective this structure emphasizes is the sovereignty of God and the future deliverance of His people from forces of evil. Knowing the structure and emphasis of a book or section will prepare and aid the interpreter to ascertain the meaning of an apocalyptic message.

3. *Interpret the book and each passage in light of their historical-cultural settings.* As with all text, careful historical-cultural and contextual analysis is a prerequisite for the accurate understanding of an apocalyptic text. Determination of the identity of all proper names, events, geographical references, and so on remains a crucial

first step. Even when such references are used symbolically, as the city of Babylon often is, knowledge of the historical city of Babylon provides important clues about its symbolic meaning.

4. *Determine the function and meaning of symbols.* Biblical symbolism is actually a special type of metaphor, and therefore each interpreter is to determine which figurative sense the symbol has in the larger context. This means that the true meaning is not to be found in our present situation but rather in the use of that symbol in its ancient setting.[2] This does not mean that prophecy and apocalyptic prediction should not be applied to the current situation or that their "fulfillment" should not be sought. Rather, it means that the interpreter should seek first the "author's intended meaning" in its original context before determining what impact the symbol has for its modern readers. This point can hardly be overstated in light of the misuse of biblical symbols in many circles today. When interpreting symbols, we want to first ask ourselves if the symbol is interpreted in the immediate context or elsewhere in the book. If so, this will provide the first line of interpretation. Next, we will want to consider if the symbol has a direct allusion to a previous or future text (such as the use of Ezekiel or Daniel in the book of Revelation). These provide specific help to the meaning of the symbol, although the final arbiter is still the immediate context. Finally, look for any possible connection between the symbol and the cultural-historical context. Almost two thousand years separate the modern reader of the book of Revelation from the historical, cultural, and political environment of the original recipients. Some of the confusion regarding the imagery of this book arrives from the fact that John wrote to people that shared a common understanding of their surrounding culture within the Roman Empire. Images of beasts, dragons, kings, and cities wielding enormous political and military power over its citizens may seem strange and foreign to the modern reader living

in North America. To the readers of John's vision in first-century Asia Minor, however, they would have picked up on the cultural connections associated with these images. Thus, it is essential that each interpretation be consistent with the way the original recipients would have understood the apocalyptic message. If, after all this, the symbol in question is still unclear, it must remain unclear. The interpreter must resist the desire to fill the void, left by a lack of understanding, with a speculative meaning that has not first been established by careful exegesis—no matter how intriguing the interpretation might seem! In such cases, the interpreter must seek to understand the surrounding context of the symbol, such as how it impacts the overall message, even if we are unable to interpret the symbol directly.

5. *Stress the theological and note the predictive with humility.* This does not mean that predictive prophecy is not as important as the theological message to the writer's own day. Rather, the future, even in apocalyptic text, was not an end in itself but a means to an end—namely, to comfort and challenge the saints. The writer wanted to turn the reader toward God, not just toward future events. Oftentimes, the theological point an apocalyptic message is making is quite understandable even when it is being conveyed through an image or symbol that is not so clear. We must not, therefore, get bogged down with speculative interpretations. How easily we forget just how poorly Israel interpreted prophecies relating to the first advent. Our perspective from which we are to interpret prophecies relating to the second advent is marginally better at best. We must remember that each era of the church through the ages has believed that Christ could return in its generation. Therefore, we need to stress the theological meaning of apocalyptic texts and hold to interpretations of fulfillment in our own day (such as those related to the reinstatement of Israel as a nation) with humility. Above all, we dare not preach such prophecies as

absolute truth. Otherwise, when they fail to come to pass, people's faith can be hurt, and the church made to look foolish. Such has occurred through the years by those who have given too much credence to the setting of specific dates for the Lord's return.

11

PARABLES

Very few portions of Scripture have received more attention than parables. Not only does the practical nature of parables make for relevant and exciting sermons, Jesus frequently taught by means of them, making parables naturally intriguing to any student of Scripture. In fact, fully a third of Jesus's teaching in the Synoptic Gospels comes in parabolic form. So then, not only does this fact make evident the importance for studying the genre, it also necessitates that we study the genre well (especially since so many have hermeneutically abused parables in the past, and continue to do so today).

Understanding the point of any parable begins by understanding the point of parables as whole. As a story or depiction that uses a common earthly example to convey or illustrate a spiritual concept, parables were intended to accomplish two things: First, parables were intended to illustrate specific truths to believers in an impactful way (Matthew 13:10–12; Mark 4:11). As relatable stories, parables can make a greater impact on our understanding of a particular truth, as well as its significance. For example, Jesus could have simply told his disciples that they should persevere in prayer, and not to give up. As it is, Jesus reinforced that truth with a story of a widow who persisted in begging an "unjust judge" to act in favor of her situation (Luke 18:1–5). Because of her continually complaining before the judge, he finally gives in to her complaint, wishing only to make her go away. Christ then explained the lesson of the parable: If an unjust judge who cares nothing for this widow can be swayed by her persistent begging, how much more will a loving heavenly Father answer those who consistently pray to Him (18:6–8)? Similarly, the Lord could have said, "Stop being self-righteous." Instead, He gave a story of a Pharisee and a tax collector who both went up to the temple to pray (18:9–14). The prideful arrogance of the Pharisee and the authentic humility of the tax collector teach a lesson against the danger of a self-righteous attitude in a simple yet unforgettable way.

Second, because they illustrate truth in an impactful way, parables are also used to confront listeners with wrongdoing in their lives. If a believer possesses basically sound moral standards and yet fails to live up to those standards, a parable can be a powerful means of exposing this discrepancy. A striking example of this is how God confronted David's own moral failure in 2 Samuel 12:1–7. Prior to this incident, David had placed Uriah in the frontlines of battle so that he would be killed and David could therefore take his wife, Bathsheba. Consequently, the prophet Nathan was sent by God to deliver a message to David in the form of a parable. He told him the story of a rich man who took a ewe lamb from a man who was poor in order to feed a houseguest that was traveling through. Instead of using one of the "many" sheep or cattle he personally owned, he took the only lamb this poor man had, and one that had been raised and cared for by him and his children. David, a man of moral principle, easily identified with the injustice that had been done to the poor man in the story, and when the parable was applied to his own behavior, he immediately repented of his wrongdoing. So then, whether it was intended to convey truth in an impactful way or correct a moral issue, parables by their very nature always called for a response on the part of the hearer. "It is told to address and capture the hearers, to bring them up short about their own actions, or to cause them to respond in some way to Jesus and His ministry."[1]

Until relatively recent times, parables were generally understood to be allegorical, and their interpretation was, therefore, a matter of identifying the "hidden" meaning of the elements in the story. For example, Augustine of Hippo, a notably brilliant scholar (AD 354–AD 430), famously interpreted the parable of the good Samaritan (Luke 10:29–37) as follows (in *Quaestiones Evangeliorum 2*): The Man going down to Jerusalem from Jericho is Adam (representing all humanity), who leaves the heavenly city of peace (Jerusalem) for the world (Jericho, which also signifies sin). The thieves (the devil and his angels) attack him and leave him "half-dead" in sin (alive on the outside but dead on the inside). The priest and the Levite are the OT law (its priesthood and ministry), which cannot help Adam in his spiritually dead condition. And the good Samaritan is Christ Himself, who takes the man (Adam) to the inn (the church), and leaves him with the innkeeper (the apostle Paul). The two denarii given to the innkeeper represented the two greatest commandments—to love God and neighbor, and the promise to return and repay the innkeeper represented Christ's second coming.

While all of this is certainly clever, one can be sure that this is not at all what Jesus intended. After all, the context clearly indicates that the point of the parable relates to our human relationships (who is my neighbor?), not our need for a Savior. As important as salvation is, it seems unlikely that these allegorical correspondences have anything to do with the original meaning of the parable.

By the turn of the twentieth century, some scholars, in recognition of these interpretive embellishments, began to argue the opposite extreme that parables are never allegorical. Accordingly, a parable has only one significant point, and other details (thieves, money, innkeeper, etc.) are simply there for the sake of telling the story. This, however, takes the caution of overly allegorizing parables much too far. Some parables, such as the parable of the vineyard in Matthew 21:33–43, clearly have several points of allegorical correspondence, and the parable of the sower in Matthew 13 and Mark 4 is directly interpreted by Jesus, with reference to the "seed" and each of the "soils," as representing allegorical meaning. The problem with the old approach was not that it interpreted allegorically, but that it did so without any indication that the proposed allegorical meaning was ever intended by Jesus. A symbol is extremely adaptable, and the true meaning of a symbol can only be determined on the basis of its contextual use and the cultural background within which it is used. A parable may use symbolic meaning, whether it is one symbolic point or several, yet its symbolism must be understood with reference to the cultural situation in first-century Palestine and in light of the particular concerns of Jesus found within the context in which the parable was spoken. The Gospel writers themselves will usually indicate the specific contextual setting of a parable, and it's critical that we pay close attention to this setting.

It is also important to note that parables often present unexpected or surprise elements meant to provoke the hearer to reexamine his or her worldview. For example, in the parable of the laborers in the vineyard (Matthew 20:1–16), it is surprising that the landowner pays each worker the same amount, regardless of the time spent working. This surprise leads us to rethink the matter of "rewards" for our "good" works. Unfortunately, much of what would have been a surprise to the original hearers of the parables hardly surprises us today, and we must therefore read each parable through the eyes of a first-century Jew if we hope to capture and appreciate the unexpected elements in the story. For instance, when we hear the parable of the tax collector and the Pharisee (Luke 18:9–14), we are not surprised at the outcome. To us, the Pharisee comes across as an arrogant, self-righteous hypocrite. But most first-century Jews considered the Pharisees to be the moral elite. Even his prayer, "I thank you that I'm not like the tax collector," would not have been regarded as hypocritical arrogance, but as genuine gratitude that God had kept him from a life of sinful wretchedness. On the other hand, first-century Palestinian Jews regarded tax collectors as being morally inept. They were not only dishonest, but traitors to their people. The outcome of the parable—that the tax collector and not the Pharisee was declared to be righteous—was shocking. It shifts from a worldview that looks at righteousness as something we achieve (which was a universal assumption) to one where righteousness means abandoning all thoughts of our own righteousness.

The single-most dominant theme found throughout the parables is the *Kingdom of God*. By using earthly examples as points of comparison, these parables commonly tell us what the Kingdom of God "is like." For example, the parable of the mustard seed (Matthew 13:31–32) begins by stating, "The kingdom of heaven is like a mustard seed, which a man took and sowed in his field . . ." While a mustard seed alone can hardly represent what the Kingdom of heaven is like, its use within the context of the parable as a whole works to illustrate something important about the nature of the Kingdom (which we will define as God's rule). Namely, it illustrates that the Kingdom, which is represented by a tiny seed that grows into a large tree, has come in a tiny, insignificant way but will result in great observation. As Ladd comments,

> The majority of modern exegetes see the emphasis of the parable in the contrast between the tiny beginning and the large end, and this certainly lies at the heart of the parable. The mustard seed, while not actually the smallest seed known, was a proverbial illustration of smallness. The burning question faced by Jesus' disciples was how the kingdom of God could actually be present in such an insignificant movement as that embodied in His ministry. The Jews expected the kingdom to be like a great tree under which the nations would find shelter (cf. Ezekiel 17:22–24). They could not understand how one could talk about the Kingdom apart from such an all-encompassing manifestation of God's rule. How could the coming glorious Kingdom have anything to do with the poor little band of Jesus disciples? Rejected by the religious leaders, welcomed by tax collectors and sinners, Jesus looked more like a deluded dreamer than the bearer of the kingdom of God. Jesus' answer is, first the tiny seed, later the

large tree. The smallness and relative insignificance of what is happening in His ministry does not exclude the secret presence of the very kingdom of God.[2]

On one hand, the parables of the Kingdom speak of the present abiding and/or the progressive unfolding ministry of the Kingdom of God. For instance, the parable of leaven (Luke 13:20–21), similar to the parable of the mustard seed, illustrates, by way of a baking metaphor, the presently progressive spread of the Kingdom from a tiny origin. On the other hand, the parables also look forward to the climactic fulfillment of God's Kingdom, when its ultimate triumph over evil is fully realized. This concept is clearly pictured by the parable of the net (Matthew 13:47–50), which pictures the Kingdom of God as a fishing net that is dragged through the sea. In the end, when the catch is sorted out, the good fish are kept and the bad fish are discarded.

Principles for Interpreting the Parables:

1. *Note the contextual setting in which the parable is placed.* This includes the immediate context (the particular situation or concern that prompted the parable) as well as the specific audience Christ was addressing. Furthermore, any discussion that follows the parable must also be considered as important clues for discovering its intended purpose and meaning.

2. *Study the structure of the parable.* Not everything that is labeled as a parable looks the same way. Some parables (usually identified as true parables) take the form of a story, while others follow a literary style closer to that of metaphor or simile. Because the parables are not all of one kind, one cannot necessarily lay down rules that will cover them all. For the many parables that follow the story genre, the interpreter must apply compositional and rhetorical techniques to discover its plot development and literary patterns. This will include the following: 1) Identifying the main characters.

Oftentimes the point of a parable is recognized by understanding the interrelation of the characters within the story plot. 2) Recognizing the topic or detail that receives the most attention. This topic is likely to be the focal point. 3) Observing any elements that occur in direct dialogue. Direct dialogue may serve to emphasize a particular feature within the story. 4) Identifying the unexpected twist in the story. Frequently the unexpected shock appears for the purpose of catching the listener's attention and forcing them to reconsider their perspective. 5) Discovering the climax, or turning point, of the story (such as the welcoming reaction of the father in the parable of the prodigal son). Normally the climax will identify the referential point that guides the reader to the basic thrust of the parable. 6) Noticing how the action shifts before and after the climax (such as the reaction of the older brother to the prodigal). 7) Paying close attention to the plot resolution. Very often the main point of a parable occurs at the end of the story.

3. *Seek to uncover the cultural-historical background of any of the elements within the parable.* Normally, unless we understand the historical context of the parable, its meaning is inaccessible. The story of every parable is told within a Mediterranean, first-century context. Thus, if we are going to catch the point of each element in the story, we must understand them within their historical-cultural perspective.

4. *Relate the point of the parables to the overall message of each Gospel, as well as Jesus's teaching as a whole.* After one has determined the message of a parable, it is important to place the message within the larger context of Jesus's teaching, as well as within the overall emphasis of the Gospel within which it is found. This will help the interpreter to avoid misunderstanding or overstating any of the points of the parable. As an example, the theological implications of the parable of the vine and branches (John 15:1–8), which has

been a point of contention between Calvinist and Arminian think-
ers, must be weighed in balance with the biblical theology of God's
sovereignty and man's responsibility that is presented throughout
John's Gospel as a whole.

5. *Do not base doctrines on the parables without further corroborative
    detail elsewhere.* Parables by their nature tend to be more illustra-
    tive than informative (though this does not mean that they never
    convey new concepts). This means that we are to focus on the ratio-
    nale of the parable's main idea and not overanalyze the support-
    ing, minor details in search for doctrinal concepts. For instance,
    the parable of the rich man and Lazarus (Luke 16:19–31) is often
    taken as proof of a compartmentalized Hades. However, such a
    doctrine is not found in Jesus's teaching in Luke nor anywhere else
    in Scripture. Therefore, the setting of the parable in Hades is better
    understood as a colorful element for telling the story rather than
    an established dogma, and must not be pressed too far. While we
    are right to recognize that the great themes of the parables carry
    theological weight, we must exercise great care in delineating the
    theological elements within a given parable.

6. *Make application of parables by relating its historical significance to
    our modern, similar situations.* The evocative power of the parable
    is as great today as it was in the first century. In fact, the great
    preachers of the past century, like Charles Spurgeon or Chuck
    Swindoll, are known for their parabolic style. "The parables reach
    down to the deepest levels of the human psyche and grip the heart
    and will."[3] Moreover, the themes of the parables speak as clearly
    today as they did in Jesus's day. Forgiveness and compassion, and
    jealousy and self-centeredness are as necessary topics for us today
    as they were in ancient times. As Osborne rightly heralds, "The
    message of divine mercy and the radical demands of the presence
    of the Kingdom should ring with clarion call in the church today."[4]

Bloomberg believes it quite helpful to include modern parallels when preaching a parable, since "they work to recreate the original dynamic, force, or effect of Jesus' original story."[5] Much of the impact that results from reading a parable hinges on its historical-cultural context. Whenever possible, the interpreter should seek a modern parallel for any parabolic story in order to better relate to its emotive thrust. For example, a modern-day story of the good Samaritan might look something like this:

A Jewish man left his home in Tel Aviv, headed toward Jerusalem, when along the way he was carjacked, beaten mercilessly, and left for dead by local street thugs. After some time, a rabbi, on his way to offer prayers at the Western Wall, drove by and saw the man, but he passed over to the other side of the road, not wanting to get involved. Later, a group of Israeli soldiers drove upon the dying man, but instead of stopping, they kept on driving. Finally, a Palestinian was walking by and saw the man lying on the roadside. He immediately came to his rescue, binding his wounds and covering the man with his own coat. He tried to help the man to his feet, but he was too weak; so he called for an ambulance, which delivered him to a local hospital a few miles down the road. Later, while in recovery, the Palestinian brought the man some food, new clothes, and some extra money for any other needs he might have.

PART 4

SEEING THE BIG PICTURE: THE THEOLOGICAL ANALYSIS OF SCRIPTURE

After we have determined the meaning of a passage, we must analyze the theological contribution the passage has first on the body of work from which it comes and second on Scripture as a whole. Essentially, we must ask, how does the passage fit into the total pattern of God's revelation? If we believe that all of Scripture has a common divine Author, then our exegetical exploration expands beyond answering the question, "What does the text mean?" to include questions about its relationship to the entire biblical canon. We are compelled to explore how each part is in continuity with, and is consistent with, the whole of biblical teaching. As a result, we simultaneously maintain the individual contributions of each biblical author while checking our interpretation against passages by other biblical authors to see how they support or pose potential problems for our interpretation. When we ask this question, however, it immediately becomes evident that another question must also be answered, namely, "What is the pattern of God's revelation?" And here lies the hermeneutical challenge: Which question should we attempt to answer first? Once again, the hermeneutical cycle—the recognition that our interpretation of any part of

Scripture is dependent on our interpretation of Scripture as a whole, while at the same time, our interpretation of the whole cannot be separated from our interpretation of the parts—becomes evident. The following chapters (12–14) illustrate the hermeneutical cycle with regard to theology.

Even though, as we have argued, exegesis must precede doctrine, interpretation rarely takes place in a theological vacuum. One will inevitably take a preliminary theological position and begin the exegetical process from a mindful commitment to that perspective. The answer to this, however, is neither deny nor ignore our theological presuppositions, but use them properly in the interpretive process. As we proceed, if we encounter biblical data that does not easily fit our framework, we must reevaluate our position in light of our newfound biblical insight. Moises Silva explains this approach quite well:

> Sometimes we make the facts fit our preconceptions and thus distort [a text]. The remedy, however, is neither to deny that we have those presuppositions nor to try to suppress them, for we would only be deceiving ourselves. We are much more likely to be conscious of those preconceptions if we deliberately seek to identify them and then use them in the exegetical process. That way, when we come across a fact that resists the direction our interpretation is taking, we are better prepared to recognize that anomaly for what it is, namely an indication that our interpretive scheme is faulty and must be modified.[1]

Knowing that our theological perspectives have a remarkable sway on our interpretation of biblical texts (whether we admit it or not), we thus believe that the broader theological question must become the initial question and concur with Silva that "exegesis stands to gain, rather than to lose, if it is consciously done within the framework of one's theology."[2] Therefore, before we ask how a biblical passage fits into the total pattern of God's revelation, we must first become aware of what we believe to be

God's pattern of revelation. This question is so important that the greater part of this section will be spent discussing it. Once the pattern of divine revelation has been tentatively determined, the question of how a particular passage fits into this pattern becomes much easier to answer.

12

THE TOTAL PATTERN OF REVELATION

When we ask the question, "What is the total pattern of God's revelation?" we are essentially asking, "How does the Bible as a whole fit together?" Scholars have debated for years whether or not it is possible to point to a unifying theme that binds the whole Bible together. Many have argued that the search for such a theme is fruitless: it is better just to accept that Scripture contains a number of different themes and then look at them individually without trying to unite them. They warn of the dangers of squeezing all parts of the Bible into a point of singularity rather than letting them speak individually in their rich variety. Indeed, that is an important warning that must be heard. Any unifying theme that is used to help us see how the Bible fits together must arise out of Scripture itself, rather than being imposed upon it; and it must be broad enough to allow each part to make its own distinct contribution. It is our deep conviction that the theme of the *Kingdom of God* satisfies both requirements.

The Kingdom of God as a central theme has become a popular approach to Bible interpretation (largely due to the contributions made by George Ladd to biblical theology); however, it is only one of many interpretive approaches for developing a central theme. Walter Kaiser, for example, a notable theologian, argues strongly that the "promise of God" lays the foundation for understanding all the major themes of the Bible (what has been termed, at times, the promise-plan of God). Another popular approach argues that God's covenants provide the central point from which all the elements of Scripture circle. These covenants, it is postulated, ultimately reveal God's plan for man's redemption and thus our salvation in Christ results as the unified theme of Scripture. While both approaches have merit, and we agree that our salvation in Christ is an immensely important concept that runs throughout the Bible, it is only part of the Bible's larger message. The greater message goes far beyond the man-centered focus of salvation to embrace the redemptive purpose and restoration of God's sovereign rule over all things. We may call this message the revelation of God's plan and purpose for the universe. Thus, we intend to argue that the central theme of Scripture is God's sovereign rule over all things and that His rule is both theologically and scripturally tied to the concept of the Kingdom of God. This rule was first invested in man, who was to rule over all the earth for God's glory. But man, in his rebellion, lost his place of rulership, and therefore God, in accordance with His eternal plan, must rescue man from the dominion of Satan, the consequences of his sin, and restore again His sovereign rule (through man) over all the earth. To establish this central theme, we shall consider Scripture in its progressive revelatory form, paying close attention to its recurring themes, and attempt to develop a common pattern (or theme) that broadly binds all the individual themes together.

Man in the Image of God (Genesis 1)

Our attempt to discover a unifying theme of the Bible must begin, naturally, "in the beginning." After God had created a world suitable for sustaining all life, God made humans uniquely in His own image: "Then God said, 'Let Us make man in Our image, according to Our likeness'" (1:26). That God made man to be like Him is clear, but in what way are we like God? This is not so clear. In fact, many theologians throughout the years have struggled to give an adequate answer as to how man was made in the likeness of God. Indeed, we can all agree that we are made different from all other earthly and heavenly creatures. Unlike animals, man is built with the mental faculty for meaningful relationships. We are able to love others, share intimacy, and desire fellowship. We have an amazing capacity for language and are highly conversational. We know what it is to share thoughts, give and take friendship, perceive a sense of brotherhood, and participate in experiences with others. Animals are incapable of experiencing those things the same way people do.

When God made us in His image, He therefore made us persons—that is, He made us with the unique ability to reason and to have relationships. The most important of which is with God Himself. In Genesis 1:28, you will notice that immediately after God had created man and woman in His image, He spoke to them: "Then God blessed them, and God said to them . . ." which He did not do with any of the animals. This not only demonstrates the close relationship God has with man, it shows the uniqueness of man in that we can hear and receive God's Word—which animals cannot do. Furthermore, we are ethical creatures. God has made man with the ability to rationalize and to make moral judgments. Of course, our moral and ethical senses have been severely marred by sin. Even so, we know intrinsically that there is a difference between right and wrong.

While all of this is true, man is like God in that he is a relational, ethical being, when interpreting the meaning of what it means to be made in God's "image," one very important aspect should not be overlooked. The fact that *tselem* (image) is applied to humans at creation indicates that they were made to be God's representatives on earth. This is understood contextually when we read the next clause in the verse, "and let them have dominion" (1:26). We are essentially God's proxy, so to speak, in the community of creation. An often-used analogy well establishes this point: just as kings set up statues of themselves throughout the borders of their land to show their sovereign dominion, so God created man to be His royal representatives on earth and His vicegerents over creation. This truth was so astonishing to the psalmist that he wrote:

When I consider Your heavens, the work of Your fingers, the moon and the stars, which You have ordained, what is man that You are mindful of him, and the son of man that You visit him? For You have made him a little lower than the angels, and You have crowned him with glory and honor. You have made him to have dominion over the works of Your hands; You have put all things under His feet, all sheep and oxen—even the beasts of the field, the birds of the air, and the fish of the sea, that pass through the paths of the seas. O Lord, our Lord, how excellent is Your name in all the earth! (Psalm 8:3–9)

Here David describes man as being crowned with "glory and honor." This precisely indicates that man was given the unique responsibility of ruling over all the earth (the works of His hands). Yet, as the writer of Hebrews observes (Hebrews 2), "now we do not yet see all things put under him." Unfortunately, Adam, instead of loving and obeying God, disobeyed Him and yielded to the lies of the serpent (Satan) (Genesis 3:1–5). Adam had been "blessed" with all sorts of trees that were "pleasant to the sight and good for food" (Genesis 2:8–9). Yet he chose to eat (after his wife, Eve) from the only tree in the garden that was forbidden (the tree of the knowledge of good and evil). Of this tree, God had said that "in the day that you eat of it you shall surely die" (2:15–17).

The Fall of Man and the Consequence of Sin (Genesis 3–11)

Even though Adam and Eve had every reason to trust and obey their Creator, they "saw" that the forbidden tree was "desirable," at least they were led to believe it was, and chose to eat from it (3:6–7). Consequently, they both died instantly right there at the tree of the knowledge of good and evil, while the taste of fruit was yet on their lips. To die does not mean to cease to exist; rather the biblical definition of death is separation (cf. Isaiah 59:2; Ephesians 2:1; Colossians 2:13). For example, the Bible often employs the phrase "cut off from the land of the living" as an expression for physical death (cf. Isaiah 53:8). Adam and Eve were now spiritually separated from God; and not only that, sin had penetrated every sphere of their being to the point that they no longer desired fellowship with the Lord. The fact that their communion with God had been destroyed by sin is clearly presented in the text: The man and the woman "heard the voice of the LORD God walking in the garden" and they "hid themselves from the presence of the LORD God," a hiding that Adam later explains was occasioned by fear (3:8–10).

In tragic irony, the one who was made to rule became a slave, namely to the devil, sin, and death. Not only so, we who are born from Adam are also born as slaves (cf. Romans 5:12; 1 Corinthians 15:21–22; John 8:34). We too are ruled by Satan (John 12:31; 16:11; Ephesians 2:1–3), sin (Romans 6:12–14), and death (Romans 5:17). Yet Adam and Eve, along with all their descendants, were given great hope. Prior to their removal from the Garden, God gave Adam and Eve a promise and a picture. The promise, provided in a most unusual way (by way of cursing the serpent), was that the "seed of the woman" would "crush" the head of the serpent, which in return would "bruise" His heel (3:15). This metaphorically spoke of the time when Jesus, the "seed of the woman," would defeat the devil (crushing his head) by dying on the cross (illustrated by bruising His heel; see John 12:27–28; Hebrews 2:14; 1 John 3:8). His death would be the ransom that sets the captives free (Mark 10:45; 1 Timothy 2:5–6; John 8:36)! The picture, on the other hand, was provided by God as a way of addressing the need for Adam and Eve's covering. As a result of their broken relationship with God, and with each other, they felt shame and attempted to cover themselves with fig leaves. However, God would provide them with more suitable clothing: skins from an animal. Animal sacrifice would later become a major part of the Bible's redemptive history. These animal sacrifices present two important concepts: (1) man's failure to please God, and (2) God's provision for his failure. Ultimately, these sacrifices pointed to the One who could permanently put sin away (Hebrews 10:1–18). The One who, through His own death, covers our shame and guilt.

The fact that Adam and Eve had fallen in sin, and subsequently the whole world with them, prepares the reader for understanding the following narratives of chapters four through six. The world that God had made "very good" had now become filled with chaos and evil (Genesis 6:1–6). So much so that God chose to cleanse the earth with a flood (v. 7). But Noah, a man of God, was graciously chosen to build an ark to preserve his family (and certain animals) from the coming calamity (v. 8). As a righteous man, he would lead the "new" world for God's glory, under God's rule (9:1–17; notice the similarities between Noah's covenant and Adam's "blessing" in Genesis 1:28–30). However, man proved to be self-centered and sought after his own glory instead. Nimrod led the charge to build a tower unto the heavens (possibly, as some have suggested, in an attempt to worship the stars[1]), so as to make a name for themselves (11:1–9). God would again intervene. This time, God confused their communication by dividing their language into multiple dialects. This divine intervention ultimately resulted in the various ethnicities (nations) that represent humanity today. At this point, the Bible becomes very concerned with one particular nation, the nation of Israel.

Abraham and His Seed (Genesis 12–50)

The next pivotal point in the biblical story centers around the man Abram (later to be called Abraham). God appeared to Abraham and called him to leave his country, and his father's household, for a land of his own (the land of Canaan) (12:1–3). Unlike Noah, the author does not indicate that there was anything particularly special about Abraham, or why God chose him. Thus, it can be inferred that he was not chosen because of his own goodness but because of God's grace. Furthermore, Abraham was promised that his descendants would become "a great nation," a nation ruled by God. God later made this point clear to Abraham through an official covenant (called the Abrahamic Covenant) when He said, "And I will establish My covenant between me and you and your descendants after you in their generations, for an everlasting covenant, to be God to you and your descendants after you" (17:7). The promise is frequently repeated throughout the Old Testament in the covenant refrain, "I will be your God and you will be my people." Finally, Abraham is promised that his descendants will be "blessed," and, in him "all the families of the earth shall be blessed." In other words, the "curse" of the fall would be nullified by the "blessing" of salvation. Right from the very start God's plan of salvation was universal; it encompassed all nations. This fact was underlined when God changed the patriarch's name from Abram (which means exalted father) to Abraham (father of multitudes) (17:5).

But if we think that this salvific blessing comes through Abraham's descendants collectively, we are mistaken. In fact, Paul, in Galatians 3, specifically states that the "seed" to which Abraham was promised, which would be the source of blessing to all (cf. Genesis 22:18), was Christ (Galatians 3:16). Thus the "seed" promise continues to build momentum. The "seed of the woman" that would defeat the devil will also reverse the curse of sin. By being "cursed" for us, in that He took our place in judgment, Christ removes the curse of sin, and we, through faith in Him, are therefore "blessed" as Abraham's children (see Galatians 3:6–14). Thus, the promises made to Abraham were the means by which God would undo the devastation wrought by Adam, and would also result in restoring God's rule on earth (the Kingdom of God). The Lord promised Abraham land, children, and blessing, of which all would result in his posterity becoming "a great nation." The blessing and dominion given to Adam, and later to Noah, are now given to Abraham. And the command given to both Adam and Noah to be "fruitful and multiply" (1:28; 9:1) is now reinstated as a promise (17:1–2).

The focus of Genesis 12 to Exodus 18 is centered on God's fulfillment of His promises to Abraham: that his descendants will be a great nation, living as God's people under God's rule. This storyline is filled with trials, tragedies, and triumphs. Although God had promised that Abraham would be a father, He intentionally waited twenty-five years until after Sarah (Abraham's wife) was too old to have children. Yet God proved His capability of bringing that which is dead back to life (see Romans 4:16–25), and by miraculous intervention, Sarah gave birth to a healthy, happy boy (Isaac). But before God enabled Sarah to have a son, the couple tragically decided to take matters into their own hands. At the request of Sarah, her maidservant (Hagar) was given to Abraham to be a surrogate (16:1–4). The result was the birth of Ishmael. But God makes it clear that His people will not arise from Ishmael, rather from Sarah's own womb (17:19; see Romans 9:6–9). Abraham and Sarah would have to trust, and eventually would come to know that nothing is impossible with God (18:1–15; cf. 21:1–7). Indeed, a lesson that Abraham did not soon forget. God, sometime after Isaac had been born, called him to do the unthinkable: to offer his son as an offering (Genesis 22:1–2). While Abraham would faithfully oblige (vv. 3–10), God at the last moment kept him from harming his son (vv. 11–12). Instead, God gave Abraham a ram as a substitute offering (vv. 12–14; which many have rightfully seen as a picture of Christ as our substitute, see Isaiah 53). Abraham did not understand why God told him to do it, and surely, he was full of grief at the thought, but he was still prepared to obey. He knew that the future of the promise depended on Isaac's survival, so he trusted that God would protect his son somehow, or even raise him from the dead (see Hebrews 11:17–19). His faith was not only evident (vv. 15–19), but was well placed!

Although Abraham was eventually provided an heir, he did not live to see the great nation that God had promised him. Instead, God would pass down these promises to Abraham's children. The first to inherit the promises, of course, is Isaac. The narrative tells us very little of the details of Isaac's life, and we must infer from this that his principle significance is seen in the repetition of the covenant promises to him and in the fact that he is living proof of the faithfulness of God to His promises made to Abraham.[2] There are some interesting parallels between the story of Abraham and that of Isaac; one of note is that his wife (Rebecca) is also infertile (25:20–21). As with Abraham, the fulfillment of God's promises was predicated on Isaac's future posterity. Yet God waited until Isaac was sixty (Genesis 25:26) before blessing him with sons. Thus the birth of twins (Esau and Jacob) must be reckoned as a supernatural birth just as Isaac's was.

Once again, God's divine choice is nestled in the text. Esau is the oldest son, and yet it is Jacob who receives the father's blessing. He is the one whose descendants will be in the line of promise and become the people of God (25:19–23). Why does God choose him? He is certainly not the obvious choice: he is the younger son, and he is far from a good person. Genesis 27, for example, describes at length the cunning character of Jacob in deceiving his then feeble and nearly blind father. He tricked Isaac into giving him the blessing that belongs to the firstborn. Jacob was a lying, conniving person. However, God's choice of people are never based on their own merit, but on His grace (see Romans 9:10–13). Thus, it will be through the children of Jacob that the Kingdom of God will be demonstrated.

After Jacob deceived his father into giving him the "blessing," he fled to the house of his uncle Laban in fear that his brother Esau would take his life. Along the way, in a dream, God had promised that He would be with Jacob, would watch over him, and that it would be through him that God would fulfill His promises to Abraham (28:10–22). Eventually, Jacob would fall in love and plan to marry Rachel, the younger daughter of Laban. To this end, an agreement was made that after seven years of working for Laban, he would give his daughter to Jacob to be his wife. However, when it came time to marry Rachel, Laban tricked Jacob into marrying his older daughter, Leah, instead (the deceiver had been deceived, 29:15–30). Consequently, Jacob agrees to work seven more years so that he can marry Rachel as well.

By these women, and two maidservants, Jacob has twelve sons (29:31–30:24). Initially, it seems almost impossible that anything good could ever originate from these twelve men. They are truly an unsightly bunch. Joseph, Rachel's firstborn, is favored by his father; and, as a result, he is hated by his brothers (37:3). It is this family dynamic that propels the story forward. Moreover, Joseph begins having dreams which depict him ruling over his family (vv. 5–8). All of this compounded was more than his brothers could take, and when an occasion arose, they plotted to take Joseph's life by leaving him stranded in a pit (vv. 12–20). Although Reuben, the oldest sibling, had planned to retrieve his brother from the pit at a later time (vv. 21–22), providence would have it that Ishmaelite traders would be passing through on their way to Egypt; so instead, Levi convinced his brothers to sell Joseph to the merchants for a profit (vv. 25–28). These Ishmaelites, after arriving in Egypt, would providentially sell Joseph as a slave to an Egyptian aristocrat, Potiphar, who was in charge of Pharaoh's prison (v. 36).

As a slave in Potiphar's house, Joseph would thrive. So much so that soon after his arrival he was appointed to oversee all of Potiphar's affairs. The Lord was with Joseph, and as a result, Potiphar's household prospered (39:2–6). Yet, more heartache was in store for Joseph as he was eventually thrown into prison on false charges (vv. 11–20). Still, the Lord was with him and provided the opportunity for Joseph to interpret the dreams of two inmates (Pharaoh's head baker and head cupbearer) (Genesis 40). This occasion eventually becomes known to Pharaoh, who is struggling to understand his own dreams, and Joseph is summoned for his help (41:14). It is quite clear at this point in the story that Joseph's circumstances were far from accidental and that the Lord was not only with Joseph, but had also purposed the unfolding events. God had not only given Joseph the ability to interpret dreams, He had divinely orchestrated the opportunity for him to interpret the dreams of the most powerful man in all of Egypt. As a result, at the age of thirty, Joseph was appointed to be a ruler of Egypt, second only to Pharaoh himself (41:37–46). His interpretation of Pharaoh's dreams warned of a severe seven-year famine that would come at the end of a seven-year stretch of rich bounty. Thus, Joseph proposed a national policy of reserving one-fifth of all the food that was produced in Egypt, so that it could be redistributed in the time of need. Not only did this please

Pharaoh, but Joseph was specifically placed in power to oversee the implementation of the policy.

The famine had reached its peak, and word had begun to spread that there was food in Egypt for a price. In hopes of securing some of this food, Jacob sent his sons (minus Benjamin) to Egypt to buy grain (42:1–5). At first, Joseph disguises his identity, partially in hopes of retrieving Benjamin (his only non-half-blooded sibling), but eventually makes himself known and he and his brothers are reconciled. While this story is full of human interest, its significance is highlighted in the dramatic scene where Joseph addresses his brothers' wrongdoing: "But now, do not therefore be grieved or angry with yourselves because you sold me here; for God sent me before you to preserve life. For these two years the famine has been in the land, and there are still five years in which there will be neither plowing nor harvesting. And God sent me before you to preserve a posterity for you in the earth, and to save your lives by a great deliverance. So now it was not you who sent me here, but God; and He has made me a father to Pharaoh, and lord of all his house, and a ruler throughout all the land of Egypt" (45:5–8). Joseph did not intend to minimize the evil treatment of his brothers (Genesis 50:20), only to emphasize the larger purpose of God in the transpiring of these events. As such, God sovereignly regulated circumstances so that Joseph would be a ruler in Egypt, and thus Jacob's family was preserved in Egypt during the famine in order that a remnant would continue to exist (v. 11). At the same time, the promise of offspring was being fulfilled, for now there were seventy persons in Jacob's family (46:6–27). Of course, they were not yet as numerous as the stars, but they were on their way to the realization of what God had promised. Furthermore, the Israelites would maintain their ancestral identity while they were in Egypt. They had an occupation as shepherds, which was detestable to Egyptians, and so they were able to live separately in Goshen (46:33–47:6).

Up to this point, some very clear theological themes have emerged: 1) Man was originally created to have dominion over all the earth, but 2) man has fallen into sin and is now desperately in need of God's grace.

3) Through Adam's fall, all people have come under the power of Satan, sin, and death. 4) Yet, God's grace will ultimately result in the "seed of the woman" (Jesus) defeating Satan, sin, and death on the cross, in order that He might deliver man and reinstate His supreme rule (the Kingdom of God) over all the earth. 5) Furthermore, Abraham is promised that through him all the word would be "blessed" and that his children would be innumerable, would inherit the land of Canaan, and would become a great nation. Thus, the promise of the coming of the Kingdom would be secured through the covenant made with Abraham. And while none of the patriarchs were perfect, they all lived in faith that the Lord would fulfill His promises in the future. Even in Egypt, Joseph arranges for his dead body to be taken with God's people when they are called to go into the Promised Land (50:22–25).

Moses and the Exodus (Exodus 1–18)

The beginning of Exodus continues where Genesis concludes, namely with Jacob's family living in Egypt. God had promised that Abraham would multiply exceedingly (Genesis 17:1), and now we read that "the people of Israel were fruitful and increased abundantly; multiplied and grew exceedingly mighty, and the land was filled with them" (1:7). Joseph and his brothers have all died, and a new Pharaoh has come to power. Having no regard for the services rendered by Joseph, this Pharaoh sees the Israelites as a threat to national security and therefore makes them slaves of the state (vv. 8–11). The purpose for their captivity was intended to stunt their rapid growth in population. Nothing, however, could ultimately disrupt the Lord's sovereign plan. In fact, the more the king tries to thwart God's blessing, the more that blessing increases (v. 12). God is at work in these events to bring about His plan, and no one, not even the power of the great Pharaoh, can stand in His way.

Even so, the matter goes from bad to worse as Pharaoh, in reaction to his inability to suppress the fruitful fertility of the Israelites, resorts to murdering all Hebrew newborn sons (vv. 15–22). This atrocity must be viewed as an attack on God's covenant. Such hostility was forewarned when God prophetically stated: "I will put enmity between you [Satan] and the women, and between your seed and her seed" (Genesis 3:15). The "seed" of the devil is not to be taken literally. Rather, it represents all those who are influenced by and act toward Satan's cause (see John 8:44–45). Those who oppose the will of God, by acting contrary to it, resemble Satan himself (as one might say, "like father, like son") and thus constitute the "seed" of the devil. From such, we should expect strong animosity toward Christ, as well as toward those who act in accordance with God's will and follow Him (cf. John 15:18–25). Satan very early tried to halt God's plan of sending a Deliverer by leading Cain in killing his brother Abel (Genesis 4:1–16); here Satan does so again by murdering innocent children—but to no avail; the Deliverer will come!

The focus narrows from the grievous situation of the Israelites in Egypt to an Israelite family whose quiet but determined reaction to the quandary they face opens the way for the Lord's deliverance (Exodus 2). The chapter relates three key events in the early life of Moses. First, there is his birth and divinely ordained survival so that he can become the deliverer of Israel (vv. 1–10). Here we read that after Moses was born, his mother, Jochebed, recognizing he was a "beautiful" child (a Hebrew word that depicts a quality of excellence, or having value and benefit), hid him three months from the Egyptians. That Moses was seen as a "beautiful" child has been explained in various ways. Stuart believes it to be a Hebrew idiom, intending to mean that she "longed to keep him."[3] Currid, however, takes it to mean that Moses was extraordinarily healthy for a Hebrew baby: "He was not going to die in infancy as so many children did in those days."[4] Mackay, at last, simply explains it that Jochebed valued the life of Moses as a precious gift from God and was moved with compassion to protect it (much like the Hebrew midwives in chapter 1).[5] While all three explanations have merit, it cannot be ruled out that God had simply put it in Jochebed's heart to see Moses as having a special part in God's plan, and thus a life that must be protected. Either way, we know that his parents were acting in faith when they hid him (cf. Hebrews 11:23). But the time came when she could no longer hide Moses (2:3), so she places him in a waterproofed basket and hides him instead in the reeds along the river bank of the Nile. It is here that he is discovered by the royal princess and rescued. As a result, Moses is saved from death and given both a Hebrew and an Egyptian upbringing in preparation for his ministry. The theological significance of Moses's deliverance lies not in a general providential care of little children, but in the overruling of the powers opposed to God's Kingdom, in that they are unable to prevail against the one chosen to mediate God's plan of salvation. Indeed, the sovereignty of God manifested itself in a most curious and ironic way. The eventual deliverer of Israel and destroyer of Egypt was rescued by Pharaoh's own daughter, raised in Pharaoh's palace, and educated in Egyptian wisdom (cf. Acts 7:22).

The next key event in Moses's life occurs when he is nearly forty years old and attempts to rescue one of his fellow countrymen from Egyptian oppression (vv. 11–15). At this point Moses was facing a personal crisis of identity: would he continue to lead the life of an Egyptian prince, filled with prestige and power, or would he act to alleviate the suffering of his own people? Hebrews tells us that "By faith Moses, when he became of age, refused to be called the son of Pharaoh's daughter" (11:24). While we do not know if this royal renunciation preceded or followed the incident at hand, it certainly is part of Moses's inner turmoil at this time. He went out to where his own people were and "looked" at their burdens (v. 11). The Hebrew word for "looked" does not describe a casual watching, but the action of one who is studying a situation intently and who is reacting to it, perhaps, with grief. Moses's feelings, which had already been aroused by the poverty, humiliation, and suffering of his own people, are stirred further as he observes an Egyptian beating a Hebrew slave. His conscience would no longer allow him to remain a spectator. After making sure he would not be seen, he kills the Egyptian and hides him in the sand (v. 12). Yet, Moses is seen, after all, and word gets out. When Pharaoh realizes that Moses is his adversary, he tries to put him to death (v. 15), but Moses flees into exile. Even Moses, the one chosen to deliver God's people, has to learn that he cannot force events forward at his own pace.

The final event is Moses's arrival in Midian and the help he extends to Jethro's daughter, which leads to his marriage and settlement in that land (vv. 16–25). Midian was centered in the northwestern part of the Arabian Peninsula, under the control of a series of semi-nomadic tribes called Midianites. It was an area outside of Egyptian control, and we may suppose that Moses moved there as speedily as he could. An interval of time now occurs between Moses's settlement and what is to follow. How long that was is not directly stated in the text. However, we know from other portions of Scripture that Moses lived in Midian for forty years prior to the burning bush episode (cf. Acts 7:30).

Back in Egypt the Israelites are crying out for help. God hears them and remembers His covenant with their forefathers (2:23–25). This does not imply that He could ever forget His promises, but rather that He is about to act on the basis of those promises. Moses was the man appointed to lead Israel out of Egypt, though the narrative stresses Moses's feelings that he was utterly incapable of being the deliverer (chapters 3–4). Moses is concerned, particularly, that the Israelites will not believe him when he returns to Egypt and claims to be God's chosen (v. 13; 4:1). He is reassured on two grounds. First, he will identify the God who has spoken to him as "I AM" and as the God of their fathers (3:14–16). The meaning and trans-lation of the Hebrew word for "I AM" has precipitated much discussion. It is often referred to in modern literature as the tetragrammaton "YHWH," and is often pronounced as Jehovah or Yahweh. Unfortunately, the original pronunciation has been lost because Orthodox Judaism, from the time of the second temple period onward, refused to pronounce the name. It was considered too sacred or holy. Whenever a Jew saw *YHWH* written, he would replace it in speech with *Adonai* (a more common Hebrew word for God). With a clear connection to the Hebrew verb "to be," the name most likely emphasizes God's eternal existence and faithful consistency (Malachi 3:6). But whatever the case might be, we may safely land on what the text emphasizes. The Lord "YHWH" appeared to Moses as the God who keeps His covenant with His people. He will fulfill His covenant promises by rescuing Israel from Egypt and by bringing them into the land of promise (3:7–10, 16–17). Hence, as Schreiner has noted, "'I AM' emphasizes that the Lord is the God of the covenant, that He is fulfilling His promises as the God of Abraham, the God of Isaac, and the God of Jacob (3:15). The Lord is the living God and always keeps His promises, and the realization of the promises is not in question, since He is the Lord over all. YHWH will be remembered and praised forever for being the covenant-keeping God. The kingdom surely will come, for the Lord always fulfills His promises."[6]

Second, Moses is given some miraculous signs, which he will be able to repeat to persuade the Israelites of his mission (v. 19). Thus, these two themes of the name of God and the signs and wonders (His mighty power) are closely woven into the redemptive event by which Israel is freed. Another important and related theme is that of the identity of Israel as the people of God (cf. 3:7). To be the covenant people of God also means that they are known by His name (Deuteronomy 28:10). Centuries later, when the nation is held in a second captivity, God promises redemption to everyone who is "called by My name" (Isaiah 43:7).

Moses returns to Egypt and convinces his brother Aaron and all the people of his God-appointed task (4:31). But when his first demands to Pharaoh are met by the imposition of even harder conditions on the captives, the people reverse their receptive disposition entirely (5:21). It is on the heels of Moses's perceived failure that God gives him one of the great covenant statements in the Bible (6:6–8). The text emphasizes the Lord's faithfulness to His covenant promises:

> *I am the Lord; I will bring you out from under the burdens of the Egyptians, I will rescue you from their bondage, and I will redeem you with an outstretched arm and with great judgments. I will take you as My people, and I will be your God. Then you shall know that I am the Lord your God who brings you out from under*

the burdens of the Egyptians. And I will bring you into the land which I swore to give to Abraham, Isaac, and Jacob; and I will give it to you as a heritage: I am the Lord.

By Israel being redeemed and freed from Egypt, Yahweh was fulfilling the promises that He had given to the patriarchs. Yahweh was Israel's God, and hence they would come to realize His deliverance and salvation in accordance with His covenantal promises.

Chapter seven begins with a reinstatement of Moses's commission from the Lord (vv. 1–7), and then, after the record of a second interview with Pharaoh, the narrative moves on to give an account of the plagues that divinely afflicted Egypt (chapters 7–12). The theological crux that arises in this portion of the Old Testament and in other similar passages (Deuteronomy 2:30; Joshua 11:20; Isaiah 6:9–10; 63:17) derives not from the fact that it is said that the human heart is hard, but that it is said that God hardens the human heart. Is it fair of God to make people resolute in their rebellion? Is this something that a loving and righteous God would do? In particular, can God harden someone's heart and then condemn them because their heart is hard? Many different approaches have been developed to try to explain this phenomenon. Some interpret this to mean that God had directly hardened Pharaoh's heart as an act of judgment for his persistent rebellion. Others contend that He does not override the will of the individual but permits the individual to harden his own heart. God allows individuals to resist His will by withdrawing any restraining influence upon them or by introducing the circumstances which He knows will lead to this defiant action on their part. They take the action themselves, but since God is the instigator, He is described as if He had done it directly. There is a level of truth in each approach.

Looking over these chapters in Exodus, we find that ten times it is directly said that God hardened Pharaoh's heart (4:21; 7:3; 9:12; 10:1, 20, 27; 11:10; 14:4, 8, 17). At other times Pharaoh hardened his own heart (8:15, 32; 9:34), or it is merely said that his heart was hardened without specifying by whom or what (7:13, 14, 22; 9:7, 35). It is surely significant that in the accounts of the first five plagues it is said that Pharaoh hardened his own heart, and that it is only beginning with the sixth plague that the Lord intervenes to harden his heart. Thus, Pharaoh's own reaction leads to the divine imposition of judgment on him, and therefore the Lord's action may be viewed as a judicial consequence of Pharaoh's rebellion. But it should also be noted that before the plague sequence begins the Lord has already declared that He will harden Pharaoh's heart. Indeed, this was something which, even before Moses had returned to Egypt, God had told him would happen (4:21). The Lord had let the situation in Egypt develop over many years so that He could intervene and display His power (9:16). It is not that God is going to induce evil into Pharaoh's heart—that was not needed; it was already there. Rather, by withdrawing any restraining influence on Pharaoh and by directly challenging his status, the Lord brought it about that the full extent of Pharaoh's stubbornness and opposition became evident. As such, God did not make Pharaoh a bad person, but rather made a bad Pharaoh the object of His power and judgment (Paul uses this text as a way of explaining God's rejection of unbelieving Israel in Romans 9; see also 1 Samuel 6:6).

Over and over, Moses faithfully appeared before Pharaoh and delivered God's command that His people should be set free. Each time, however, Pharaoh replies with contempt: "Who is the Lord, that I should obey Him and let Israel go?" (5:2). His rhetorical and irreverent inquiry will soon be answered. In the end, God will have sent ten terrible plagues against Egypt. These plagues demonstrate the Lord's mighty power over all Egyptian deities (12:12), including Pharaoh himself. Nine of the plagues will prove Pharaoh's extreme renitency toward God, but the tenth and final plague breaks his resistance. On one dreadful night, God passes through the land in Egypt and every Egyptian firstborn son is killed. The threat of death was not limited to Egyptians alone but to all of Egypt's residents. It was sinners that deserved God's judgment of death (Ezekiel 18:20; Romans 3:23), and this included the Hebrews as well. But God graciously provides them with a way of escape. Each family is to kill a lamb instead and put its blood on the external door-frame of their house. Moses tells them, "For the Lord will pass through to strike the Egyptians, and when He sees the blood on the lintel and on the two doorposts, the Lord will pass over the door and will not allow the destroyer to enter your houses to strike you" (12:23). The fact that Pharaoh would not allow Israel, God's firstborn son, to leave Egypt, means that the firstborn sons of Egyptian families must forfeit their lives unless they are protected by sacrificial blood (4:2–3; 11:5; 12:29). Furthermore, as a result of God having preserved Israel's firstborn sons, they now belong to Him in a special way and must be set apart to Him for His use (13:1–2).

Through this great act of deliverance, the Israelites are being taught an important principle: God's salvation comes by way of substitution. His people deserve to die for their sin, but another will die instead. We are being prepared for a greater act of deliverance, of which the Passover is only a shadow. Just as the Passover lamb died in the place of others, so Jesus died as a substitute for our sin. This point was well made when John the Baptist said of Jesus, "Behold, the Lamb of God, which takes away the sin of the world" (John 1:29). Surely it is beyond mere coincidence that Jesus died at Passover time (Matthew 26:19; John 19:31). The deliverance of the Israelites from Egypt points forward to the greater deliverance Jesus achieved on the cross, as Paul explicitly states, "Christ, our Passover, was sacrificed for us" (1 Corinthians 5:7). Thus, God instructs Moses to establish the feast of the Passover as a memorial forever (Exodus 12:14–20). This shows how important the Passover is in patterning the redemptive work of God, in that by the shedding of blood, His people are delivered from slavery and escape the coming judgment.

No sooner did the Israelites leave Goshen than Pharaoh have second thoughts and decided to pursue them with his mighty army. When they had caught up to them, the soldiers found the defenseless Israelites cornered at Pi Hahiroth, whose location is presently unknown. Realizing their dire circumstances, the Israelites hurled bitter accusation against Moses for having led them there, to which he responded, "Do not be afraid. Stand still, and see the salvation of the Lord, which He will accomplish for you today. For the Egyptians whom you see today, you shall see again no more forever. The Lord will fight for you, and you shall hold your peace" (14:13–14). Just as God had delivered the Israelites from Egyptian bondage, He would likewise defend them against the Egyptian army. This was God's war, any-way, not theirs. That is, this war was undertaken by the Lord in defense of His own reputation, promises, and self-interest (Exodus 14:10–14; see also, for example, 15:3; Deuteronomy 1:30; 3:22; 20:4). Here, in Israel's hope-less situation, an opportunity arose for the Lord to make clear that He is the almighty God. He therefore commanded Moses to part the "Red Sea" (probably a stretch of water at the northern end of the Suez Gulf), an act that would exalt Him above Pharaoh and testify to Egypt that He alone is the Lord. The glowing cloud that would lead the way would symbolize God's presence and His role as the divine provider and protector of Israel.

The Mosaic (Sinaitic) Covenant (Exodus 19–Numbers 10)

The significance of the Exodus provides the important context for bringing Israel to the place, both spiritually and geographically, of enter-ing into covenant fellowship with God. This was not, however, a covenant that made Israel the people of God. That had already been established through God's covenant with Abraham. Rather, the covenant about to be implemented was one that established the ground rules for maintaining a proper relationship with God, who is holy, and the channel for receiving and enjoying God's blessings. What is obvious, obedience to the covenant was never intended in any way to be a means of salvation, but rather the expectation of those who had already come to experience God's salvation. Furthermore, God had promised Abraham that his people would become a great nation, so now God will constitute the very essence of what makes them great: His rule over them.

Three months after the Exodus, Israel arrived at the mountain where the Lord had earlier said He would meet them (19:1–2; see 3:12). With

Moses as His mediator, God reminded them how He had defeated the Egyptians, delivered His own people, and brought them to Himself, that is to the place of Mt. Sinai (v. 4). Now, on condition of their obedience to His forthcoming covenant, He was prepared to make them His special possession, a precious gem, as it were, that he had selected from among all the nations (v. 5). The role they were to play should they accede would be one of intercession between the Lord and the peoples of the earth. They would become a royal priesthood, a holy nation (v. 6). "Just as any priest bridged the gap between the transcendent God and His earthbound creatures, so Israel, already God's 'son,' would become a mediator between the infallible one and all the nations that needed to be reconciled to Him."[7] This is probably not meant to insinuate that the Israelites were to be missional, as with the New Testament church. Nowhere was Israel instructed to bring the message of the love of God to other nations. Other nations would be attracted to Yahweh when they saw the blessings that belong to Israel as the chosen and consecrated people of the Lord.

When Moses communicated this astounding offer to the people, they immediately responded in the affirmative: "All that the Lord has spoken we will do" (vv. 7–8). The Lord then commanded Moses to prepare the people for a forthcoming encounter with Him as the two parties—the Lord and Israel—would come together to officially make their covenantal agreement (vv. 9–15). Such an encounter was by no means between equals. In fact, the holiness of God differs so greatly from the carnality of humanity that the Israelites could not even look on His radiant glory. In language wholly inadequate to describe the divine manifestation, Moses spoke of it in terms of cosmic imagery: thunder, lightning, clouds, smoke, and earthquake (vv. 16–19). The usual theological term for this kind of visitation is *theophany*, a display of the Lord's presence short of the revelation of His actual person. The Israelites stood at the foot of the mountain, trembling as they stared up at the terrifying scene above. The whole mountain seemed ablaze with God's presence, and it shook as He thundered forth His response to Israel's offer to make a covenant with Him. Only Moses could stand between, and so he shuttled back and forth between Israel at the foot of the mountain and the Lord God in the impenetrable heights of Sinai. The task of communicating between the two lay with him, for if the Lord spoke directly to the people they would die (vv. 16–25; see also Deuteronomy 4:33; 5:4–5, 24–25).

The revelation God shared with Moses on the mountaintop was a collection of laws that are referred to collectively as the *Book of the Covenant* (20:2–23:33), the first part of which is the *Decalogue* or Ten Commandments. The Decalogue is the constitution of the covenant community, as it were, and the remaining laws are amendments or clarifications of those commandments. In fact, the Book of the Covenant begins and ends with a focus on the first two commandments, thus establishing their importance as the foundation of the entire covenant relationship. In recent times scholars have drawn attention to the fact that the laws of the Decalogue are of one type or form (apodictic) whereas the others are of a different kind (casuistic). In other words, the Decalogue are laws that lay down moral principles which are general to all life, whereas the laws that follow the Decalogue are the application of those moral principles within a specific context. Moreover, it is clear in light of ancient Near Eastern (particularly Hittite) models that the book of the Covenant (as well as in Deuteronomy) is best described as a suzerain-vassal treaty, one in which a great king (here, God Himself) makes a covenant with a lesser king or subject (here, Israel). In this covenantal form the will of the greater is imposed on the lesser, but the latter stands to gain great benefit if he accepts and obeys the terms of the covenant. The important relationship between the Mosaic covenant and this covenantal structure has already been considered in chapter 7 above, and thus we direct the reader there for further insight.

It seems that Moses first ascended alone to the presence of the Lord (24:1–2), where he received the Decalogue and the Book of the Covenant by God's gracious revelation. He then descended to the people with the "words" (commandments) and presented them to the assembly, which swore to obey them (v. 3). After writing down all these terms, Moses erected an altar (representing the Lord) and twelve pillars (representing Israel's twelve tribes). He then sprinkled the blood of a sacrifice on the altar and pillars, thereby symbolizing God's covenant union with His people (vv. 4–8). Moses, Aaron, Aaron's sons, and seventy elders then met the Lord in a display of His glory and shared with Him the covenant banquet (a formal meal that testified publicly to the binding nature of the agreements to which the contracting parties had sworn) (vv. 9–11). Afterward, Moses ascended once more to Sinai's summit, where he encountered the ineffably awesome presence of God (vv. 12–17). The Lord there gave him a duplicate set of the Commandments and Book of the Covenant (v. 12), one that was identical to what Moses had already written. One copy was to be retained by the Lord, as it were, and the other by Israel, for it was traditional in the ancient world for both covenant parties to have a copy of their mutual agreement. After the whole arrangement had been consummated on the mountain, Moses returned to the people below (v. 18).

Now that the Lord had made a covenant with Israel and, as part of it, had commanded Israel to appear before Him three times a year (23:14–17), a place for those occasions (and more) must be built—according to strict specifications (25:1–8). This place was called the tabernacle, which means dwelling, and would come to represent the dwelling presence of God. The tabernacle consisted of an outer courtyard and a tent-like structure that was separated into two sections: "the Holy Place" and "the Most Holy Place" (or "Holy of Holies"). Inside the courtyard stood an altar, called the "brazen altar," and a shiny bronze laver basin for the priests to wash themselves before entering the tabernacle. Inside the Holy Place were three important pieces of furniture: the table of showbread, the lampstand, and the altar of incense. Each piece of furniture served to illustrate in some way God's provision for and presence with His people. It is also believed by many that each piece illustrates or points to Christ. He is the bread of life (John 6:35), the light of the world (John 8:12), and the one who intercedes on behalf of all believers (Romans 8:34; Hebrews 7:25). Dividing the Holy Place from the Most Holy Place was a "veil," or curtain, which served to block the entrance to the Holy of Holies. Inside the Most Holy Place stood just one piece of furniture: the Ark of the Covenant. It was a chest, about 130 cm long and 60 cm wide and high, which housed the stone tablets on which God had inscribed the Ten Commandments. Above it was a separate lid called the "Mercy Seat," or literally the "atonement cover." At either end sat a golden cherub angel, whose wings spread horizontally over the cover to form the throne of the invisible God. God tells Moses, "There I will meet with you, and I will speak with you from above the mercy seat, from between the two cherubim which are on the ark of the Testimony, about everything which I will give you in commandment to the children of Israel" (25:22). After the construction of the tabernacle, God's "glory" fills the place and afterward continues to abide with Israel in the form of a cloud by day and a pillar of fire by night (40:34–38). Thus, as it was with Adam and Eve in the Garden of Eden, God is dwelling among His people once again.

Exodus concludes with Yahweh's presence among the people of Israel. Despite Israel's predisposition toward sin and rebellion, the Lord dwells among His people via the tabernacle. Leviticus continues as part of the Mosaic Covenant, which deals directly with the prospect of how the Lord can continue to live in the midst of Israel. Or a better way of putting it may be that Leviticus describes how Israel, a sinful people, may live in the Lord's presence.

Exodus 19:4–6 describe Israel as a "holy nation," one set apart by the Lord to be His special people. Having accepted this role by affirming the Sinai Covenant, Israel became God's vassal, His minister to mediate His saving grace to all nations. To be a "holy" nation required Israel to have a means whereby that holiness could be maintained. Therefore, there needed to be a set of guidelines stipulating every aspect of that relationship between the nation and her God. In this sense, holiness as a position intersects with holiness as a condition. With the former, holiness means merely the establishment of a relationship whereby a person or even an object or institution is set apart for a particular function. It has no necessary ethical or moral corollary. In the latter sense, holiness comes to embody purity and righteousness, for God's own personal holiness entails not only His remoteness and uniqueness but also His moral perfection. People whom He sanctifies and declares holy must also therefore exhibit moral uprightness. Fundamentally, Leviticus describes the means by which Israel may approach God to offer appropriate homage and to cultivate and maintain the relationship brought about by the covenant. Since Israel (with all the human race) was inherently evil by virtue of the Fall, there must be a divinely appointed apparatus or system to make possible the purification of the people and all they touch so that they might be qualified to approach and serve the Lord.

This system of purity revolved around five designated offerings that served as God's gracious provision for how one could regain and sustain fellowship with Him: the burnt offering, the meal offering, the peace offering, the sin offering, and the trespass offering. Whatever the Israelites may have thought of it at the time, the unceasing sacrifice of animals and the never-ending glow of fire at the altar of sacrifice no doubt was intended to burn into the hearts of every person an awareness of their own sin— an object lesson that was to be an age-long picture of the coming sacrifice of Messiah. The sacrifices pointed to Him and were fulfilled in Him (see Hebrews 10:1–14). Not only did God make provision for individual Israelites, He also established provisions for the corporate people of the Lord to deal with the matter of national alienation.

The death of Aaron's two sons (Leviticus 10:1–2) provided the impetus for instruction to Aaron about approaching the Holy One. He could do so even to the extent of entering the Most Holy Place but only once a year, on the day he would present there the sacrificial blood for national atonement. Properly attired, he would enter the outer room of the tabernacle, the Holy Place, with a sin offering and a burnt offering. He would also set apart two goats and a ram for sacrifice; a bull, as well, had to be slain for Aaron's own atonement. Afterward, one of the goats was to be selected as a sin offering and the other as a "scapegoat." The former would symbolize the propitiation for sin—that is, it being covered, and the other represented expiation, the removal of sin. Both of these were on behalf of the whole people.

The blood of the slain goat, like that of the bull, must be brought into the Most Holy Place and sprinkled on the Ark of the Covenant (16:14–15), representative of God's very throne. By this act not only the people but also the tabernacle and all its furnishings would become purified. The live goat must then be driven into the wild, bearing with him the aggregate sins of all Israel (16:22). Once he left the tabernacle, Aaron must bathe himself, change his clothes, and then offer up sin and burnt offerings on the great bronze altar in the courtyard. The parts of the animals not consumed on the altar must be taken outside the camp and burned (16:27–28).

This sacred ritual was to take place on the tenth day of the seventh month of each year, a day known as *Yom Kippur* (Day of Atonement). It was to be a day of complete rest (Sabbath), when the whole nation could undertake intense introspection and, in light of its collective sin, seek and receive atoning grace so as to enter the new year in perfect fellowship with the Lord. These sacrifices enabled in some measure a relationship with God, but it was never a permanent one. They never fully dealt with sin. Instead, they point beyond themselves to the perfect sacrifice that Christ would offer through His death on the cross. His death deals with sin once and for all; it never needs to be repeated. It opens up the way into God's presence "beyond the veil" to all who trust in Him. When Christ died, the curtain in the temple (the permanent structure in Jerusalem, which later replaced the tabernacle) was torn in two by God (Mark 15:58). The symbolism is powerful: the door to God's presence is now wide open for all who will go in (Hebrews 10:19–20). So again, all through the Bible God provides a substitute to die in the place of others. The different sacrifices in the Old Testament point ahead to the perfect sacrifice offered by Jesus when He died on the cross:

- A sacrifice for an individual: Adam and Eve (Genesis 3).

- A sacrifice for a family: the Passover (Exodus 12).

- A sacrifice for a nation: The Day of Atonement (Leviticus 16).

- A sacrifice for the world: the death of Jesus (John 1:29; 1 John 2:2).

The Conquest and Settlement of Canaan (Numbers 10–1 Samuel 7)

Once the law had been given and the tabernacle established, the Israelites were able to live as God's people under God's rule and enjoy the blessings and benefits that came as a result of living in God's presence. Nevertheless, they were a people without a land. Thus, the next section of the history of the Bible is focused on their entrance and settlement in the Promised Land. In the book of Numbers, after their time of preparation at Mount Sinai, we find the Israelites ready to set out on their journey to Canaan. The rabble from Egypt is now organized and is beginning to look like an impressive army. And when they set out, God marches in front of them in a pillar of cloud (Numbers 10:11–12). Surely nothing can go wrong now. We could have expected them to reach their destination in a matter of months, but in actuality, it takes them forty years.

The journey from Sinai to the border of Canaan consisted of two major stages—many miles and a few weeks to Kadesh Barnea (Numbers 10:11–14:45), and a few miles and many years from there to the plains of Moab (22:1). The difference is the crisis of unbelief and rebellion that took place at Kadesh Barnea, a spiritual malaise that sentenced Israel to aimless migration in hostile deserts. The crisis was already foreshadowed in the trek from Sinai to Kadesh Barnea, for in that short time the people repeatedly complained and resisted Moses's leadership.

After arriving at Kadesh Barnea, a place located in the Paran desert just south of Canaan, Moses sent out a reconnaissance party of twelve men—one from each tribe—to explore Canaan in order to determine the feasibility of conquest and the nature of Canaan's resources (13:1–20). The spies, having scoped out the land for forty days, report back that it is a land "flowing with milk and honey" and that the people who live there are "strong" and "the cities are fortified and very large" (13:27–28). They exclaimed: "The land through which we have gone as spies is a land that devours its inhabitants, and all the people whom we saw in it are men of great stature. There we saw the giants (the descendants of Anak came from the giants); and we were like grasshoppers in our own sight, and so we were in their sight" (vv. 32–33). The reaction of the people was predictable:

> So all the congregation lifted up their voices and cried, and the people wept that night. And all the children of Israel complained against Moses and Aaron, and the whole congregation said to them, "If only we had died in the land of Egypt! Or if only we had died in this wilderness! Why has the Lord brought us to this land to fall by the sword, that our wives and children should become victims? Would it not be better for us to return to Egypt?" So they said to one another, "Let us select a leader and return to Egypt."
> (Numbers 14:1–4)

Despite Joshua's and Caleb's pleading with the people to trust in the Lord, the Israelites were terrified and refused to enter the land, convinced that they would be destroyed. God responds by judging them. At first, the Lord threatens to destroy the people and make a great nation of Moses and his descendants (14:12). But again, as in Exodus, Moses intercedes for the people, reminding the Lord that His own reputation would be tarnished if He destroyed Israel (14:13–20). The Lord's name and presence was inextricably entwined with Israel's fate, so if He annihilated them, the Lord's power and presence among His people would be questioned by surrounding nations. Moses, therefore, reminded the Lord of His great name and character, for He is a God who is "longsuffering and abundant in mercy, forgiving iniquity and transgression; but He by no means clears the guilty, visiting the iniquity of the fathers on the children to the third and fourth generation. Pardon the iniquity of this people, I pray, according to the greatness of Your mercy, just as You have forgiven this people, from Egypt even until now" (14:18–19). Israel's betrayal warranted their judgment and annihilation, but the Lord, in response to Moses's intercession and as a revelation of His saving love, spared them. Even so, due to their obstinacy as a result of unbelief, no one over the age of twenty, except for Joshua and Caleb, would enter into the Promised Land. Only after the older generation had died off, would He then lead their children, the ones that they were so afraid would be mistreated, into the land of Canaan to possess it.

Indeed, other rebellions are recorded, and it becomes clear that Israel is incapable of keeping the covenant. The positive side of this bleak fact is that man's failure, though it may incite dire consequences, never prevails against the faithfulness of God. Each time the Israelites falter in faith, the grace and covenant faithfulness of God is highlighted, and we are made to look to the future when the problem of human sin will be truly overcome in one surprisingly victorious redeeming act. This event, as an example, is foreshadowed in the wilderness when a plague of deadly snakes is sent as judgment on the people's grumbling. Moses cries out to God for mercy and is commanded to set a bronze snake on a pole in the midst of the camp. Anyone who is bitten has only to look at the bronze snake to be saved from death (Numbers 21:4–9; see John 3:14–15). There is no obvious logic to this as a remedy for deadly venom, but as a response of faith to a word of promise, it illustrates man's remedy for sin (Christ death for us), and our only prerequisite for help: we must believe (John 3:16–17). In these events of the wilderness wanderings, we see an emerging pattern of Israel's rejection of the covenant, and God's unrelenting faithfulness to keep it.

Forty years after the Exodus the new generation now stands in the plains of Moab, on the east side of the Jordan, ready to enter the Promised Land. The book of Deuteronomy records Moses's words to the nation as it prepares for conquest. It is generally recognized that Deuteronomy is written in the form of a treaty covenant and represents a renewal of the covenant to the new generation about to move under a new leader, Joshua.[8] The first section recounts the period of Israel's history that is covered in the book of Numbers. It emphasizes the greatness and goodness of God as He performs mighty deeds to fulfill His promises to Israel. It also recounts the faithlessness and rebellion of the people in the wilderness (Deuteronomy 1–3). Next, the Lord assures Joshua that He will go before him and fight for His people (3:21–22; 28). In addition to God's promise to be with the Israelites, Deuteronomy repeats the stipulations of the covenant that are to be obeyed (Deuteronomy 4–26). These stipulations provide the foundation for covenant faithfulness, which is summarized in these words: "Hear, O Israel: The Lord our God, the Lord is one! You shall love the Lord your God with all your heart, with all your soul, and with all your strength" (Deuteronomy 6:4–5). These regulations for holy living are covered by sanctions—that is, what happens if you obey and what happens if you do not.[9] These blessings and curses are scattered throughout the book, but a comprehensive collection of them is found in Deuteronomy 28. "Thus, the book emphasizes the goodness of God in His choice of Israel and the covenant blessings that He gives to His people. It also points repeatedly to Israel's responsibility to live consistently as the holy people of God. Should the nation refuse those responsibilities, it will in turn be denied the blessings. Such rebellion not only deserves the withdrawal of the blessings but also invites the curses."[10]

As the new leader, Joshua is tasked with leading the people in conquest. The theological thrust of the book of Joshua can be grasped from a reading of the first and the last two chapters. As promised, and with hardly a challenge, Israel enters the land of Canaan (23:1–13). In the end, they are left in no doubt that the conquest is not a victory they can claim for themselves. They are powerless, but God is mighty. That is seen most clearly in the sage of Jericho, when God causes the walls to collapse before them. The only reason they possess the land is that the Lord has fought for them. Although there is still some territory to be acquired (23:4–5), the promises are deemed as fulfilled: "You know with all your heart and soul that not one of all the good promises the Lord your God gave you has failed. Every promise has been fulfilled; not one has failed Joshua" (23:14, ESV; see also 21:43–45).

The book of Joshua highlights the successful possession of the land. The very next book, the book of Judges, however, concentrates on the blemishes of this achievement. In many places the Israelites retain their conquered foes for forced labor (Judges 1:27–36). The Lord rebukes them for making covenants with the Canaanites and reminds them that these foreigners will become a snare to them (Judges 2:2–3). The theme of the book is set out in Judges 2:11–23:

> *Then the children of Israel did evil in the sight of the Lord, and served the Baals; and they forsook the Lord God of their fathers, who had brought them out of the land of Egypt; and they followed other gods from among the gods of the people who were all around them, and they bowed down to them; and they provoked the Lord to anger. They forsook the Lord and served Baal and the Ashtoreths. And the anger of the Lord was hot against Israel. So He delivered them into the hands of plunderers who despoiled them; and He sold them into the hands of their enemies all around, so that they could no longer stand before their enemies. Wherever they went out, the hand of the Lord was against them for calamity, as the Lord had said, and as the Lord had sworn to them. And they were greatly distressed. Nevertheless, the Lord raised up judges who delivered them out of the hand of those who plundered them. Yet they would not listen to their judges, but they played the harlot with other gods, and bowed down to them. They turned quickly from the way in which their fathers walked, in obeying the commandments of the Lord; they did not do so. And when the Lord raised up judges for them, the Lord was with the judge and delivered them out of the hand of their enemies all the days of the judge; for the Lord was moved to pity by their groaning because of those who oppressed them and harassed them. And it came to pass, when the judge was dead, that they reverted and behaved more corruptly than their fathers, by following other gods, to serve*

them and bow down to them. They did not cease from their own doings nor from their stubborn way. Then the anger of the Lord was hot against Israel; and He said, "Because this nation has transgressed My covenant which I commanded their fathers, and has not heeded My voice, I also will no longer drive out before them any of the nations which Joshua left when he died, so that through them I may test Israel, whether they will keep the ways of the Lord, to walk in them as their fathers kept them, or not." Therefore the Lord left those nations, without driving them out immediately; nor did He deliver them into the hand of Joshua.

After the Israelites take general possession of the land the pattern of events becomes a repetitive cycle. The people rebel against the Lord and indulge in religious syncretism (the mixing of pagan ideas with their own) and even apostasy.[11] Consequently, God punishes them by allowing foreigners to invade and oppress them. Then, as they cry out under their affliction, God sends judges to save them from their enemies (2:14–23). Thus, as Goldsworthy has well noted,

This crucial period in Israel's history reinforces the salvation pattern established in the Exodus. Although the Israelites do well physically in the Promised Land their disobedience prevents their enjoyment of the promised blessings. They repeatedly enter into a kind of captivity and, unlike the Egyptian captivity, the reason for it is obviously their sinful rejection of the Lord. But then the Lord's covenant faithfulness and love leads to their salvation through some saving act of God through a timely chosen deliverer. The giving of the Spirit to the judges indicates that what the Israelites cannot do for themselves, God does for them through a chosen, Spirit empowered human being.[12]

13

The Total Pattern of Revelation (Part 2)

The Rise and Fall of the Nation of Israel
(1 Samuel 8–2 Chronicles 36)[1]

When trouble arises in Israel and the possession of their Land is threatened, they naturally look for help, but not necessarily for the right kind of help. After Gideon's success against the Midianites, the Israelites press to have him establish a dynasty of kings. Gideon rejects this on the grounds that the Lord alone is King (Judges 8:22–23). After the death of Gideon, one of his sons, Abimelech, succeeds in being made a ruler for a short period, probably over only a relatively small region (chapter 9). For the most part, however, the judges continued to rule the people. The book of Judges concludes with a reference to instability and chaos in the land as due to the lack of a king (21:25).

During the time of the prophet and judge Samuel, some disastrous encounters with the Philistines lead to the resurgence of Israel's desire for a king. And while Samuel rejects the notion of a king, as Gideon did before, the idea of kingship was established long before this and the Israelites might seem justified in their request. Jacob, for example, prophesied that a kingly ruler would one day come from the tribe of Judah, with no suggestion that this would not be God's will (see Genesis 49:8–10). Also, written into the statutes and ordinances of Deuteronomy is the provision of a king (Deuteronomy 17:14–20). Strict guidelines are given which clearly distinguish between the usual type of pagan despotic ruler and the king whose rule reflects the covenant relationship with the living God. Israel's kings must fear the Lord, keep His law, and refrain from lifting their hearts above their fellowmen. In other words, kingship for Israel is defined by the covenant. Unfortunately, the people do not see it that way, and rather than taking the covenant as the model of kingship, they undoubtedly desire the benefits that appear to come from the autocratic rule of the Canaanite and Philistine kings.[2] Thus, the request for a king, which Samuel at first refuses, is born of the desire to imitate the pagan nations. This was indeed a rejection of the covenant model and, therefore, a rejection of God's rule over them (1 Samuel 8:4–8). Thus, we may assume that God tells Samuel to comply with the peoples' request partially because it was always God's will to rule Israel through a king, and partially for teaching them the hard way the reality of living outside of God's rule. So Samuel warns the people that the kind of king they are asking for would not in any way turn out to be what they had hoped for (vv. 10–18).

When Saul is chosen publicly by the casting of lots, there is no indication that he will end up a failure. In fact, he is full of promise and begins his reign by acting the part of a Savior-King. Though chosen prematurely, Saul was still used by God to deliver His people. The Holy Spirit came on him, and with a hastily gathered militia he marched to Jabesh-Gilead and defeated the Ammonites. In this important victory, Saul was ready to recognize the hand of the Lord (11:12–15). This type of leadership prompted Samuel to step aside, but he warns the people that it is up to them and Saul to follow the Lord. If they do, all will be well (12:14–15). Unfortunately, they do not, and before you know it, Saul has forsaken the Word of the Lord. Saul's first major blunder occurs while the Israelites are at war with the Philistines. Having retreated to Gilgal, he decided to take upon himself the office of priest and offer sacrifices to God. But as soon as he had done so, Samuel arrived. Saul tries in vain to excuse his inappropriate behavior, yet Samuel tells him that because he had rejected the Lord, the Lord would reject him and his kingdom will be taken from him (13:8–14). Later, after a victorious defeat of the Amalekites, Saul ignores God's restriction of keeping any of the spoil from battle (15:1–31). Thus, Saul shows himself to be very opposite of the kingly qualities found in Deuteronomy 17. Again, Samuel reminds Saul that because he has rejected the Word of the Lord, the Lord rejects him and will soon give his kingdom to a more preferable candidate (vv. 26–28).

While Saul yet lives and reigns as king, a man after God's own heart is being prepared unaware to be Israel's next leader (1 Samuel 13:14). Samuel is sent by God to the house of Jesse to anoint David, out of all his brothers (16:13), as Saul's replacement. The Spirit of the Lord departed Saul and now rested upon David (16:13–14). God's presence with him was demonstrated very early on when he defeated Goliath, the mighty Philistine champion, single-handed (chapter 17). As all Israel retreats in terror from the mighty giant, God's newly anointed, who appears weak and insignificant, fights for his people, knowing that the battle is the Lord's (17:45–47). David stands alone as the one in the place of the many, and through him God works salvation for Israel.

Understandably, David is the prize of the nation, resulting in Saul becoming increasingly jealous, to the point that he desires to have David killed. Rejected and despised, David flees from society and gathers a band of misfits around him. Yet so overwhelming is his sense of the king being anointed by God that he refuses on at least two occasions to lift his hand against Saul. He is prepared to leave it to the Lord to remove His anointed from office (24:1–7; 26:6–12). Assuredly, in God's time, David will be vindicated in the eyes of the people and will be exalted as king of Israel. Saul's grasp on the kingdom (and his sanity) slips, and eventually he dies on Mount Gilboa in a battle with the Philistines (chapter 31). The transition from Saul's rule to David's is not especially smooth. Nevertheless,

David is soon proclaimed king at the age of thirty. At the Lord's command he launches a successful campaign against the Philistines and secures the borders of Israel. He also captures the Jebusite stronghold of Jerusalem and makes it his capital (2 Samuel 5). He brings the Ark of the Covenant to Jerusalem (chapter 6) and then decides to build a permanent sanctuary for it (7:12–13). However, the prophet Nathan brings the Word of the Lord forbidding David to build Him a temple.

The highlight of David's life was God's revelation to him of His covenant purposes. Moreover, this covenant (referred to as the Davidic Covenant) is the utmost importance for understanding the theology that surrounds the most notable of all the kings. The time had now come for the reality of what up to this point had only been promised (Genesis 49:10; Numbers 24:17; 1 Samuel 16:1–13). The impetus for the covenant revelation was, ironically, David's desire to build a substantial temple for the Lord, not just a temporary tabernacle He had already installed–for why should David dwell in a magnificent palace while the Lord dwells in a common tent? Through the prophet Nathan, however, the Lord made clear that rather than David making a house for Him, He would make one for David, that is, a royal dynasty (2 Samuel 7:11). David's name would become great (7:9), and Israel, the nation over which he ruled, would forever be established in the land (7:10). Furthermore, David shall have a son (Solomon) who shall indeed build the temple and whose throne will be established forever (7:4–12). The continuity of this covenant with the covenant made with Abraham can be seen in their respective summaries. "I will be your God, and you shall be my people" sums up God's purpose in the covenant with Abraham and after him, with David (Genesis 17:7–8; 26:12; Exodus 6:7; see Jeremiah 7:23; 11:4; 30:22). Next the promise concerning David's son, the one whose kingdom will be established "forever," continues with the immensely important Messianic designation, "I will be His father, and He shall be My son" (2 Samuel 7:14). Thus, David's son is also the Son of God (a future king far greater than himself), and therefore it is ultimately in God's Son (Jesus) that the Kingdom of God is established forever (7:16).

From 2 Samuel 7 onward, the Bible anticipates the arrival of God's King, the Son of David. The Kingdom of God must be established by Him, the Messiah (meaning anointed one). An example of such anticipation is captured in Psalm 2:

> *Why do the nations rage and the peoples plot in vain? The kings of the earth set themselves, and the rulers take counsel together, against the Lord and against his Anointed, saying, "Let us burst their bonds apart and cast away their cords from us." He who sits in the heavens laughs; the Lord holds them in derision. Then He will speak to them in His wrath, and terrify them in his fury, saying, "As for me, I have set my King on Zion, my holy hill." I will tell of the decree: The Lord said to me, "You are my Son; today I have begotten you. Ask of me, and I will make the nations your heritage, and the ends of the earth your possession. You shall break them with a rod of iron and dash them in pieces like a potter's vessel." Now therefore, O kings, be wise; be warned, O rulers of the earth. Serve the Lord with fear, and rejoice with trembling. Kiss the Son, lest He be angry, and you perish in the way, for His wrath is quickly kindled. Blessed are all who take refuge in him.*

This psalm particularly focuses on the fact that, in spite of the efforts by the rulers of this world, God's Son, as an inheritance, will one day rule the nations as its King (see also Psalm 110).

Solomon succeeds his father, David, to the throne around the year 970 BC. The first and obvious point to note about Solomon is that as the son of David he fulfills an immediate sense of Nathan's prediction that the house of God would be built by such a son. But Solomon must be remembered for more than his temple-building activity. In fact, he is an enigma, for "he was both the perfecter of Israel's glory and the architect of its destruction."[3] The problem of the throne succession having been settled in Solomon's favor, the narrator deals at once with two apparently contradictory aspects of Solomon's behavior. First, we are told of the marriage alliance with the king of Egypt (1 Kings 3:1), which becomes a cause of stumbling in that it is the first stage of the apostasy described in chapter 11 (vv. 1–13). Second, we are told of Solomon's desire and noble request for wisdom, which receives God's commendation.

The wisdom of Solomon and the splendor of his kingdom go hand in hand, and both are seen as undergirding national prosperity and safety: "Judah and Israel dwelt in safety, each man under his vine and his fig tree, from Dan as far as Beersheba, all the days of Solomon" (4:25). So, the writer sums up the situation in a way that suggests that the prosperity of Solomon's reign is indicative of the fulfillment of the promises to Abraham. The people are in the land, they are safe, and the land yields its fruit in bountiful blessing.

The fact that wisdom characterized Solomon's reign demands that we try to understand the significance of wisdom in biblical theology. The king who rules wisely is not only concerned with intelligent decisions which promote justice (3:16–28), but he also achieves prosperity and peace in the land according to the covenant promise (4:20–28). At the heart of his wisdom is the revelation of God and His covenant.

Job, Proverbs, and Ecclesiastes are the main books of the Old Testament that deal with the search of knowledge and the establishment of wisdom. They start from the framework of revelation and a fear of or reverence for the Lord. From the standpoint of a believer, they explore the issues of the human experience. The world and human life have meaning because God not only preserves His creation from chaos, but also because He has shown that He is restoring all things to their rightful relationships. The book of Proverbs invites us to examine our experiences and to find in them the underlying relationships that make life coherent and meaningful. The wise person tries to understand the realities of this life and to yield to the knowledge that brings about a fruitful life with God. The individual proverbs are not detailed expressions of the law handed down by God, but rather are human reflections on individual experiences in light of God's truth. Thus, they show that being human as God intended means learning to think and act in a godly way. It means that, in revelation, God gives the framework for godly thinking, but He will not do our thinking for us. We are responsible for the decisions we make as we seek to be wise (to think in a godly way) and to avoid being foolish (to think in a godless way). Decisions are wise when they are made in the light of the life which God provides and chooses for us.

David's heart was to bring the ark to Jerusalem and to make the city the focal point of the covenant relation with God. All the promises of God concerning His relationship to His people and the land He gives them are concentrated in Jerusalem, or Zion. Solomon now builds the temple as the permanent dwelling place of God in the holy city. Its glory is described in detail in 1 Kings 5–7, but the theology of the temple is concentrated in Solomon's dedicatory prayer (1 Kings 8). Through the temple and its ministry, the covenant relationship is maintained (vv. 15–53). Even the Gentiles who came to believe in the Lord could look to the temple in faith and find there that the God of Israel was their God also (8:41–43). The temple, therefore, is a witness to all the nations that God dwells in Israel and that He is found by all through the name He has revealed.

In spite of all of these positive points, Solomon's reign and character, of course, are blemished. Solomon had begun to marry foreign wives and, to accommodate his wives and the religious traditions they represented, he established pagan shrines throughout the land (11:1–8). Consequently, his moral failures evoked a severe reprimand from the Lord (vv. 9–13). The covenant with David's dynasty would stand, but all the tribes except Judah (David's own tribe) would be torn away from the kingdom to form a separate entity. God would delay this judgment for David's sake until after Solomon dies, but then He causes a civil war to break out and the kingdom begins to implode.

Soon after Solomon's son, Rehoboam, comes to the throne, the ten northern and eastern tribes rebel against him and set up their own kingdom under Jeroboam (who served over Solomon's workforce; see 1 Kings 11:28). Israel had been united for 120 years under Saul, David, and Solomon, but now it is divided. The northern kingdom is, confusingly, called Israel, with its capital in Shechem and, later, in Samaria. The southern kingdom, Judah, has Jerusalem as its capital. There are occasional good kings in Judah, but the general direction of the history of both kingdoms is downward.

The decline is obvious in the north from the very beginning. Jeroboam is concerned that his people will continue to want to go to Jerusalem in the southern kingdom to meet with God at the temple. Thus, he establishes two alternative shrines, at Bethel and Dan, and puts a golden calf in each, saying, "Here are your gods, O Israel, which brought you up out of the land of Egypt" (12:28). Aaron had made the same imbecilic statement after he and the people had made another golden calf while Moses was on Mount Sinai receiving the law from God (Exodus 32:4). This idolatrous worship is the besetting sin of Israel throughout its existence. It is only a matter of time before God acts in judgment.

The end comes in 722 BC, two hundred years after the kingdoms divided. The Assyrians attack Samaria and eventually destroy it. There is no doubt why this happens: "And this occurred because the people of Israel had sinned against the Lord their God, who had brought them out of the land of Egypt" (2 Kings 17:7, ESV). The ten northern tribes will never have a separate existence again.

The southern kingdom of Judah fares no better. Its sad story of decline is told in the second half of 2 Kings and also in 2 Chronicles. Even though they have the temple in their midst, the people turn to other gods. There are periods when they are more obedient to God, in particular under King Josiah, who promotes religious reform after he finds a copy of the law in the temple. But the change does not go far enough, or deep enough, to deflect God's anger. The people have broken His covenant and they must be punished. God had warned them before they entered the land that they would not be allowed to stay if they broke His covenant. He keeps His word by sending the Babylonians to defeat Judah in 597 BC, who take some of the inhabitants into exile. The judgment is extended soon afterward, in 586 BC, when the city and its temple are destroyed and many more Israelites are taken to Babylon. The golden age they had enjoyed under Solomon is nothing but a distant memory. There is very little evidence that they are God's people; they are not in God's place, but in exile, and they face the curse of God's judgment rather than His blessing. It is as if the fall of man has happened all over again. God had warned them before they entered the Promised Land that they would be evicted if they did not obey Him (Deuteronomy 28:25, 63–64; Joshua 23:12–13). Even still they have rejected His rule, and, as a result, they have now been banished from His presence.

The Word of the Lord as Spoken by the Prophets

Written within the terms of the covenant at Sinai were clear warnings against any and all persistent covenant disloyalty. To inform His people of blatant infractions, as well as their pending consequences, God sent faithful men known as prophets to deliver His messages. For the purpose of our discussion we may divide the prophets of Israel into two main groups: the "non"-writing prophets (or the "former" prophets) and the "writing" prophets (or the "latter" prophets). At first, God was content to preserve His prophetic revelation within the context of wider historical narratives. But eventually it became necessary, starting (most likely) with Obadiah, to preserve their oracles in a more formal way (within individual books).

The "former" prophets, then, are to be understood within the framework of Israel's history, as essential components for understanding the theological significance of Israel's history, particularly as it relates to the total pattern of God's revelation. Moses was the definitive prophet of this era. It was Moses who mediated the declared purpose of God to save Israel out of Egypt, and who was at the same time God's instrument in carrying out this purpose. Later, it was Moses who received the law at Sinai on behalf of the people, in order that they might be constituted as the people of God's Kingdom. The entire history of the fulfillment of God's promises to Abraham, as it is worked out from Moses to Solomon, is regulated by the Kingdom ideals contained in the Sinaitic covenant. In other words, all future generations were to live in the light of that covenant if they wished to remain in the land and enjoy God's blessings there. If they did not obey His law, they would face His judgment and would ultimately be exiled from the land.

All the prophets after Moses stand as the watchdogs of the society of God's people, working always within the framework of the Sinaitic covenant.[4] The prophets hold the law as a mirror so that individuals, as well as the whole nation, may see how they have transgressed. They call people back to faithful obedience to the covenant and, when necessary, denounce the unbelief and disobedience of their day. The first great prophets after Moses were Elijah and Elisha, who were both active in the northern kingdom of Israel in the ninth century BC. Much of their ministries involved public confrontations with the kings of Israel. They called the kings to live according to God's law, and to repent of their idolatry and lack of trust in the Lord. Israel's spiritual state is dire during this period. Under the reign of King Ahab there is widespread apostasy. Baal is worshiped throughout the land, and consequently, many of God's prophets are being sentenced to death. Elijah challenges the prophets of Baal to a public showdown on Mount Carmel, resulting in a resounding victory for the one true God. But, even then, most of the people refuse to worship the Lord. A dejected Elijah speaks to God, "The children of Israel have forsaken Your covenant, torn down Your altars, and killed Your prophets with the sword, I alone am left" (1 Kings 19:10). God reassures him, "I have reserved seven thousand in Israel, all whose knees have not bowed to Baal" (19:18). Seven thousand is better than one, but it still represents a very small portion of the entire nation. And yet, despite the abundant wickedness of their day, Elijah and Elisha still seem optimistic that there is time for the people to return to the

Lord before His judgment comes. As time passes, however, the prophets come to see that judgment is inevitable.

Furthermore, the latter, or "written," prophets may be divided into three subcategories: pre-exilic prophets (the prophets that ministered to Israel before they were taken into exile), exilic prophets (prophets that ministered to Israel while they were in exile), and post-exilic prophets (prophets that ministered to Israel after they returned from exile). There are three essential themes in the oracles of these latter prophets. First, there is the covenant of Sinai which remains the rule of faith and behavior. This God-given law stands as the expression of God's holy character, and as such it is the point of reference when the prophets interpret events as God's dealings with Israel. Second, the prophets are the dutiful mediators of the message of judgment. The act of covenant breaking, likewise, provides a reference point to the accusations against various forms of evildoing, and lays the basis for the pronouncement of impending judgment. Insofar as these prophets are still orientated to God's faithfulness and mercy, there is a conditional element to their woeful messages, which indicates that repentance and faithful obedience may yet avert the judgment. More and more, however, the prophets present a picture of terrible and final judgment. This aspect partly reflects the reality of the situation in that history gave no grounds for optimism. Given the pattern of rebellion that is easily discerned from the very moment Israel is delivered from Egyptian captivity, there is little basis for confidence in the outcome unless this sinful bent of human character is taken care of. Consequently, we notice a growing sense of the inevitable curse and self-destruction of the covenant people, and even the most concentrated efforts at reform are powerless to correct the situation.

The form of the judgment to come is described in various ways, but it is essential that we discern two relatable, yet distinct emphases. One is to depict a rather immediate and local judgment of God. In the northern kingdom of Israel, the approaching doom is pinpointed as the Assyrian invasion, which subsequently brought about the end of that nation in 722

BC. In Judah the fate of Israel is cited as both a warning and example, and a similar fate at the hands of Babylon is predicted (Isaiah 39; Jeremiah 1:13–16; 20:5–6; 22:24–27). The other emphasis is to portray judgment as something which is of universal or cosmic proportions. While we must be careful not to oversimplify the prophetic message, it is necessary to discern a distinct development in emphasis particularly in the prophetic view of eschatology or the end-times.

The third major element in the prophetic message as a whole is the declaration that God is faithful to the covenant, and on that basis, He will save a remnant to be His own true possession. Like the judgment oracles, the salvation oracles depict two relatable but distinct aspects of saving restoration. God will restore the covenant people to their inheritance, and He will also restore the whole universe to a glory which has not been known since man was rejected from Eden (cf. Isaiah 65:17–25). The pattern of future hope, to which all the writing prophets contributed, may be best illustrated as a replay of past history but with significant differences. As Goldsworthy notes,

> All the hope for the future is expressed in terms of a return to the Kingdom structures revealed in the history of Israel from the Exodus to Solomon. The great difference is that none of the weaknesses of the past will be present. In short, sin and its effects will be eradicated. The prophets depict a continuity from the past to the future as well as a distinction between them. All that God has revealed about the Kingdom through Israel's history remains valid. But is modified to the extent that the new view of the Kingdom leaves no place for a further disruption and decline. The restored Kingdom will be in the context of a new heaven and a new earth, and all this new creation of God will be permanent, perfect and glorious.[5]

So, whereas their history proclaimed the failure of Israel, the prophets proclaimed the future of Israel. They spoke of good times ahead in terms of action replay. There will be a new exodus, a new covenant, a new nation, a new Jerusalem, a new temple, a new King, and even a new creation. God will not rebuild the model, but He will establish that to which it pointed, the real thing, the perfect Kingdom: God's people in God's place, under God's rule, enjoying God's blessings. The prophets spoke of the ultimate fulfillment of these Kingdom promises.

A New Exodus and a New Nation. Although God had brought a terrible judgment on His people, He would not destroy them completely. A remnant would be preserved, out of whom God would create a new nation: "The remnant will return, the remnant of Jacob, to the Mighty God. For though your people O Israel, be as the sand of the sea, a remnant of them will return. The destruction decreed shall overflow with righteousness" (Isaiah 10:20–21). Isaiah is even instructed to call one of his sons "Shear-Jashub," which means "a remnant will return," to underline the message (cf. Isaiah 7:3). The plight of the people of Judah as exiles in Babylon is similar to that of the Israelites when they were slaves in Egypt. As God rescued them then, so He will rescue them again. There will be a new exodus: "Therefore behold, the days are coming, says the Lord, that it shall no more be said, 'The Lord lives who brought up the children of Israel from the land of Egypt,' but 'The Lord lives who brought up the children of Israel from the land of the north and from all the lands where He had driven them.' For I will bring them back into their land which I gave to their fathers" (Jeremiah 16:14–15).

Furthermore, Isaiah stresses that the new exodus will be achieved by a mysterious figure he calls "the Servant." Sometimes the servant is identified as the nation of Israel (e.g., 44:1–2). But in other passages it is clear that He is an individual who will be used by God to rescue the remnant of Israel (e.g., 49:5–6; 52:13–53:12). He will achieve this rescue via His own death. God uses what is known as the prophetic perfect tense, speaking of a future event as if it had already taken place, because it is so certain: "But

He was wounded for our transgressions, He was bruised for our iniquities; The chastisement for our peace was upon Him, And by His stripes we are healed. All we like sheep have gone astray; We have turned, every one, to his own way; And the Lord has laid on Him the iniquity of us all" (Isaiah 53:5–6). The individual is the True Servant who dies for the remnant of Israel, so that God's people can be rescued from their sin. He will face their punishment, in their place, so they can be forgiven and a new Israel constituted (compare Exodus 19:5–6 with 1 Peter 2:9; see Galatians 2:23–31). This prophecy was to be fulfilled when Jesus died on the cross. He had said of Himself: *For even the Son of Man did not come to be served, but to serve, and to give his life a ransom for many* (Mark 10:45; see 1 Peter 2:22–25).

A New Nation Under a New Covenant. The Servant's role, however, extends beyond Israel. Just as Israel was to be a kingdom of priests, channeling the blessing of His rule to the nations (Exodus 19:6), likewise God says to the Servant, "It is too small a thing that You should be My servant to raise up the tribes of Jacob, and to restore the preserved ones of Israel; I will give You as a light to the Gentiles, that You should be my salvation to the end of the earth" (Isaiah 49:6). The promise to Abraham, a blessing to the nations, will be realized in and through the atoning work of Jesus. Men and women from all peoples will benefit when God acts to save Israel (Isaiah 60:1–3). What is more, the prophets predict that the return of a renewed people will also constitute a people whose hearts are changed and to whom a new spirit has been given (see Jeremiah 32:39–42):

> *Behold, the days are coming, says the Lord, when I will make a new covenant with the house of Israel and with the house of Judah, not according to the covenant that I made with their fathers in the day that I took them by the hand to lead them out of the land of Egypt, My covenant which they broke, though I was a husband to them, says the Lord. But this is the covenant that I will make with the house of Israel after those days, says the Lord: I will put My law in their minds, and write it on their hearts; and I will be their*

God, and they shall be My people. No more shall every man teach
his neighbor, and every man his brother, saying, "Know the Lord,"
for they all shall know Me, from the least of them to the greatest of
them, says the Lord. For I will forgive their iniquity, and their sin I
will remember no more. (Jeremiah 31:31–34)

The fundamental flaw with the Old Covenant was that Israel, due to man's inherent sin problem, was incapable of keeping its stipulations (v. 32). Thus, the covenant curses inevitably came upon Israel and cumulated in their exile. The New Covenant remedies this problem, however, for God promises to put "My law in their minds" and to "write it on their hearts" (v. 33). This is how the purpose of the covenant, which is fellowship with God, will be achieved: "I will be their God, and they shall be My people" (v. 33). The New Covenant, then, makes provision so that the people of God have a desire from within to keep God's commands.

The promise of a "new heart" and a "new spirit" is also found in Ezekiel 36:26–27: "I will give you a new heart and put a new spirit within you; I will take the heart of stone out of your flesh and give you a heart of flesh. I will put My Spirit within you and cause you to walk in My statutes, and you will keep My judgments and do them." Under the Old Covenant Israel was beleaguered by a heart of stone. In the New Covenant God plants His Spirit within His people, and as a result they received a heart of flesh, a new heart, and a new spirit (see also Ezekiel 11:19). The gift of the Spirit enables the people of God to keep God's law. The failure to obey, which began with Adam in the garden, is then remedied by the New Covenant.

It should also be noted that Israel's new heart is directly connected with their return from exile, as we see clearly in Jeremiah 32:

I will give them one heart and one way, that they may fear Me
forever, for the good of them and their children after them. And I
will make an everlasting covenant with them, that I will not turn
away from doing them good; but I will put My fear in their hearts

so that they will not depart from Me. Yes, I will rejoice over them to do them good, and I will assuredly plant them in this land, with all My heart and with all My soul. "For thus says the Lord: 'Just as I have brought all this great calamity on this people, so I will bring on them all the good that I have promised them.'" (39–42)

When the New Covenant arrives, Israel will be planted in the land and will not turn away from the Lord again. Incidentally, we see from this passage that Israel's return to the land in 538 BC does not fulfill this prophecy, for Israel did not ultimately return to the Lord after this time, and they have still not done so to this day.

The understanding of the fulfillment of this New Covenant begins to take final shape within the context of Jesus's ministry. When He took the cup at the Last Supper, Jesus said, "This cup is the New Covenant in my blood, which is poured out for you" (Luke 22:20). Jesus's death was the inauguration of the New Covenant. His blood was shed for the sins of the whole world, and thus all may benefit from this covenant. Yet, the benefits come not by physical birth, as with the Old Covenant, but rather by our new birth; we "must be born again" (John 3:3–5). In other words, we must receive God's Holy Spirit on the account of our faith in Jesus's death on the cross for the forgiveness of our sins (John 3:15–18).

In the Old Testament we see that the Spirit is poured out on prophets, kings, and other leaders. There is a recognition, however, that the Spirit is not distributed to all. Moses voices the hope that in the future the Spirit will be poured out more generally, responding to Joshua's concerns about some who had prophesied within the camp: "Oh, that all the Lord's people were prophets and that the Lord would put His Spirit upon them!" (Numbers 11:29). Joel's prophecy represents the fulfillment of Moses's desire: "And it shall come to pass afterward That I will pour out My Spirit on all flesh; Your sons and your daughters shall prophesy, Your old men shall dream dreams, Your young men shall see visions. And also on My menservants and on My maidservants I will pour out My Spirit in those days" (Joel 2:28–29). Peter proclaims that Joel's prophecy was fulfilled on the Day of Pentecost (Acts 2:16–17). Distinctive about Joel's prophecy is that the Spirit is poured out upon "all flesh": young and old, male and female. The comprehensiveness and the universality of the Spirit's work in the New Covenant represents a striking contrast to the Old Covenant (cf. 2 Corinthians 3:4–18). In addition, it is sometimes said that there is an "already but not yet" component in the fulfillment of the New Covenant promises. The "not yet" is that though the Spirit regenerates and indwells every New Covenant member, they are not yet completely transformed. Their obedience, though genuine and supernatural, is not yet perfect. Complete sanctification and holiness will be theirs on the final day, on the day of redemption (see 1 Thessalonians 5:23–24). Even still, all New Covenant members are "already" regenerated by the Holy Spirit and are in the process of being made holy (cf. Ephesians 1:7–14).

A King to Rule the New Earth. The prophet Isaiah, possibly more than any other prophet, looks forward to the proclamation of the good news of the renewed presence of the Lord and the reestablishment of His Kingdom (Isaiah 40:9; 52:7; 61:1). As suggested above, the theme of the Kingdom of God goes back to the first chapter of the Bible with God's appointment of mankind to be His vice-regent over all the earth. God's glory and honor were to be reflected in all of creation through the righteous dominion of the ones created in His image and likeness (see Psalm 8). Furthermore, God's determination to establish the monarchy and His promise to establish the throne of David's Son forever (2 Samuel 7) should raise the expectation that the Kingdom was somehow to relate to God's original intention for humanity and creation. The Father–Son relationship between God and the Davidic King is consistent with the pattern of relationship suggested by Genesis 2. Several royal Psalms suggest that the Davidic Kingdom was expected to be not only unending, but also universal as humanity's reign was intended to be according to Genesis 1. Psalm 2 speaks of the futility of the resistance of the kings of the earth to God's anointed King and builds on the Father–Son relationship to affirm that upon request the King will be granted the nations and the ends of the earth for His inheritance. Psalm 72 appeals to God to grant the Davidic King dominion "from sea to sea, and from the River to the ends of the earth" (v. 8), and longs for the day when "all kings shall fall down before Him" and "all nations shall serve Him" (v. 11).

Like some of the royal psalms, Zechariah too makes it clear that he is not only looking forward to the restoration of the Kingdom, but he also expects the Kingdom to have universal influence (8:22–23; 9:10; 14:14–19). The establishment of the Kingdom results in "many peoples and strong nations" coming "to seek the Lord of hosts in Jerusalem" (8:22). Then their humble King will come to them and "speak peace to the nations," and "His dominion shall be from sea to sea, and from the River to the ends of the earth" (9:10; cf. Psalm 72:8). Daniel's vision of the human-like figure who is given "dominion and glory and a kingdom, that all peoples, nations, and languages should serve Him," further affirms that the Kingdom of the Son of Man "is an everlasting dominion, which shall not pass away . . . one which shall not be destroyed" (Daniel 7:14; see 2 Samuel 7:12–16). Unlike any previous global domination, the Kingdom of God's Son will not lose its power and influence over time, and through this Kingdom glory and honor will redound to the One to whom it is properly due, rather than to those whose arrogance foolishly leads them to wear such a status pretentiously.

The universal reign of the Davidic King could be understood in more than one way, of course. For some they only see the extermination or at least the violent subjugation of the pagan nations. Texts such as Zechariah 9 and others, however, describe the coming of God's Kingdom as something that would bring great blessing to other nations. Isaiah 49 is crucial for understanding the restoration of Israel and its relationship to the future of other nations. There it seems the Servant of the Lord has a two-pronged commission: First to bring Jacob back and gather Israel to the Lord—that is, "to raise up the tribes of Jacob and restore the preserved ones of Israel" (49:5–6). Secondly, to serve "as a light for the Gentiles," so that God's "salvation may reach to the ends of all the earth." That is when "kings shall see and arise; princes, also shall worship, because of the Lord who is faithful" (v. 7). Here it becomes clear how God's original intention for humanity is realized through God's Servant as He establishes God's unending reign of righteousness over all creation. This brings tremendous blessing to all the nations and to all of creation (cf. Psalm 67:1–4). In order for that purpose to be realized, however, Israel must first be restored so that its Kingdom might bring blessing to all nations in fulfillment of the promises to Abraham (Genesis 22:18), while simultaneously achieving the original intention for humanity and creation as indicated in Genesis 1.

The time of fulfillment will be marked by great blessing for the whole world. With God's rule established, everything falls into place once more. There is a return to the blessings of Eden; peace and prosperity will abound: "The plowman shall overtake the reaper, and the treader of grapes him who sows seed. The mountains shall drip with sweet wine, and all the hills flow with it" (Amos 9:13–14). Furthermore, "the wolf also shall dwell with the lamb, the leopard shall lie down with the young goat, the calf and the young lion and the fatling together, and a little child shall lead them" (Isaiah 11:6).

The Return and Restoration of Israel (Ezra–Nehemiah)

In 538 BC, six decades after the exile had begun, it finally looks as if the prophecies of hope are about to be fulfilled. Cyrus of Persia defeats the Babylonians and issues an edict that allows the exiles to return and rebuild their temple. The restoration of the nation, however, is not the triumphant success that the prophets had promised. Only a small number make the journey back to their homeland, and when they try to make a settlement there, they are faced with great opposition. Eventually a new temple is built, and under Ezra's leadership, the centrality of God's law as the regulator of all life is reaffirmed.

Soon afterward, Nehemiah leads a party to rebuild the walls of Jerusalem. Some of the promises have been fulfilled, at least in part, but it is clear that this is not the time of final fulfillment. Those who can remember the good old days before the exile, or have heard tales of them from the previous generation, realize that the new temple is far less impressive than the old one and that the prophets had foretold something much better. When the foundation for the new temple is laid, some of the younger generation shout for joy. But those who are older and wiser weep (Ezra 3:11–13). They know that this cannot be the new temple Ezekiel prophesied, a temple far less than Solomon's. And the people clearly do not have new hearts: the book of Nehemiah ends in disappointment as he laments the fact that God's law is disobeyed, despite Ezra's efforts (Nehemiah 13).

Three prophets, Haggai, Zachariah, and Malachi, prophesy at this time (the post-exilic prophets). Their message is much the same as that of their predecessors before the exile. They too have to condemn their hearers for breaking the covenant and warn of coming judgment. But they also point to a time in the future when God will act to fulfill His promises so that His people may enjoy all the blessings of the covenant. In all of this, it is evident that this cannot be the new exodus that the prophets spoke of. Spiritually speaking, God's people are still in exile, waiting for the Lord to return to them and fulfill all His promises of salvation. God's Kingdom still has not come, because God's King has not come. But the last of the prophets insist that He will appear, preceded by a messenger: "Behold, I send My messenger, and he will prepare the way before Me. And the Lord, whom you seek, will suddenly come to His temple, Even the Messenger of the covenant, in whom you delight. Behold, He is coming" (Malachi 3:1).

The Gospel of the Kingdom

That the Old Testament anticipates the New, and is fulfilled in the New, is underlined by many general statements throughout the New Testament:

> *God, who at various times and in various ways spoke in time past*
> *to the fathers by the prophets, has in these last days spoken to us by*

His son, whom He has appointed heir of all things, through whom also He made the worlds. (Hebrews 1:1–2)

For all the promises of God in Him [Christ] are yes, and in Him Amen. (2 Corinthians 1:20)

And we declare to you glad tidings—that promise which was made to the fathers. God has fulfilled this for us their children, in that He has raised up Jesus. (Acts 13:32–33a)

And beginning at Moses and all the prophets, He expounded to them in all the Scriptures the things concerning Himself. (Luke 24:27)

It is important that we understand very clearly that this fact of the Old Testament's progression toward a fulfillment in the New is not merely an invitation to understand Jesus Christ as the end of the process. It is also a demand that the Bible as a whole be understood in the light of the gospel.

It should be realized at the outset that when we speak of Jesus Christ as the key to interpretation we mean to speak of Jesus Christ as He is entirely revealed to us in Scripture. It is neither helpful nor sufficient to stress the ethics of the man Jesus of Nazareth apart from His divine attributes, or out of context of the saving acts of God (as many liberal interpreters do). Nor is it permissible to emphasize the supernatural presence of the Lord with the believer out of context of the meaning of the historical humanity of God in the flesh (as some evangelicals do). Obviously, we need to be clear about the gospel itself if we are to be clear about the significance of Christ for interpreting the Bible.

If you were to ask the question, "What is the gospel?" to ten different Christians, you are liable to get ten different answers. Perhaps none of them will be entirely wrong, but the vast differences will suggest a certain confusion. The liberal Christian, for example, often stresses the humility of Jesus: Jesus was a good man, in fact the only truly good man. The gospel of the "good man" is usually reduced to some example for us to follow, a demonstration inviting us to try to do likewise. There is obviously some truth in this view. On the other hand, the evangelical often stresses the divinity of Jesus. The Christ is the supernatural Son of God who is alive today in the hearts of all believers. The gospel of the "divine Christ" tends to emphasize the supernaturally changed life of all who believe. And there is obviously some truth in that. While in no way are we suggesting that these two views are extremes, each containing some level of the truth, which calls for a middle road or a balanced approach in which we borrow a little from each extreme. Rather, it is a plea for the interpreter to draw their understanding of the gospel from the total perspective of biblical revelation.

Essentially, the gospel is a declaration of what God has done for us in Jesus Christ, rather than (as it is often implied) what God does in us, although both are essential aspects of the believer's salvation and must not be separated too neatly. It is the objective historical facts of the coming of Jesus in the flesh and the divinely given interpretation of those facts. When Peter preached the gospel at Pentecost, he was quick to divert attention from what God had done in the apostles by the outpouring of the Holy Spirit, and to concentrate on the facts concerning Jesus of Nazareth (Acts 2:14–36). The facts are those of the incarnation, the perfect life of Jesus, and of His dying and rising from the grave. The interpretation of those facts are that they have taken place "for our trespasses" and "for our justification" (cf. Romans 4:25). In these simple statements of fact, along with their divine interpretation, we sum up the breadth and depth of biblical revelation.

In referring to the birth of Jesus as incarnation we take seriously the biblical assertion that this was no mere man, nor even a man with some divine qualities. The baby in the manger was at one and the same time, and one and the same person, both Son of God and Son of Man—both fully divine and fully human, the God-man (Isaiah 7:14; cf. Matthew 1:23; Isaiah 9:6; John 1:1–14; John 10:30–33; John 20:27–29). Without the recognition that Jesus Christ was truly God and truly man we cannot maintain the gospel as "good news" nor as the power of God for salvation. If Jesus is not God, He would not have been born perfect, for no mere man, due to the inherent sin nature, could ever be born perfect, "no not one." And if Jesus was not perfect, He would not have been qualified to be man's Savior. This is why belief in the incarnation (and virgin birth) is not merely a theoretical matter.

The gospel is saying that, what man cannot do in order to be accepted by God, God Himself has done for us in the person of Jesus Christ. To be acceptable to God we must present to Him a life of perfect and unceasing obedience to His will. The gospel declares that Jesus has done this for us. The holy law of God was lived out perfectly by Christ on our behalf, and its penalty was paid in its entirety for us by His death on the cross. This living and dying of Christ for us, and our reliance upon Him, is the basis of our acceptance with God (John 3:16; Acts 10:43; Ephesians 1:7; 2:8). Only the God-man, Jesus Christ, could both live the true sinless human life and rise victoriously over death after paying the penalty for man's sin. We cannot understand how the one person, Jesus Christ, contained two distinguishable yet inseparable natures. No more could the apostles understand it, yet they were driven to accept the fact as integral to the gospel.

So then, in summary, the gospel is what God has done for us in Christ for our salvation. And as the two natures of Christ must be distinguished, so also we must distinguish what God does for us from that which God does in and through us. Likewise, as we must not separate the two natures of Christ, neither must we separate the facts of the gospel from the fruit of the gospel. It is by the gospel that we are born again (1 Peter 1:23–25), and it is the gospel which produces the sanctified or Spirit-filled life within us (Colossians 1:56).

Truly, the salvation of man from sin and judgment is an epic part of the gospel and can hardly be overemphasized. But the "good news" of Jesus Christ entails much more than this. Its power goes well beyond the deliverance of mankind; it proclaims the restoration of God's rule over all things once again.

At the center of Jesus's preaching was the declaration that "the kingdom of God is at hand" (Mark 1:14–15). Matthew particularly calls this "the gospel of the Kingdom" (Matthew 4:23; 9:35; 24:14). The theme of the gospel, then, is intrinsically connected with the theme of the Kingdom of God, and this idea of kingdom is not something completely new. That it is "at hand" presupposes some kind of fulfillment, and the term "Kingdom of God" must have meant something to those who heard Jesus speak (even though it is not of itself an Old Testament term). The unavoidable conclusion from the New Testament evidence is that the gospel fulfills the Old Testament hope of the coming of the Kingdom of God.

The Gospels and the book of Acts, despite all their diversity, have something in common. All of them proclaim that the King has come and that Jesus of Nazareth is the Son of Man, the Son of God, the Messiah, the final Prophet, the true Israel, and the Lord of all. Jesus fulfills the promise made to David that his dynasty would never end, that a king would always sit on the Davidic throne (Luke 1:31–33; cf. 2 Samuel 7:12–14; Isaiah 9:7). By virtue of His resurrection and exaltation He is now seated at God's right hand and reigns from heaven (Acts 2:32–33, 36; 7:55–56).

The Kingdom prophesied in the Old Testament has come, for the King has come. The day of fulfillment has arrived in Jesus's ministry, death, and resurrection. The age to come has invaded history, for Jesus is risen from the dead. The presence of the Kingdom manifests itself in Jesus's healings, exorcisms, and other miracles (cf. Luke 11:20). These miracles anticipated the new creation that is coming, the day when all that is wrong with the world will be made right. By virtue of Jesus's death, salvation is available for all those who have defied the King's lordship; but the day of forgiveness will only last for a limited time, for the King will return to the earth and finish what He has started. Then the devil and his cohorts will be destroyed forever, through the crushing blow (cf. Genesis 3:15) already delivered at Jesus's death and resurrection.

Luke particularly emphasizes, though the theme is not absent from Matthew and Mark, that the Kingdom advances through the power of the Holy Spirit. The gospel of the Kingdom will be herald to the ends of the earth (Matthew 24:14; Luke 24:44–49), and Acts testifies that such a mission is carried out through the work of the Holy Spirit (Acts 1:8), empowering and strengthening disciples to testify to the gospel of Jesus Christ. The people of God consist of all those who belong to Jesus Christ. All those who accept the apostolic testimony about the Christ are members of God's Kingdom. The restored and new Israel is not limited to the Jewish people. Gentiles who repent of their sins and put their faith in Jesus Christ belong to the new people of God. Luke particularly emphasizes in Acts the expansion of the people of God. The promise of the outpouring of the Holy Spirit on God's people has come upon the Gentiles as well, manifesting their divine acceptance (Acts 8; 10). The inclusion of the Gentiles fulfills the universal blessings promised to Abraham and the other patriarchs. Those who are members of the Kingdom repent of their sins and put their faith in Jesus Christ. They submit to Jesus's lordship and His reign as disciples (Matthew 16:24). True disciples are obedient to God and do what Jesus commands them to do (John 8:31). They live a new life as members of the Kingdom, bearing fruit that is pleasant to God (John 15:8).

Kingdom Themes in the Epistles of Paul

It is quite obvious to any student of Scripture that Paul's epistles play a significant role in the development of New Testament theology, since nearly half of the New Testament canon in terms of books come from Paul. While it is necessary for the student to read each letter individually and construct the theology of each epistle separately, for the purpose of our study in developing a unified theme of the Bible, we will examine all the letters together in order that we might unfold Paul's theology as a whole.

Unlike the Synoptic Gospels and Acts, Paul does not typically use the word "Kingdom" to describe the fulfillment of the Old Testament promises. While the term is not entirely absent, as we will see, the eschatological promises of the Old Testament are instead usually considered by Paul to be fulfilled in Christ more generally. If we examine Paul's theology closely, it becomes evident that there is an "already but not yet" dimension to the fulfillment. God's promises have been realized in Jesus Christ, and yet they have not reached their final consummation. In other words, God's saving promises have "already" been inaugurated but "not yet" consummated. Such a theme runs like a thread through all of Paul's theology. Whether we think of Christology, the salvific work accomplished by Christ, the new life that Christians live, the new people of God, or the new heaven and earth, an eschatological tension characterizes Paul's thought.

The New David. Throughout his epistles Paul uses the expression "Son of God" (or "the Son") seventeen times in reference to Jesus. Incidentally, the Davidic King is also identified as God's "Son" (2 Samuel 7:14; Psalm 2:7, 12; Isaiah 9:6). Moreover, Paul often describes Jesus as God's Son when considering His death on the cross (Romans 5:10; 8:3, 32; Galatians 2:20; 4:4). Here in these passages the obedience of the Son is highlighted; Christ fulfilled the Father's will by dying for sinners. Consequently, Jesus is now the exalted and reigning Son of God, fulfilling the promise of the covenant with David (Romans 1:4; Ephesians 1:19–23; Philippians 2:8–10). As God's Son, He will subject Himself to the Father on the last day, when all things will be placed under His sovereign rule (1 Corinthians 15:28). In the meantime, believers enjoy fellowship with the Son (1 Corinthians 1:9; Ephesians 4:13) and await His second coming (1 Thessalonians 1:10). Furthermore, according to Paul, Jesus is the unique and distinctive Son of God (Romans 1:3–4) who preexisted with the Father (Colossians 2:9). Thus, as the Son of God, Jesus clearly enjoys a special relationship with God the Father.

The fulfillment of redemptive history is especially emphasized with the exaltation of Jesus as Lord. For example, Paul consistently uses various Old Testament texts where Yahweh's sovereignty is featured, and applies them directly to Jesus. The hymn in Philippians 2 provides a striking example of this. Jesus, even though He could claim equality with God, did not take advantage of His equality with the Father while He was on earth. He did not utilize the extent of His divine power, even though He was Himself "in the form of God." Rather, He took on humanity and humbled Himself, even to the extent of suffering and dying on a cross (2:7–8). Therefore, God granted Him the name above all names and exalted Him as Lord of all, so that every knee will bow before Jesus and every tongue confess Him as Lord (2:9–11). Paul certainly alludes here to Isaiah 45:23, which proclaims that every knee will bow before Yahweh and every tongue profess allegiance to Him. Paul makes a similar connection in Romans 10:13, where he asserts that "whoever calls on the name of the Lord shall be saved." The Lord here clearly is Jesus (Romans 10:9), where one must confess Him as Lord and believe on Him to be saved. Paul cites Joel 2:32, where the Lord upon whom one must call certainly is Yahweh, and so there is no doubt that Jesus shares the same status as God (2 Corinthians 4:5).

As Lord and Creator, Jesus deserves the same homage as Yahweh (1 Corinthians 8:5–6; see John 1:3, 10; Hebrews 1:2). Indeed, Paul links "name" with Christ's lordship and stresses the deity of Christ by reaching back to the Old Testament (e.g., Romans 14:9–11; 1 Corinthians 1:2, 10; 5:4; 6:11; Ephesians 5:20; Philippians 2:19; Colossians 3:17; 2 Thessalonians 1:12; 3:6; cf. Ephesians 1:20–23; Colossians 3:23). The transcendence of the Lord is evident in many other texts as well. He is the Lord of glory (1 Corinthians 2:8); the One who gives grace and peace (2 Corinthians 1:2; 13:14; Galatians 1:3; Philippians 1:2; 1 Thessalonians 1:1), mercy (2 Timothy 1:16, 18), understanding (2 Timothy 2:7); delivers from afflictions (2 Timothy 4:17); provides strength to resist temptation (2 Thessalonians 3:3); and is coming again to judge the righteous and wicked (1 Corinthians 1:7; 4:5; Ephesians 6:8; Philippians 3:20; 4:5; Colossians 3:24; 1 Thessalonians 3:13; 4:15–16; 5:23; 2 Thessalonians 1:7; 2:1, 8; 1 Timothy 6:14–15; 2 Timothy 4:8, 14). Prayer is directed to Him (2 Corinthians 12:7–10; 1 Thessalonians 3:11–12; 2 Thessalonians 2:16; 3:5), songs are sung to Him (Ephesians 5:19), and He is to be trusted (Ephesians 1:15; Philippians 1:14; 2 Corinthians 3:16) and rejoiced in (Philippians 3:1; cf. 1 Corinthians 1:31; 2 Corinthians 10:17).

Furthermore, it was Paul's recognition of Jesus's glory that made it possible for him to accept that Jesus was the Christ and to heed the call to preach the gospel message to all nations and not just the Jews. The ultimate Davidic King is reigning, so Israel's restoration has begun and the time has come for salvation to go to "the ends of the earth" (notice how this was the assumption of the disciples in Acts 1:6). When Paul summarizes his understanding of the gospel in Romans 1:1–6, he does so in terms of its relationship with the Davidic promises: Jesus is not only the "seed of David" like every other Davidic king, but, unlike any other king, He is exalted to the long-awaited, glorious, and universal phase of the promised Kingdom by reason of His resurrection and Spirit-declared enthronement. That such is Paul's understanding of the significance of the resurrection, and His current status of Davidic king, is made clear by the logical connection between Romans 1:4 and Romans 1:5. Since Jesus has been "declared to be the Son of God with power," the time has come to bring about the "obedience to the faith among all the nations for His name."

A significant portion of Pauline Christology centers around the fact that Jesus reigns as the Christ, the new and better David. Such a theme is also connected to Jesus as the new and better Adam, who not only succeeds where Adam fell, but also regains what Adam had lost. We have an implicit connection here with Genesis 3:15, for a promise was given that an offspring of the woman would triumph over the serpent, suggesting there would be a second Adam, who would succeed where the first Adam failed. The first Adam brought death into the world, but the last Adam—Christ (1 Corinthians 15:45)—brought life by virtue of His resurrection from the dead (1 Corinthians 15:21–22). The resurrection of the Christ signals the dawning of the new creation, for Christ at His resurrection conquered both sin and death (Ramen 6:8–10). The first Adam was responsible for the entrance of death and sin into the world (Romans 5:12–19), but Jesus, the second Adam, the last Adam, conquered the two-headed foe

(Romans 5:12–19). He cleaned up the mess that Adam spawned and more, for human beings will not only return to their pre-fallen state, they now enjoy the righteousness and life given to them by the last Adam. The first Adam chose to act independent of God by transgressing His command in the garden (Genesis 3:1–6). But the last Adam was the obedient one (Romans 5:19; Philippians 2:8), surrendering His life on the cross in the place of Adam's helpless descendants.

Jesus is not only the last Adam and the new David, He is also the off-spring of Abraham. Indeed, Paul argues that He is the only true offspring of Abraham (Galatians 3:16). The promise of land, offspring, and blessing given to Abraham are fulfilled in Christ (cf. Romans 4:13–25). Hence, the only way to belong to Abraham is if one is united with Christ (Galatians 3:29). The promise to bless the whole world, both Jews and Gentiles, would become a reality through Jesus Christ, who was the true Son of Abraham. Ethnicity did not guarantee participation in the blessing of Abraham. Gentiles who belong to Jesus Christ are the circumcised in heart and are therefore the true Jews (Romans 2:26–29; Philippians 3:3; Colossians 2:11). In Christ the *eschaton* has dawned, for the worldwide blessings promised to Abraham are now becoming a reality.

The connection between Jesus as the fulfillment of the Davidic promise and the fulfillment of the promised blessings to Abraham is clearly made in comparing such passages as Galatians 3:26–29 and Romans 8:14–17. Having established that we are made "sons of God through faith in Jesus Christ," and that as sons, "we are Abraham's seed and heirs accord-ing to the promise," Paul builds on such a concept by expounding on the believer's inheritance in Romans 8. In verse 17, Paul profoundly states that we are not only the heirs of God, but are also "Joint heirs with Christ." Jesus, as Son of God, was promised the whole world as an inheritance (cf. Psalm 2). Christ, the Son of God, will one day rule the nations, and we, as his brothers (Hebrews 2:10–11), will one day rule over all the earth with Him: "If indeed we suffer with Him, that we also be glorified together" (see Ephesians 1:15–23; 2:4–7; 2 Timothy 2:12).

The fact that Jesus reigns contributes significantly to the "already not yet" theme in Paul's writings. Jesus as the Davidic Messiah now reigns from heaven. He is the exalted Christ, and yet His enemies are not yet completely routed. The final destruction of Satan and death is still to come, so that believers await the fulfillment of the prophecy of Psalms 110:1, where everything will be placed under Jesus's feet (cf. 1 Corinthians 15:24–28). The same theme appears in Ephesians 1:20–22. Jesus was enthroned at His resurrection as Lord of all, so that all demonic beings are now subservient to His authority (see Colossians 2:10). Jesus is the Messianic King, the sovereign One sitting on God's right hand, ruling even now from heaven. However, Jesus's physical rule on earth and our reigning with Him as kings and priests (Revelation 5:10) are yet to come. One day Jesus will rule both heaven and earth. His presence on earth, as the new temple, will permanently establish His universal lordship "to the ends of the earth." The consummation of His rule will finalize God's plan to restore all things to their intended purpose (Romans 8:18–29): God's people, made in His image, ruling over the works of His hand.

The People of God. The idea of the people of God stands as one of the central themes of the Bible. It is prominently featured as the middle affirmation of the often-repeated tripartite declaration: "I will be your God, you shall be my people, and I will dwell in the midst of you." This important confessional statement begins in Genesis 17:7 and stretches all the way to the book of Revelation (21:4) in the New Testament. God will adopt a people to be His very own in a very distinct way. It would seem that both Israel in the Old Testament and the believing church of the New Testament are intended to form, in some way, one harmonious body, since the identical designation, "My people," is used of both Israel and the church in both Testaments. What is certain, "the people of God" is the continuity term for the unified people of God across both Testaments.

The biblical idea of the people of God finds its first formal expression in the book of Exodus. Previously in the patriarchal narratives God had revealed Himself as *El Shaddai* (or "the mighty God"). But now in the exodus experience, as the enlarged family of Jacob prepared for nation-hood, God would reveal Himself as *Yahweh* (I Am). Already God had announced that He would be a personal God to Israel (Genesis 17:7). This affirmation was repeated in Exodus 6:3, as God declared that as He had originally appeared to Abraham, Isaac, and Jacob, now He will be known to His people by the newly revealed name, the great "I Am." Not only did God declare, "I am the Lord," but with five "I wills," He declared that He would be the same one who would intervene for them (Exodus 6:6–7). The Lord enumerated these five divine acts:

> *I will bring you out from under the yoke of the Egyptians.*
>
> *I will free you from being slaves to them, and. . .*
>
> *I will redeem you with an outstretched arm and with Mighty acts. . .*
>
> *I will take you as my own people, and. . .*
>
> *I will be your God.*

From all of this we learn that the idea of the people of God, as well as what constitutes the people of God, is at the heart of biblical faith.

Moreover, this uniquely owned people who had pride of possession with God were destined to become a "kingdom of priests and a holy nation" (Exodus 19:6). The problem, however, with this designated identity was that it was predicated on the obedience of Israel to God's holy law. Israel, due to a hardened heart, was resistant in following God's commandments. It is not surprising, then, that these words are not repeated anywhere else in the Old Testament. In fact, we do not hear of them again until they are used to describe believers in 1 Peter 2:9–10. Israel, time after time, was drawn away from God's presence to serve other gods. Accordingly, they forfeited any immediate role as a "peculiar treasure." This role would only be delayed, however, not rescinded. The same concept, which would be reinstated among the people of God later in 1 Peter 2:9 and Revelation

1:6; 5:10, would designate those who accept the Savior as the priesthood of all believers. However, even in Israel's day, the whole congregation was destined originally to be kings and priests to God and a nation set apart to God as "holy."

The idea of Israel's divine favor, evidenced by the increase of their numbers and by the covenantal promise that God would walk with them, is again expressed in Leviticus (26:9–13). Once again God promised: "I will set My tabernacle among you . . . I will walk among you and be your God, and you shall be My people" (vv. 11–12). What should be noticed is the recurring connection between God's presence and God's people. Here God not only constitutes Israel as His people, He further sets them apart as those whom He chooses to dwell among. What had begun as a promise to Abraham, that God would make him into a great nation, continued to that climactic moment at Mount Sinai during the "day of the assembly," when God formally constituted Israel as His people (Exodus 19:5–6; Deuteronomy 9:10; 10:4). Afterward, Israel is called "God's people" about ten times; and another three hundred instances, the "people" appear with the pronominal suffix "My." Likewise, Yahweh is also called the "God of Israel," and frequently the prophets described Israel as God's "wife" or "bride" (Isaiah 54:5–8; 62:5; Jeremiah 2:2). Israel is also referred to at times as God's "son" (cf. Hosea 11:1).

Despite the fact that the concept of "the people of God" referred predominantly to the Israelites throughout the Old Testament, it was by no means limited to them alone. In messianic times, "Many nations shall be joined to the Lord, in that day, and they shall become My people," the Lord taught through the prophet Zechariah (2:11). In like manner, Isaiah had taught that the Lord Himself would say, "Blessed is Egypt, My people, and Assyria the work of My hands, and Israel My inheritance" (19:24–25). And was this not what Solomon had prayed for at the dedication of the temple—that "all peoples of the earth may know Your name and fear You, as do Your own people Israel" (1 Kings 8:43; Isaiah 56:6–8). Thus, even before

New Testament times, the concept of the people of God encompasses both believing Israel and believing Gentiles outside that nation.

The eschatological character of the people of God manifests itself in Paul's theology of the church. Paul conceives of the church as God's new temple, as the body of Christ, and as the new Israel. Paul uses the term *ekklesia* ("assembly" or "church") sixty-two times. He uses this term to describe God's people both universally (as in "the church of God," 1 Corinthians 10:32) and geographically (as in "the church of God that is at Corinth," 1 Corinthians 1:2). For Paul, then, the local congregation represents the whole church in a particular location.

What was the assembly of Israel in the Old Testament, that is, the Lord's assembly or God's assembly, is now made up of both Jews and Gentiles who believe in Jesus Christ. The churches of the Gentiles (Romans 16:4) are now the assemblies of the Lord. Just as Israel was beloved (Deuteronomy 33:12; Isaiah 44:2; Jeremiah 11:15), so the church of God is beloved (Romans 9:24–25; 1 Thessalonians 1:4). Just as Israel was the elect people of God, so now the church is God's elect people (Romans 9–11). And just as Israel was frequently referred to as the bride of God, the same metaphor carries through to the New Testament where both Paul and John reflect on the nature of the church as the bride of Christ, a metaphor that carries along until the end of the book of Revelation (12:2, 9; 22:17; cf., Ephesians 5:22–23). Furthermore, the church's identity with Israel is revealed when Gentiles are referred to as having a common ancestry with the people of Israel (1 Corinthians 10:1). Prophecies originally given to Israel are often fulfilled as well in Gentile believers because they are integrated into Israel (1 Peter 2:1–10) and are Abraham's children through Christ (Galatians 3:6–9, 16; Romans 4:9–25). Believers in Christ are "true" Jews and the "true" circumcision (Romans 2:28–29; Philippians 3:3).

Since the laws that separate Jews and Gentiles have been abolished (Ephesians 2:15), they are now united together in Christ (Ephesians 2:11–22). They have been reconciled to Christ and to one another through the cross. Hence, Gentiles are fellow citizens with Jews in the people of God. The mystery hidden in the Old Testament is now revealed: Jews and Gentiles are co-heirs and members of the same body through the gospel (Ephesian 3:5–6). Gentiles are now part of the true Israel because they are united to Christ, who is the true Israel of God, in contrast to Israel "according to the flesh" (1 Corinthians 10:18), which is separated from God. Gentiles have been grafted into the olive tree of God's people (Romans 11:17–24).

Identifying believers in Christ as the true Israel does not preclude a future for ethnic Israel, however. Indeed, in Romans 9:11, Paul promises a future salvation for Israel. Ethnic Jews who trust in Christ will be grafted back into the olive tree (11:23–24). All Israel will be saved (11:26). They will become part of the church of the Lord, part of God's assembly when they are converted, so that they are united with Gentile believers in Christ. So then, as Kaiser notes, "The contemporary doctrine of the church must be anchored in the unity and singularity of the people of God of all ages. The gifts and calling that this people of God have are from God. Therefore, all attempts to isolate Israel from the church in every sense runs counter to the direct challenge of Scripture. On the other hand, all reports of Israel's death and demise as the people of God in every sense are, as Mark Twain quipped in another connection, certainly premature—and I might add, non-biblical!"[6]

The unity of the people of God is signified through the church being described as Christ's body (1 Corinthians 12:27; Ephesians 1:23; 4:12; 5:23; Colossians 1:24). Believers are one body in Christ (Romans 12:5). Paul often uses the image of the body without designating it specifically as the body of Christ (Romans 12:4; 1 Corinthians 12:13–17; Ephesians 3:6; 4:4, 16; Colossians 2:19; 3:15), though in context the relation to Christ is implicit or obvious. What is clear is that the church as Christ's body, as those who are incorporated into Christ, represents Christ to the world. The church is to live out her life in holiness and godliness as the radiant bride of Christ and herald the good news of salvation to the ends of the earth so that others who live in the darkness of sin may be transformed from Satan's kingdom to the Kingdom of the Lord.

Furthermore, all believers are "baptized into one body" (1 Corinthians 12:13) and are therefore one in Christ (Romans 12:5; 1 Corinthians 12:12, 20; Ephesians 2:16; 4:4; Colossians 3:5). Because the body is united in Christ, no member of the body is inferior or superior to another (1 Corinthians 12:14–26). Disputations over food and the importance of days, which particularly divided Jews and Gentiles, become occasions in which Paul exhorts the church to love one another, to desist from judging and condemning one another, and to seek to understand the perspective of those with whom they disagree (Romans 14–15; 1 Corinthians 8–10). The importance of unity is highlighted in the letter to the Philippians, the entirety of which can be understood as a call to unity (1:27–2:5; 4:2–3).

Moreover, each member of the church plays a crucial role, for they are endowed with spiritual gifts (Romans 12:3–8; 1 Corinthians 12–14; Ephesians 4:7–16). These gifts are not to be used for showing off one's spirituality. They are rather for the purpose of edifying and strengthening fellow believers in the faith (1 Corinthians 12:7; 14:1–19; Ephesians 4:12–16). The participation of every member does not mean that there is not a place for leaders or for official ministries in the churches. Some are called to be elders (otherwise called bishops or pastors, Ephesians 4:11; Philippians 1:1; 1 Timothy 3:1–7; 5:17–22; Titus 1:5–9) and deacons (Philippians 1:1; 1 Timothy 3:8–13; cf., Romans 16:1–2). Some have mistakenly taught that structure and offices do not coexist with the work of the Spirit and manifestation of gifts. However, the two, when worked out scripturally, are not contradictory but complementary.

We also see the eschatological character of Pauline thought relative to the church as God's temple. In the Old Testament, God dwelt in the tabernacle and the temple. In the New Testament, John emphasizes that Jesus is the new temple (John 2:12–22; 4:21–23), that the temple has been replaced by Jesus Himself. According to Paul, the Old Testament teaching on the temple anticipates and points to Jesus dwelling in the church. The indwelling Spirit signifies that the church is God's temple (1 Corinthians 3:16). As the temple, the church is holy (1 Corinthians 3:17), and those who defile it will themselves be destroyed (cf. Leviticus 10:1–3). Thus, the Old Testament promises of the Lord dwelling with His people (Exodus 29:4–5; Leviticus 26:12) through the tabernacle are now realized in the church as God's temple. Clearly the church, then, reflects the glory of God, for the true and living God dwells in the church, as He did in the temple under the old covenant. As such, believers must refrain from what is unclean and refuse to imitate the evil practices by unbelievers (2 Corinthians 6:17), cleansing themselves "from all filthiness of the flesh and spirit, perfecting holiness in the fear of God" (2 Corinthians 7:1).

In summary, the Old Testament promise from the beginning was that blessing would reach the whole world and include all people. This promise is fulfilled in Jesus Christ. The blessings promised to Israel now belong to the new and true Israel, composed of Jews and Gentiles, in Christ. Hence, the church is now God's assembly, His gathered people. The divisions between Jew and Gentiles have been erased through Christ's death so that now Gentiles are fellow members with Jews in God's temple—that is, the church. The church as Christ's body and God's temple communicates God's presence to the world. The unity of the church is a major Pauline theme, for love is the signature of the people of God and the evidence that the Spirit resides in the church. The people of the church celebrate its new life together in baptism and the Lord's Supper, and the Lord grants gifts to the church for the building up of one another in love. Leaders in particular are called upon to guard the gospel and to teach it faithfully, for love in the church will be severely repressed if error becomes predominant.

The New World. The climactic victory of the coming age and the realization of the fulfillment of the covenant formula "I will be your God, you shall be My people" emphasize God's commitment to be present with His community via the catchword "dwell." "Behold, the tabernacle of God is with man, and He will dwell with them, and they shall be His people"

(Revelations 21:3). Such a statement echoes an earlier statement in John's Gospel, "The Word became flesh and dwelt among us" (John 1:14), and the much earlier promise of His presence, "I will walk among you and be your God, and you shall be My people" (Leviticus 26:12). The reality of God's presence with His people is graphically captured in the wilderness tabernacle and later in the temple. The term most associated with the wilderness structure is "dwell" (Exodus 25:8–9). By this designation, Israel was led to understand that through this structure, God was among them. So ingrained was the understanding of Yahweh's presence in the temple that by the late seventh century it became a source of false security (cf. Jeremiah 7:4). The significance of Ezekiel's temple is exemplified in the exclamation that also ends the book, "The Lord Is there" (Ezekiel 48:35). "Tabernacle" and "temple" were clearly symbols of God's presence with His people (Exodus 40:34; 1 Kings 8:10–12).

When the tabernacle and the temple are viewed typologically, then the antitype is the incarnation, where God is present in Jesus Christ and indeed has taken up residence among us (John 1:14). A further New Testament correspondence with the Old Testament is the concept that the Holy Spirit, not unlike the cloud filling the tabernacle or temple, has come to fill the body of God's people, the church. God has taken up residence in the church, the community of God's people (1 Corinthians 3:16–17; 2 Corinthians 6:16). God's desire to take a people for Himself is a commitment to be present with them, a point made in both Testaments.

The Old Testament often emphasizes the place, the land, where Yahweh dwells with His people and where His promises will be fulfilled. Yet, when we read the New Testament, there is little to be read in reference to the land promises. Paul, in fact, emphasizes the salvation that awaits God's people, the future in final redemption, and their final sanctification. The physical dimension of salvation certainly is not abandoned, for the resurrection of the body is a major theme in Paul's writings (Roman 6:5; 8–9; cf. 8:11; 1 Corinthians 15:1–58; 2 Corinthians 4:14; Philippians 3:10; 1 Thessalonians 4:13–18). Paul does not abandon the Old Testament hope of a physical resurrection (Job 19:25–26; Isaiah 26:19; Daniel 12:2) for a trans-physical or ethereal future. When Jesus returns, believers will be raised from the dead and glorified (1 Corinthians 15:26; see John 5:29). The return of Jesus signals the consummation of God's promises and the realization of all that has been pledged to them. Paul does not emphasize, however, the location, the place where believers will reside. It is not that he abandons such a promise. We saw previously that believers will inherit the Kingdom, and the Kingdom includes the notion of a realm, a place where believers will rule, even though the Kingdom is heavenly (2 Timothy 4:18; see Daniel 2:44; 7:13–14, 27).

Clearly, Paul is aware of a future reward and inheritance, and yet he does not tie it closely or specifically to the land. A reference to the physicality of the promises is not entirely absent, however, for Abraham is said to be "heir of the world" (Romans 4:13), and believers, as the children of Abraham, will obtain the same inheritance (Galatians 3:29). Furthermore, in Romans 8:18–25, the transformation of all creation is featured. The old creation was subject to frustration and futility because of the sin of Adam and Eve in the garden. The bondage and the corruption of the present creation are temporary. A new day is coming when all of creation will be liberated from its present condition. A new creation, free from disease, death, and sin will replace it. The promises of the land are not limited to Canaan, then, but are now focused on Christ, on the redemption and salvation that He has accomplished, and on the restoration of a new heaven and earth. When Paul contemplates the future resurrection and its importance, he concludes the entire discussion by relaying why the resurrection matters to believers, saying, "And thus we shall always be with the Lord" (1 Thessalonians 4:17). The focus is not on the resurrection itself, important as that is, but rather on the experience of enjoying the Lord forever. The blessings of salvation and the inheritance are to be prized, but what makes them praiseworthy is the exaltation of God through Jesus Christ and our endless access and worship of Him (Romans 5:11). Hence, when

Jesus returns, believers will marvel and be astonished in His presence (2 Thessalonians 1:10).

In summary, when Paul thinks of the final inheritance, he focuses on a person instead of a place, on fellowship with God in Christ instead of the new universe that is coming. But this comment should not be taken too far. As Schreiner rightly concludes,

> A creation free from groaning and futility is envisioned (Romans 8:18–25). Christians will be heirs of the entire world (Romans 4:13). A new Jerusalem is coming (Galatians 4:26), and believers even now are members of the heavenly Jerusalem. Believers will be raised from the dead and inhabit the new world that is coming. All will confess that Jesus is Lord (Philippians 2:11), and every enemy in the universe will be pacified (Colossians 1:20). God will be 'all in all' (1 Corinthians 15:28), and those who do not know God or who disobeyed the gospel will be excluded from God's presence forever (2 Thessalonians 1:6–10). The long-promised Kingdom will be finally consummated, and believers will enjoy God in Christ forever in the new and transformed world that He has created (cf. John 14:6).[7]

So then, we conclude this section with the following overview of the Bible: God originally created humans in His image to rule over the works of His hands (cf. Genesis 1:32; Psalm 8). But mankind lost their dominion after Adam and Eve, prompted by Satan's solicitation, transgressed God's commandment of not eating from the tree of the knowledge of good and evil (Genesis 3; Romans 5:11). Consequently, all humans have now come under the dominion of Satan, sin, and death. Yet God in His great wisdom and mercy sent His Son to the earth to be our second Adam. To do for man what man could not possibly do for himself. Through His perfect obedience to the law and by His substitutionary death, burial, and resurrection, Christ restored for man what Adam had lost. The crown of "glory and honor" had befallen man. But Christ, for our sake, was "crowned with glory and honor" when He was resurrected from the dead (see Hebrews 2). Due to His obedience unto death, even the death of the cross, God highly exalted Christ and gave Him a name which is above every name (Philippians 2). Thus Jesus, who now sits in the highest seat in the heavens (Hebrews 1:3), will one day rule all nations in fulfillment of the promise given to David (Psalm 2; Isaiah 24:21–23; Revelation 11:5). Moreover, all who belong to Him will one day rule with Him (Romans 8:16–17; 2 Timothy 2:12; Revelation 5:10) and live again as God's people under God's rule for God's glory: such is the Kingdom of God! Having laid down the broad strokes for constructing a consistent and unified theme of Scripture, we are now better prepared for developing a clearer portrait of Bible theology, utilizing proper theological methodology.

14

DOING THEOLOGY

Chapters one through eleven focused primarily on establishing proper methodology for determining the original intended meaning of a text, a task that is commonly and generally referred to as *exegesis*. In this section (Theological Analysis) we began the switch from the meaning of a text to the significance a text will add to its overall body of work, first to the book from which it is derived and second to Scripture as a whole.

For a thorough and well-balanced understanding of Bible theology, an interpreter must engage in at least four basic theological disciplines: biblical theology, historical theology, systematic theology, and practical (or pastoral) theology. What follows looks at each of these both individually and how they interrelate with one another.

Biblical Theology

Biblical theology seeks to understand how God has revealed His Word historically and organically. Biblical theology examines the theology of individual biblical books (e.g., Isaiah, the Gospel of Matthew), as well as relatable collection of books (corpus) within the Bible (e.g., the Pentateuch, the Gospels, Paul's letters), and then traces out themes as they develop across the diverse sections of the Bible in order of determining how these unifying themes draw the Bible together. There are two types of enquiry: the search for unifying or central themes behind the Testaments and the attempt to trace a particular theme (such as the temple, or kingdom) through the various stages of the biblical canon.

When it comes to the practice of biblical theology, at least four priorities are essential:

1. *Read the Bible progressively as a historically developing collection of documents.* God did not provide His people with all of the Bible at once. There is a progression to His revelation, and reading the whole back into the part, detached from its progressive flow, may seriously distort a text by obscuring its true significance in the unfolding of redemptive history. This requires studying the Bible in its historical-chronological sequence, as well as trying to understand the theological nature of the sequence.

2. *Presuppose that the Bible is both coherent and cohesive.* The Bible has many human authors but one divine Author, and He never contradicts Himself. Biblical theology uncovers and articulates the unity of all the biblical texts taken together.

3. *Work inductively from the text—from individual books and from themes that run through the Bible as a whole.* Although readers can never entirely divorce themselves from their own backgrounds, students of biblical theology recognize that their subject matter is exclusively the Bible. They therefore try to use categories and pursue priorities that the text itself sets.

4. *Make theological connections primarily from recurring themes.* One way to do this is to trace the trajectory of themes straight through the Bible.

Biblical theology often focuses on the turning and climatic points within the Bible's storyline, and its most pivotal concern is tied to how the New Testament uses the Old Testament, observing how later biblical authors refer to previous Scriptures (more discussion on this below). Above all, the themes that unite the various parts of Scripture must emerge from within and not be opposed from without; that is, they should be drawn out of the text rather than out of the interpreter's imagination and should truly sum up the other major sub-themes of Scripture. It has been our endeavor to demonstrate such in our theological survey in the previous chapters (12 and 13).

Areas of Concern within the Discipline of Biblical Theology

Continuity vs. Discontinuity. All agree that the relationship between the Old Testament and the New Testament is a central issue for any proper biblical theology. The basic problem here is in relation to the unity and diversity of Scripture: each Testament must have its autonomous place within the larger unity of Scripture. Yet the balance between the two remains difficult to attain. Many have taught that the Old and New Testaments should remain separate. Marcion was the first to demand a radical dichotomy, removing from the canon not only the Old Testament books, but also any New Testament work that relates itself to the Old Testament in some way. In more modern times, both Adolf von Harnack and Rudolf Bultmann have stressed a discontinuity between the Testaments. For both men, this leads to a promissory approach to biblical theology. The Old Testament is the presupposition of the New, in that the failure of the covenant hope of Israel led to a new religion centering on the promissory hope of justification.

This negative tone, however, has not been influential. For one, biblical scholars tend to agree that a removal of "fulfillment" from the biblical concept of "promise" is arbitrary, unnecessary, and inadequate. Moreover, as Osborne notes, the "New Testament background is also loosed from its historical moorings and flounders in a sea of mythical irrelevance."[1] In the final analysis it is impossible to separate the two Testaments, and any truly biblical theology must begin with the recognition of unity and demonstrate such. The simple fact that there are at least 257 quotes and over 1,100 illusions shows the extent to which the latter built on the former. In terms of vocabulary, themes, religious emphasis, and worship, the two depend on one another. In terms of redemptive history, a clear typological relationship of promise-fulfillment exists between the Testaments, and any concept of the progress of revelation in history (the backbone of biblical theology) must build on this deeper interdependence. To this end, the stern words of John Bright must be underscored:

> Let it be repeated: No hermeneutic can be accounted satisfactory that does not allow the preacher to operate with any and all Old Testament texts and to bring them to word in their Christian significance, yet without in any way twisting or departing from their plane sense. A hermeneutic that silences parts of the Old Testament, or enables us to hear only the easy parts, or arbitrarily imposes meaning upon the text, or uses it as the vehicle for a sermon, the content of which is really drawn from the New Testament, will not do. Equally, an uncritical procedure that betrays the preacher into imposing Old Testament institutions, directives, and attitudes directly on the Christian will not do . . . we must be prepared to hear each text in its plain intention, yet in its Christian significance.[2]

The issues involved in the debate between continuity and discontinuity are complex, but, in reality, almost every theological construct (covenant, dispensational, or otherwise) recognizes some areas of continuity and some areas of discontinuity. Every evangelical theology would recognize that the animal sacrifices have been discontinued on the account of Christ's "once for all" sacrifice of Himself (Hebrews 10:11–12). Likewise, every evangelical theology would recognize that the moral aspects of the law continue to be in force today. For the interpreter, as it relates to a biblical theology, the task at hand is to determine just how much of the Bible should be understood as a continuity and how much should be understood as a discontinuity, especially as it relates to the wider themes within

Scripture: the covenants, the law, the people of God, the nation of Israel, etc.

As a word of caution, it may be tempting to buy into a particular system of theology and then try to read the biblical data through the lens of that system. However, it is far better to try to understand the Bible on its own terms and affirm continuity where it exists and discontinuity where it exists.

Typology, Sensus Plenior ("fuller meaning"), and the Analogia Fidei ("analogy of faith").[3] Typology, according to S. G. Sowers, is "the interpretation of earlier events, persons, and institutions in biblical history which become proleptic entities, or 'types,' anticipating later events, persons, and institutions, which are their antitypes."[4] Thus, typology is rooted in the recognition that history has a divine purpose, that purpose being ordained by an intending Being who controls it and intimates within it where it is going (Ephesians 1:9–10), and that biblical events, at times, are indicative of where history is moving. As we have already observed, Israel's prophets projected their hope for the future in the form of analogies from the past, which built Israel's tradition of expectation. What God had done in the past was an indication of the greater deeds God would perform in the future. When Israel faced exile, the hope of deliverance from Babylon was cast in the language of the exodus. And the hope for a final redemptive work of God was often juxtaposed in the same way. Out of these parallels we come to see Christ as the ultimate fulfillment of Israel's redemptive progress. Israel's past was constantly redirected toward the coming deliverance of God's anointed, the Christ, who was to carry out Israel's ultimate "exodus" (Luke 9:31).

Typology, then, is necessary for understanding the significance of Old Testament history. Likewise, it is crucial for recognizing the Christological fulfillment of many Old Testament passages and themes. Note, for example, how the author of Hebrews specifically informs us that the Old Testament sacrificial system was a type or "shadow of the good things to come" (10:1), and proceeds to show how the sacrificial system clearly pointed beyond itself to a more perfect sacrifice (Hebrews 8:10). Old Testament predictive prophecy often has a built-in indication that there is both a typological fulfillment in the immediate future and a more complete fulfillment in the distant future. For example, 2 Samuel 7:12–16 has a preliminary reference to Solomon, but the language of the passage indicates the coming of a person who would far exceed Solomon in his accomplishment of the dominion of God, and so Hebrews 1:5 could quote this passage as referring to Jesus Christ. Thus, if later revelation reflects or points to earlier texts or events through typology, especially from the standpoint of the complete revelation in Christ, we might expect to find a "fuller sense" in those text than would have been evident to the first hearers. "*Sensus plenior*" is thus simply another way of looking at how later revelation relates to earlier revelation. By showing how the later revelation reflects and completes the earlier (typology), the earlier revelation itself can be seen to take on an expanded meaning (*sensus plenior*), which is evident to us, but would not have been evident to its first readers.[5]

Furthermore, typology implies that the later revelation can only be understood in relation to the earlier, just as earlier revelation is ultimately understood only in the light of later revelation. As L. Goppelt points out, "Typology demonstrates not only the nature of the new in comparison with the old, but it also shows that the new is founded directly and solely in redemptive history."[6] It is therefore not surprising that the New Testament understands many of the events and institutions of the Old Testament to be "types." This is explicitly stated in a few texts (1 Corinthians 10:6, 11; Romans 5:14; Hebrews 9:24; 1 Peter 3:21), but is also implied in many other passages. Thus, the New Testament writers understood Christianity as the fulfillment of Old Testament expectation and understood the Old Testament as pointing to Jesus. When Jesus declared that He had to die and be raised on the third day "according to the Scriptures," He established an essential relationship between His redemptive act for His people and the expectation of the Old Testament. "If the New Testament fulfills the

Old Testament tradition, then we cannot understand the New Testament entirely apart from the typological expectations of the Old Testament."[7]

To some, this may sound suspiciously like reading things into the text that are not there. And, indeed, this can happen. However, true *sensus plenior* is organically related to the historical meaning. That is, it should be a "fuller" sense, not an entirely "other" sense. To illustrate this concept, many have used the metaphor of a seed. Just looking at an apple seed, for example, one could not see a full end result, although one could tell that the seed is intended to grow into something bigger, and from a later standpoint one can look back and see how the seed gradually grew into a full-grown apple tree. But the meaning of the seed is only fulfilled in the apple tree, not in the seed itself. Thus, the meaning of Genesis 3:15, which prophesied that the seed of the woman would crush the head of the serpent, is only fulfilled in the New Testament recognition of Christ's victory over Satan.

One way in which an "organic" relationship between the original meaning and the fuller meaning may be recognized is by making the distinction between "sense" and "reference." The reference relates to the specific object that is in the author's immediate purview. The sense, on the other hand, refers to the meaning of the sentence that transcends the immediate situation. The linguistic context defines the sense, whereas the historical context defines the reference. For example, in Psalm 2:7 the Lord says, "You are My Son, today I have begotten You." The sense of this is that the person being addressed shares a special relationship with the person speaking, and on the day of speaking, the speaker has either established or reaffirmed that relationship. The sense would be determined by the context. But the immediate reference within the psalm, the one to whom the sentence is directed, is David (cf. Acts 4:25), a king of Israel, whose special representative relationship to God was being addressed. But, as the prophetic word of the Lord, it ultimately refers to the special relationship of God the Father to Jesus the Son, the ultimate King of Israel (cf. Hebrews 1:5). So, while the linguistic sense remains the same, the little referent (like the seed) has grown into a much greater referent (like the apple tree). Thus, recognizing a fuller sense within a text is not just discovering some resemblance, but determining whether a text, or its larger context, points forward to a future development outside of its immediate context. For instance, Genesis 3:15 clearly looks to a future development.

Furthermore, Jesus taught His disciples that the Old Testament looked forward to His death, resurrection, and exaltation, as well as the preaching of the gospel to the Gentiles. Since the New Testament writers do not cover everything in the Old Testament, we may expect some areas where the typology of *sensus plenior* has not been indicated in the New Testament. But identifying types can be tricky, since we are going beyond the ordinary use of language. We have warrant from the New Testament, however, and also an indication of what qualifies as a genuine type. If we look at New Testament examples of typology, we can find three basic components:

1. To be identified as a type, the redemptive-historical function of an event, person or institution must be clear and show an organic relationship to the latter redemptive history that it foreshadows.

2. The nature of the type must be derived out of the main message of the material, not in some incidental detail.

3. The antitype (fulfillment) must be greater than the type.

An example of a type or fuller sense that is not spelled out in the New Testament is found in the story of Joseph. It has often been noted that Joseph in Genesis behaves in a very Christ-like manner, and has found a general consensus that he serves (to some degree) as a type of Christ. But the New Testament nowhere draws that conclusion. May we? Let us apply the three tests. First, it is without question that the story of Joseph is of great redemptive-historical significance. The purpose of the story in Genesis is to show how God preserved His people, saving them from famine, and furthered the fulfillment of the Abrahamic promises. This is certainly organically related to the deliverance that Christ solidified for His people, since He was the ultimate fulfillment of the Abrahamic promise, according to Paul.

Second, the main events of the central details resemble the activity and character of Christ. As Christ was betrayed by His own people and given over to Gentiles, so Joseph was betrayed by his brothers and sold to Gentiles. As Christ endured humiliation and death to rescue His people, so Joseph was enslaved and then imprisoned so that he could rescue his people. As Christ's faithfulness was rewarded with exaltation to the right hand of God, Joseph's faithfulness was rewarded with exultation to the right hand of Pharaoh. And in both cases the wicked deeds done against them were things that God had purposed for good (compare Genesis 50:20 with Acts 2:23). In these respects, the story of Joseph is typologically representative of Christ. The story taught the Israelites what God was doing. On the other hand, incidental details such as the animal blood on Joseph's coat, Joseph leaving his garments in the hand of Potiphar's wife, and his use of a cup in Benjamin's sack are probably not to be seen as having any fuller sense. But Joseph's life as a whole prefigures the ultimate Servant of God. Finally, of course, Christ's deliverance is much greater than Joseph's.

If we allow for the meaning of a text to move beyond what may be established by grammatical-historical exegesis, then the specter of relativism begins to arise. Is there any means of control over fuller meaning? Part of this control has already been discussed. The immediate, original meaning of a text (the linguistic sense) must be organically related to any further extensive meaning, and all meaning must be related to the redemptive-historical purpose of God. The other primary control is the overall consistency and self-interpretation of Scripture. This is sometimes called interpretation according to "the analogy of Scripture" (*analogue Scripturae*) or "the analogy of faith" (*analogia fidai*). Augustine's maxim that "Scripture is interpreted by Scripture" is simply to say that God determines the meaning of His own words. This is not an opening up of a Pandora's box, or what Samuel Sandmel referred to as "parallelomania," but a control on meaning. It confines the meaning of any text to that which fits the rest of Scripture.

This results in two obvious, yet important hermeneutical principles. First, obscure passages of Scripture should be interpreted in light of the clear passages. Second, whenever a New Testament writer explicitly interprets an Old Testament text, this interpretation is true.

The first of these principles is rather universally acknowledged, although not universally practiced, and falls under general interpretive practices for any text. Generally speaking, all interpretations begin as an hypothesis that accepts some things which appear to be clear and then proceed to build on that base. We must be careful here, however, since a text might be deemed "obscure" only because a putatively "clear" text has been misunderstood. But if the interpreter is aware of this danger and maintains humility with respect to the interpretation, he or she can make progress up the hermeneutical spiral by using the clear text to control or interpret the meaning of the obscure one.

The second principle is that, while the New Testament writers do not always interpret exhaustively, they do interpret correctly. This bears mentioning because some Christians think that, while it is proper to understand the New Testament in light of the Old Testament background, it is quite improper to understand the older revelation in light of the later revelation. But as McCartney and Clayton pointedly state, "This is both ridiculous, from a general hermeneutical point of view, and perverse, from a theological one. If God is the author of the whole [Bible], of both the history and the text, then surely the latter is latent in all the former, and meaning in the former is expanded by the appearance of the latter. Was Peter in error in the way he used Joel 2 or Psalm 16 in his [sermon] at Pentecost (found in Act 2)?"[8] Of course, not!

So the analogy of faith for Christians dictates that both the obscure text must be understood in light of clear text, and that the New Testament gives the correct understanding of the Old Testament. But it also serves to indicate that the meaning of any part of the Bible must be understood in the context of the Bible as a whole. This principle is sometimes called "canonical interpretation." Texts that might have been understood in one way, if they occurred in isolation from Scripture, are shown by their inclusion in Scripture to have a fuller typological meaning.

The story of Moses striking the rock in the wilderness is an excellent case in point (Exodus 17). Apart from Paul's reference to the rock in 1 Corinthians 10, we would have no indication that the rock had any typological meaning. Here the totality of Scripture provides the context. The relationship of the rock with Christ clarifies the reason for God's anger with Moses for striking the rock a second time, for Christ would come to die once and for all. Moses's impatient disobedience, then, resulted in his dislodging of some of the symbolism of the rock, though it is doubtful that he realized the full typological symbolism of his actions. This kind of exegesis does not exhibit an absolute methodological control, then, but rather operates by a "faith" control that depends on hermeneutical sensitivity and submission to God for its results. *Sensus plenior* does not negate our earlier assertion that it is the human author's meaning which is the basis for discovering the meaning of a text, but it does recognize that God's intent, especially in the Old Testament, often went beyond anything that the Old Testament writers themselves would have envisioned.

In summary, the meaning of any text is based on the way the text functioned in its original linguistic and cultural context. Since any text is understood according to its human context, the Bible must also be understood likewise. Grammatical-historical exegesis is the means in finding the author's original, immediate meaning of a biblical text. This task involves the study of the verbal elements of the discourse (words and syntax) within their place of context, the necessity of studying a text in its historical-cultural setting, and the identification of a text's genre. However, grammatical-historical exegesis establishes only the initial base, not the total meaning of a scriptural text, not only because of the historical transcendence of all biblical texts, but also and more importantly because history was going somewhere and Scripture speaks of the progressive unfolding of God's redemptive plan. The older revelation, predicated on divine authorship, anticipates and points to the later revelation. Thus, Paul can understand "seed" in Galatians 3:16 as pointing toward Christ, because ultimately there is only one true Seed of Abraham, only one individual who truly qualifies as the inheritor of the promises, and that is Jesus Christ. The principles we have noted are as follows:

1. The divinely intended meaning of any text must be organically related to the human author's original meaning. The human author's meaning is understood within his grammatical-historical context, and this is our initial access to the larger divine meaning.

2. The divinely intended meaning must be consistent with the total revelation of Scripture. Furthermore, an individual interpreter must always hold his perceptions of the divine meaning tentatively, subject to what is directly taught in Scripture.

3. The divinely intended meaning must in some way point to (but not necessarily speak directly about) God's redemptive purpose in Christ; that is, it must find its place in redemptive history and be Christologically focused.

Historical Theology

Historical theology is the basic enquiry into how others in the past have understood the Bible. In other words, what Christians have thought in the past about exegesis and theology, and, more specifically, how Christian doctrine has developed over the centuries, especially in response to false teachings. Historical theology, then, is concerned primarily with opinions in periods earlier than our own: biblical perspectives that are not tightly tethered to twenty-first-century agendas. That does not mean they (or we!) are necessarily right; rather, it means we recognize that all of us have a great deal to learn.

Church history is of vital importance to historical theology since it gives theology a context in which it was produced and defined. Systematic theology (discussed below) attempts to create statements of faith regarding the major theologies within our Bible (biblical theology). Historical theology, then, embodies both of these concepts as a way of informing theologians as to what has been believed, and what corrections, improvements, or adherence need to be made in the present based on that information. The systematician should remember, critically, that it is nearly impossible to "do theology" as if it has never been done before. Historical theology, then, is used both as an instructional tool (for systematic theology) and as a critical tool (highlighting various important topics through history as key elements of the Christian faith).

Furthermore, carefully studying the history of interpretation is a helpful tool in freeing us from unwitting slavery to our biases. It induces humility, clears our minds of unwarranted assumptions, exposes faulty interpretations that others have long since (and rightly) dismissed, and reminds us that responsibly interpreting the Bible must never be a solitary task. That being said, a word of caution is in order: while the ancient creeds and the history of exegesis and theology are invaluable, we must remember that they do not have the ultimate authority of the Bible itself. One must never become so enamored with secondary opinions that they lose sight of what the Bible actually teaches. Reading the history of interpretation, as important as it may be, must never replace or usurp the Bible itself.

Systematic Theology

Systematic theology seeks to answer the question, "What does the whole bible teach about a certain topic?" It is concerned with how the whole Bible logically coheres in systems of thought. It often organizes truth under headings such as the doctrines of God (theology proper), the Bible (bibliology), humans (anthropology), sin (hamartiology), Christ (Christology), the Holy Spirit (Pneumatology), salvation (soteriology), the church (ecclesiology), and the end-times (eschatology). In essence every discipline and methodology discussed thus far must be used in constructing a systematic theology. Most commonly, we begin the theological process with the traditional views inherited (preunderstandings) from our chosen theological community (Methodist, Presbyterian, Baptist, Pentecostal, etc.). Then we begin to trace a particular issue (such as the atonement or eschatology) through Scripture inductively (biblical theology), determining which passages speak to the issue. At this stage exegetical study searches for the exact nuances in each passage that addresses the doctrine and begins to organize the passages in order to determine which aspect of the doctrine each passage teaches. Biblical theology collates the results and determines the belief on the issue, while systematic theology organizes the material in a rather logical order as a self-consistent whole. In other words, systematic theology is the proper goal of biblical study and teaching. Every hermeneutical aspect must be put into practice in constructing such a theology.

The Bible's unity makes systematic theology not only possible, but necessary. The biblical data must, however, control systematic theology. It is especially important not to "go beyond what is written," for some Christian truths include within their sweep substantial areas of unknown things. For instance, there are important things we do not know about Jesus's incarnation, about the Trinity, and about God's sovereignty and human responsibility. To pretend we know more than we do generates shoddy theology that can prove misleading and dangerous. A large part of orthodoxy resides in listening carefully and humbly to all of Scripture and then properly relating passage with passage, truth with truth.

Furthermore, some think that their exegesis neutrally and objectively discovers the text's meaning and thus they build their systematic theology on such discoveries. In reality, systematic theology profoundly influences one's exegesis. Without realizing it, many people develop their own lists of favorite passages of the Bible that then become their controlling framework for interpreting the rest of the Bible; to a large degree this accounts for conflicting exegesis among Christians. This problem may develop in at least two ways: First, one may unwittingly overemphasize certain biblical truths at the expense of others, subordinating or even explaining away passages that do not easily "fit" the slightly distorted structure that results. For example, how one understands justification in Romans may control how one understands apostasy in Hebrews (and vice versa). Second, one may self-consciously adopt a certain structure by which to integrate all the books of the Bible with the result that they automatically classify and explain some passages and themes artificially or too narrowly. Even worse is using parts of the Bible to support one's systematic theology without considering how the whole Bible fits together (biblical theology).

Practical Theology

Practical theology answers the question, "How should humans respond to God's revelation?" Sometimes that is clearly spelled out in Scripture; other times it builds on inferences of what Scripture says. At the risk of stating the obvious, practical theology practically applies the other four disciplines—so much so that the other disciplines are in danger of being sterile and even dishonoring to God unless tied in some sense to the responses He rightly demands of us. Practical theology addresses various and diverse issues such as culture, ethics, evangelism, marriage and family, money, politics, church practices, worship, and much more.

Practical theology, essentially being a hermeneutical theology, requires contextual sensibility and sensitivity. Dealing critically with imposed theologies and ethics, it encourages students of the Bible to evaluate the inherited understandings that guide our interpretations and actions and to become transmitters of theology into people's real lives. To be "doers of the word and not hearers only." More on the practical application of Scripture will be discussed in the following chapters.

Theological Methods and Their Verification

In our day, theological systems abound; in fact, entire books (such as *The Moody Handbook of Theology*) have been written on the vast amount of theological methods that have permeated biblical scholarship.

Familiarizing yourself with many of these is worthwhile, but for the sake of our focused study on hermeneutics, we shall limit our considerations to the so-called dogmatic theologies in hopes of answering the question, "What model best identifies and is best represented by the total pattern of God's revelation?"

The term "dogmatic theology" seems to have been used first by the Lutheran humanist George Calixtus (1586–1656). However, by the end of the eighteenth century it was in fairly common use among all theologians even though the connotations of the term "dogmatic" were varied. The term is widely used by modern theologians in reference to an official or "dogmatic" theology recognized by an organized church body, such as the Roman Catholic Church, Dutch Reformed Church, etc., and that is how we shall use it here. We cannot hope to examine all of these, but we shall further discuss the theological models that have had the biggest impact on biblical interpretation: the Roman Catholic Model, the Lutheran Model, the Covenant Theology Model, the Dispensational Model, and the Progressive Covenantal Model.

The Roman Catholic Model. While Roman Catholic theology has a number of doctrines in common with conservative Protestant theology (the Trinity, deity of Christ, etc.), there are many deviations from biblical orthodoxy. A fundamental difference is the authority of tradition in addition to the authority of the Bible. In its outworking, tradition in a sense supersedes the authority of the Bible because tradition and church councils make decrees that countermand and/or add to the explicit teachings of Scripture. Their use of the Apocrypha as canonical material is a further deviation. The place of Mary in Roman Catholic theology removes Christ from His rightful place as sole mediator between God and men (1 Timothy 2:5). Also, the entire system of sacraments is a genuine rejection of the true grace of God in salvation apart from works (Ephesians 2:8–9). Salvation in Roman Catholic theology is not by grace through faith alone but a complex adherence to the sacraments and rituals as legislated by the church hierarchy.

Because of the adherence to popes and other ecclesiastical hierarchy, the Roman Catholic model has put very little emphasis on biblical theology as an inductive approach. However, their overarching views tend to show more of a continuity model within their theology, emphasizing many areas where the Old Testament plays an important role over people today. As one Catholic writer noted, "[All] Scripture is a deep font for the Church's worship and prayer life. Since the Second Vatican Council, the Church has provided for an expanded use of Sacred Scriptures in the Liturgy of the Word at Mass, in the celebration of the other sacraments and the devotional life of the Church, and in its urgings to the laity to celebrate Morning and Evening Prayer which incorporates recitation of the Psalms. It continues to instruct the faithful and call them to faithfulness in their covenant with God."[9]

The Lutheran Model. The Lutheran model derives its name and perspectives from the sixteenth-century theologian and reformer, Martin Luther. Luther believed that for a proper understanding of Scripture one must carefully distinguish between two parallel and ever-present truths of Scripture: law and gospel. According to Luther, the law reflects the holiness of God's character; were He to dispense with it, He would become an amoral rather than holy God. The gospel is the good news of God's grace, which is God's response to the fact that man can never meet the standard of holiness that the law demands. For Lutheran theologians, law and gospel reveal two integral aspects of God's personality: holiness and grace. Thus they see law and gospel as inseparable parts of redemptive history, from the story of Adam and Eve's sin to the close of this age.

Law and gospel have continuing purposes in the lives of both believers and unbelievers. For the unbeliever, the law condemns, accuses, and shows him his need for the Lord. For the believer, the law continues to demonstrate the need for grace and provides guidelines for daily living. The gospel shows the unbeliever a way to escape from condemnation, while it motivates the believer to keep God's moral law. The careful difference between (but maintenance of) both law and gospel has become an important hermeneutical tool and hallmark of Orthodox Lutheran preaching. The Lutheran position strongly emphasizes biblical continuity. God continues to respond to humans with both law and grace as He has from the beginning of human history. Law and grace are not two different epochs in God's dealing with humanity, but are integral parts of all His relationships.

The Covenant Theology Model. The Reformed position, championed by the Lutherans, was both reinvigorated and revamped by the French theologian, John Calvin. By the mid-sixteenth century, the reformed movement had become splintered and disagreements were both extensive and numerous (on views such as the use of sacraments). But by the end of the century, Calvin, who is arguably the most influential reformed theologian of his time, had left a unifying and lasting impression on Reformed theology. Among many other doctrinal influences came a conceptual overview and interpretive framework for understanding the overall structures of the Bible, commonly known today as "covenant theology."

Covenant theology, like the Lutheran model, emphasizes continuity rather than discontinuity in redemptive history. Covenant theologians view all biblical history as covered by two overarching covenants, a covenant of works (until the Fall) and the covenant of grace (from the Fall to the present). The covenant of works is described as an agreement between God and Adam that promised Adam life for perfect obedience and death as the penalty for disobedience. The covenant of grace is the agreement between God and a sinner in which God promises salvation through faith, and the sinner pledges a life of faith and obedience. All Old Testament, New Testament, and contemporary believers are part of the covenant of grace.

Reformed theology, from which covenant theology developed, has historically viewed the church as existing from the beginning of human history to the end of the world. Unlike dispensational theology, which we will discuss next, covenant theology asserts that when Israel as a nation rejected Christ, the church replaced Israel as God's chosen people. They believe that the temporal, physical promises given to Israel in the Old Testament may now be spiritually applied to the church. Moreover, most covenant theologians do not believe God has promised that He will physically restore Israel as a nation to the land of Palestine. Marten Woudstra, a covenant theologian, says that when we interpret the relationship between the Old Testament and the New Testament properly, "our concerns with an earthly restoration of Israel to the land of the fathers will diminish to the vanishing point."[10] Bruce Walkte also says that "Kingdom promises are comprehensively fulfilled in the church, not in restoring national Israel." He notes: "No clear passage teaches the restoration of national Israel; its reverse side is imprinted with the hard fact that national Israel and its law have been permanently replaced by the church and the New Covenant."[11]

The Dispensational Model. There have been several stages in the development of dispensationalism. The movement itself was initiated by John Nelson Darby and the British Plymouth Brethren, but it went through various stages of growth until it reached its dominant form (early twentieth century) through the influence of two men: C. I. Scofield and Lewis Sperry Chafer. In 1965, Charles Ryrie wrote *Dispensationalism Today*, and two years later the *New Scofield Reference Bible* was published. Both books modified a number of the teachings of earlier dispensationalism. Some theologians have referred to Ryrie's theology as "essentialist dispensationalism" since it identified certain essential features that he believed distinguish dispensationalism from covenant theology.

From the 1990s to the present, the dispensational movement has morphed into a rather "post-essentialist" model, commonly referred to as "progressive" dispensationalism. It is considered "post-essentialist" because the heterogeneity among both dispensationalist and covenant theologians has made it increasingly difficult to identify the "essential" differences that consistently differentiate one group from the other.

One of the cardinal characteristics of dispensationalism has been its continual reevaluation and dedicated use of Scripture to correct its theory. In fact, a dispensationalist study group continues to meet regularly to this day, at the annual meeting of the Evangelical Theological Society, to clarify and modify its theory. As a result of this continued study, many of the beliefs that were harshly criticized in earlier periods of dispensationalism have been either revised or withdrawn from completely. Therefore, this discussion will begin with a brief overview of dispensationalism as it was taught during the middle of the twentieth century and then clarify the changes that have occurred since then.

Scofield defined a dispensation as a "period of time during which man is tested in respect of obedience to some specific revelation of the will of God." The pattern of redemptive history was seen as three regularly recurring stages: (1) God gives human beings a specific set of responsibilities or patterns for obedience, (2) humankind fails to live up to that set of responsibilities, and (3) God responds in mercy by giving a different set of responsibilities—that is, a new dispensation. Dispensationalists historically have recognized between four and nine dispensations, though the usual number is seven. The following are typical descriptions of the seven dispensations as summarized in Charles C. Ryrie's *Dispensationalism*, but there are many variations within this school of thought:[12]

- *Dispensation of Innocence.* This dispensation included the time when Adam and Eve were in a state of innocence, before the Fall, and terminated at the time they sinned through disobedience. In this dispensation the key person was Adam, whose responsibilities involved maintaining the garden and not eating of the tree of the knowledge of good and evil. He failed the test about eating, and, as a result, "far-reaching judgments" were pronounced on him, his wife, and, consequently, all mankind (Genesis 1:28–3:6).

- *Dispensation of Conscience.* During this period, "obedience to the dictates of conscience was man's chief stewardship responsibility."

262

It ended as humans became increasingly wicked and God brought judgment through the flood (Genesis 4:1–8:14).

- *Dispensation of Government.* During this dispensation, God gave humankind the right to capital punishment, "which in the very nature of the case gave man the authority to govern others." Instead of spreading and filling the earth, humanity expressed its rebellion by building the tower of Babel. God's judgment came, and this dispensation ended, through the confusion of languages (Genesis 8:15–11:9).

- *Dispensation of Promise.* This interval covered the time of the patriarchs; its name derives from God's promise to Abraham of a land, an heir, and subsequent blessings. Both Abraham and Isaac are responsible for many moral failures during this time, and after Jacob led the people to Egypt, the judgment of slavery was brought upon the Israelites (Genesis 11:10–Exodus 18:27).

- *Dispensation of Law.* This period lasted from the giving of the Mosaic covenant at Mount Sinai until the death of Christ. During this time, God gave commandments covering all phases of life and activity. Israel's failure to abide by these commandments finally led to division within the monarchy and eventually exile from the Promised Land (Exodus 18:27–Acts 1:26).

- *Dispensation of Grace.* During this dispensation (which includes our present day), man's responsibility is to accept God's gift of righteousness. This age will end with humanity's rejection of God's gracious gift, leading to the tribulation (Acts 2–Revelation 19:21).

- *Dispensation of Kingdom.* During the millennial Kingdom, humanity's responsibility will be obedience to the personal rule of Christ. At the end of this period a final rebellion will erupt and end in final judgment. The best-known biblical passage describing this is Revelation 20 (Revelation 20–21).

One point of debate has been whether the dispensational regulations represent various means of salvation or various guidelines for obedient living after salvation. A common belief among dispensational laypeople (as well as some non-dispensationalists) is that the dispensations of law and grace represent alternative means of salvation. This belief is based, in part, on a note in the original *Scofield Reference Bible*. The note accompanying John 1:17 stated:

> As a dispensation, grace begins with the death and resurrection of Christ (Romans 3:24–26; 4:24–25). The point of testing is no longer legal obedience as the condition of salvation, but acceptance or rejection of Christ, with good works as a result of salvation.

This statement is admittedly poorly worded and did lead to the misunderstanding that dispensationalism recognizes at least two means of salvation. However, there is now a strong consensus that Scofield himself and other dispensationalist writers affirmed elsewhere that salvation was by grace in the Old Testament, and that no one was ever justified by works. The *New Scofield Reference Bible* clarifies that there has always been but one means of salvation. Thus, dispensational theologians presently believe that the commands given during the various dispensations were guidelines for godly living given after salvation rather than means of earning salvation. In the last fifty years, dispensational teaching has significantly changed with regard to at least four beliefs: the postponed-Kingdom theory; the nature of the two Kingdoms (the Kingdom of God and the Kingdom of Heaven); the assertion of two entirely separate peoples of God (Israel and the church); and the notion of two covenants, one for Israel and one for the church.

The postponed-Kingdom theory is the belief that at His first coming Christ intended to set up an earthly kingdom with Israel at its center. When the people of Israel rejected Him, Christ withdrew the offer of an earthly kingdom, created instead a spiritual kingdom (the church), and postponed the coming of an earthly kingdom with Israel at its center until His second coming. Most dispensational theologians now recognize that if Christ had been accepted by the Jews of His time, the crucifixion and resurrection would never have occurred. Walter Kaiser Jr., who does not identify himself as a dispensationalist, reviews the passages that were previously interpreted as the basis for the postponed-Kingdom theory to demonstrate that these verses, interpreted in context, simply affirm that God's offer would first be given to the Jews and then to the Gentiles[13] (see Matthew 21:43).

In the mid-twentieth century dispensationalist also generally believed in two Kingdoms. These included an eternal Kingdom, known as the Kingdom of God, and an earthly kingdom, known as the Kingdom of Heaven. It is now recognized that these two terms are used synonymously in Scripture, and that both can refer to a temporal and eternal Kingdom, as well as a present and future Kingdom (see Matthew 19:23–24).

A third belief that has changed is the notion that there are two entirely separate peoples of God, His heavenly people (the church) and His earthly people (the Jews). However, most scholars now recognize that the biblical language will not support such a strict dichotomy. The phrase "people of God" refers to both Israel and those outside Israel. Robert Saucy reflects the contemporary dispensationalist view on the issue when he says: "In the final since it is perhaps best to say that the people of God is one people, since all will be related to Him through the same covenant salvation. But the affirmation of this fundamental unity in relation to God through Christ does not eliminate the distinctiveness of Israel as a special nation called of God for a unique ministry in the world as a nation among nations."[14]

A fourth belief that has changed is the dispensational idea of two covenants, one for Israel and one for the church. Although several scriptural passages promised a New Covenant (Jeremiah 31:31–34; Ezekiel 36:26–27), dispensationalist today do not believe that the Old Covenant was for Israel and the New Covenant is for the church. Bruce Ware, for example, summarizes the characteristics of the New Covenant that distinguish it from the Old:[15]

1. A new model of implementation (the law is written in their minds rather than on tablets of stone) by the indwelling work of the Holy Spirit (John 14:17).

2. A new result: "All will know me."

3. A new basis: full and final forgiveness (thus, animal sacrifices are no longer necessary).

4. A new scope of inclusion (from the least to the greatest).

5. The Holy Spirit comes on all believers, not just on select ones.

6. The Holy Spirit's coming is permanent, not temporary.

7. The Holy Spirit's coming is not just to accomplish certain tasks but to enable all believers to live in covenant faithfulness.

Thus, the New Covenant includes all post-Pentecostal believers, whether Jew or Gentile.

In summary, dispensational theologians place more emphasis on discontinuity than do covenant theologians. While dispensationalists agree that salvation has always been by grace, they also believe that significant changes regarding God's commands for obedient living occurred across the dispensations. Although contemporary dispensational theologians now stress the continuity between dispensations more than they have in the past, earlier dispensational theologians emphasized the difference between dispensations. Humanity's responsibilities within each dispensation were seen as a different type of test resulting from the previous one. Thus, when human beings failed to obey God after receiving the responsibility of following conscience (second dispensation), God gave them the responsibility of obedience through government. On the flip side, covenant theologians place more emphasis on the additive rather than the disjunctive nature of the covenants. For example, the post-flood Noachian covenant was consistent with the pre-flood covenant; it's simply supplied more details of the grace relationship. Similarly, the Mosaic covenant did not abolish the Abrahamic one but rather added to it (Galatians 3:17–22). So then, starting from exactly the same biblical data and very similar views of inspiration and revelation, dispensational and covenantal theologians arrive at somewhat different views of the nature of redemptive history, views consequently reflected in their theological analysis of the Bible.

The Progressive Covenantalism Model. In recent years a number of theologians have sensed the need for a mediating position between dispensationalism and covenant theology, especially arising from the discipline of biblical theology. Peter Gentry and Stephen J. Wellum, in *Kingdom Through Covenant*, proposed a slightly different way of thinking through the narrative plot structure of the Bible in contrast to the current views. Although they benefited much from dispensational and covenant theology, they successfully hashed out an alternative view which answers some of these disputes. They called this mediating position "progressive covenantalism."

The term "progressive" seeks to underscore the unfolding nature of God's revelation over time, while "covenantalism" emphasizes that God's one redemptive plan for His one people unfolds through the covenants and that all of the covenants find their fulfillment and terminus in Christ. The creation covenant (some would use the word "mandate" instead of covenant) lays a foundation that continues in all the covenants and is fulfilled in Christ and His redemptive work. God's plan, then, moves from creation in Adam to consummation in Christ. On the relationship of Israel and the church,

1. God has one people, yet there is a distinction between Israel and the church by their respective covenants—the church is new in a redemptive-historical sense precisely because she is the community of the New Covenant.

2. The Israel-church relationship must be interpreted Christologically: the church is not directly the "new Israel" or her replacement. Rather, in Christ, the church is God's new creation, comprised of believing Jews and Gentiles. Because Jesus is the true and faithful seed of Abraham who inherits the promises by His work, only those who are in Christ receive the "blessing" of Abraham. Thus, in union with Christ, the church is God's new covenant people in continuity with the elect in all ages, but different from Israel in its nature and structure. The church is a new redemptive-historical reality, and is therefore linked to Israel only indirectly through its relationship with Jesus. Thus one may describe the church as the "true Israel," but it's continuity with "rejected Israel" is found in the representative figure of Jesus, who bridges salvation-history even while fulfilling it.

The progressive covenantalism model, then, while strongly arguing for the unity of God's promised plan culminating in the New Covenant, does not blur the distinction between Israel as a nation (her nature and structure) and the church as a spiritual entity, which is made up of all nations and people (unlike covenant theology). The focus on the new covenant is not to exclude the other covenants since in God's plan each covenant is significant (unlike dispensationalism). But, in order to discern that significance, each covenant must be placed in its own covenantal location, within the terms of the covenant(s) that precede and/or follow it, before we can rightly discern how God's entire plan is fulfilled in Christ. The theory postulates that by doing this, we interpret Scripture on its own terms and discover God's glorious plan unveiled before our eyes. We learn how in Christ all of God's promises are "yes and amen" (2 Corinthians 1:20).

The second-century Christian theologian Irenaeus of Lyons once compared the interpretation of the Bible to that of putting together a grand mosaic, or like assembling Homeric verses into their correct and coherent plot structure. Gnostic allegorizes, Irenaeus argued, had scattered the gems of the scriptural mosaic and configured them again to form an alien portrait. In rereading the Bible, moreover, they had come up with the wrong storyline, one foreign to the Church's Rule of Faith, the central dramatic narrative of salvation history that was the very substance of the biblical revelation. What made the Gnostics' exegesis so damaging was not that it was subjective as such, but that its subjectivity was fated to telling the world a wholly different story of creation and redemption. For all their hermeneutical sophistication, they had missed the very point of divine revelation that permeated the scriptural witness of the prophets and apostles, a mystery that could be fathomed only within the context of a "*Christocentric*" hermeneutic.

Irenaeus, for all his troubles with the Gnostics, could hardly have imagined the changes in the landscape of biblical interpretation eighteen centuries later. And yet the question still remains, "How does one assess the degree of tentativeness and authority of various theological constructions, or the validity of a particular dogmatic model?" This of course has vexed scholars for centuries, especially in terms of debate with other paradigm communities (such as Arminianism vs. Calvinism, dispensationalism vs. covenant theology). Both sides believe that their doctoral formulation is correct and neither will budge. Moreover, the layperson is rightly confused, since both sound viable when taken separately. A likely story goes as follows: Two friends, one a Calvinist and one a moderate Arminian, were discussing their respective views, and one asked the question, "What is the basic difference between my position and yours?" To which the other friend responded, "Mine is biblical!" But how do we know which one is in fact "biblical"?

The first step in validating a theological construction is to see whether it fits the biblical data (is it coherent): Does it provide a better map for biblical theology than any other theological system? This also concerns the explanatory success of the system, whether it actually portrays the teaching of Scripture and has clarity, that is, makes the complex doctrines understandable.

The second step is to ascertain whether the dogmatic assertion is a true model of the biblical material taken as a whole (is it comprehensive): Does it account for all the systems of Scripture on the issue, or does it merely arise from selected portions? Furthermore, the interpreter must compare any other theological model with competing models to see whether the others are in fact more comprehensive.

Third, does the model fit together and form a viable pattern (is it consistent)? If some portions contradict others, this calls for a reexamination and modification; if there is inconsistency throughout, the theological model may be fatally flawed.

And finally, have many different schools of thought accepted the validity of the assertion? If several traditions have recognized the truth of a theological construction, this demonstrates that it is not merely the logical outgrowth of a particular tradition but transcends the interest of party lines. Such a phenomenon has a greater chance of validity.

PART 5

THE PRACTICAL USE OF SCRIPTURE

In the previous chapters our primary focus was on answering two basic questions: First, "How do we determine the meaning of a given text (the practice of traditional hermeneutics)?" And second, "What significance does this text have for understanding the Bible as a whole?" Yet for the Christian, the process of interpretation is incomplete if it stops at the level of meaning. One must then ask: "Does the text at hand apply to them personally in some practical way?" Hermeneutics is not an end in itself. Indeed, the Scriptures constitute God's revelation to His people—His very Word in written form. As God's people we eagerly strive to understand and respond to His message. Yet, that message, needless to say, must be understood accurately if it is going to be practiced faithfully. Since our approach to hermeneutics governs what we come to learn about the Bible, a proper hermeneutic is essential if we are going to apply the Bible's content appropriately. It enables us to discover the knowledge and insight that God wants us to have so that we may appropriately respond to Him. Therefore, in the following chapters we will consider some of the ways that Christians can make proper use of the Bible, as well as some principles to guide us in applying the Bible's message to our lives.

First and foremost, the purpose of the Bible is to make people "wise unto salvation" (2 Timothy 3:15). After a person has received this salvation, then we are told, "All Scripture is given by inspiration of God, and is profitable for doctrine, for reproof, for correction, for instruction in righteousness, that the man of God may be complete, thoroughly equipped for every good work" (3:16–17). Most of the material in our Bible speaks to believers, and specifically to their growth in knowledge and holiness. Doctrine and theology have as their aim transforming sinners into saints and bringing immature Christians into spiritual maturity. The Bible and its study is a prime requisite for every Christian who desires to lead an effective and genuine Christian life.

15

USING THE BIBLE
FOR SPIRITUAL GROWTH

Using the Bible as a Devotional

In any given passage, God may provide conviction or encouragement in a particular direction. While technically this may not be the original intent of the text, it can be a valid conclusion so long as it is inferred from its original meaning. The authority of the conclusion rests on the reader's own sensitivity to the Holy Spirit and on the consistency of their conclusion with the rest of biblical teaching. Indeed, the method cannot guarantee conclusions with divine authority, but it does allow for God to speak through His Word in this manner.

While it may sound redundant at this point, it bears repeating: in using the Bible for devotional purposes, one must base the devotional meaning derived upon sound exegetical principles. Oftentimes, our intense desire to find something practical and devotional in Scripture leaves us susceptible of unintentionally obscuring the genuine meaning of a passage. Much too frequently a devotional message is developed out of a passage at the expense of its contextual and historical meaning. Never should we handle a passage of Scripture in such a way as to distort the original meaning simply because we wish to find something edifying, or, perhaps, we are called upon to teach and feel the pressure to deliver a word of encouragement. "Let the truths of God's Word be its own blessedness."[1]

Furthermore, a methodological devotional approach that moves through a book of Scripture chapter by chapter is ideal. Not only does this method raise contextual awareness, it helps to guard the interpreter against misuses of Scripture. D. A. Carson gives the following critique of which we strongly affirm:

> Devotional guides tend to offer short, personal readings from the Bible, sometimes only a verse or two, followed by several paragraphs of edifying exposition. Doubtless they provide personal help for believers with private needs, fears, and hopes. But they do not provide the framework of what the Bible says—the "plotline" or "story line"—the big picture that makes sense of all the little bits of the Bible. Wrongly used, such devotional guides may ultimately engender the profoundly wrong-headed view that God exists to sort out many problems; they may foster profoundly mistaken interpretations of some Scriptures, simply because the handful of passages they treat are no longer placed within the framework of the big picture, which is gradually fading from view. Only systematic and repeated reading of the whole Bible can meet these challenges.[2]

Various plans for reading through the entire Bible in a given time frame are readily available and can provide guidance and accountability for daily reading. If the daily text is read from a good study Bible that provides interpretive notes when needed, historical-cultural studies can also be implemented in the devotional time without being overly distracting. And finally, exegetically sound devotional guides are also available resources. When choosing a devotional guide, you will want to review several and choose one that incorporates sound exegetical methodology into the daily readings. A guide that emphasizes reading more than one verse of Scripture at a time is generally preferable to devotional aids that treat single verses out of context. Also, always remember that the Scripture is primary and the guide is secondary. Carson rightly places Scripture above all other text, and we wholeheartedly agree with his adjure: "If you must skip something, skip this book; read the Bible instead."

Using the Bible for Individual and Corporate Worship

Since the Bible derived from God Himself and records His mighty deeds and glorious attributes, His people naturally discover in its passages motivation and direction for worship.[3] Worship is the result of God's people responding appropriately to God's revelation of Himself. When believers learn from their study of the Bible who God is and what He has accomplished on their behalf through Jesus's supreme sacrifice on the cross, their hearts naturally well up in praise and adoration.[4]

In many places throughout the Psalms, the reader is drawn into such an experience. For example, one psalmist writes:

> *The Lord is my light and my salvation; whom shall I fear? The Lord is the strength of my life; of whom shall I be afraid? When the wicked came against me to eat up my flesh, my enemies and foes, they stumbled and fell. Though an army may encamp against me, my heart shall not fear; though war should rise against me, in this I will be confident. One thing I have desired of the Lord, that will I seek: that I may dwell in the house of the Lord all the days of my life, to behold the beauty of the Lord, and to inquire in His temple. (Psalm 19:27–4)*

In other places the psalmist expressly seeks to worship God and to elicit from his readers their own adoration of His majesty:

> *I will praise You with my whole heart; before the gods I will sing praises to You. I will worship toward Your holy temple, and praise*

Your name for Your lovingkindness and Your truth; For You have magnified Your word above all Your name. In the day when I cried out, You answered me, And made me bold with strength in my soul. All the kings of the earth shall praise You, O Lord, when they hear the words of Your mouth. (Psalm 138:1–4)

Praise the Lord, all you Gentiles! Laud Him, all you peoples! For His merciful kindness is great toward us, And the truth of the Lord endures forever. Praise the Lord! (Psalm 117)

The Israelites recognized these poetic texts as part of the sacred Scriptures, and since the beginning of the church, Christians have joined them in praising God through these treasured hymns.[5] Furthermore, in using prayers or anthems, the early Christians sought to lift up their readers to praise and adore their God. Paul says,

Now to Him who is able to do exceedingly abundantly above all that we ask or think, according to the power that works in us, to Him be glory in the church by Christ Jesus to all generations, forever and ever. Amen. (Ephesians 3:20–21)

It is not surprising that believers throughout church history have responded to what they have read in unique spontaneous worship. "In one sense, believers function as a worshiping community to announce to the unbelieving world 'How Great Thou Art.'"[6] From what they discover in the Bible, believers can obey the divine injunction: "Therefore by Him let us continually offer the sacrifice of praise to God, that is, the fruit of our lips, giving thanks to His name" (Hebrews 13:15). At another time, Paul instructs believers directly to "Let the word of Christ dwell in you richly in all wisdom, teaching and admonishing one another in psalms and hymns and spiritual songs, singing with grace in your hearts to the Lord" (Colossians 3:16). For Christians, then, the Scriptures attest God's presence, activity, and love, particularly as expressed in His Son, Jesus Christ.

They bring to our attention, in a concrete and vivid manner, God's personal and loving commitment to His people.[7] And as such, the Scriptures move us to worship both individually and corporately.

Corporate worship, as part of the liturgy of the Christian Church, has historically incorporated text from the Bible. A familiar example of this is how *The Book of Common Prayer* of the Protestant Episcopal Church incorporates portions of the Bible extensively for guiding its congregants in corporate worship. Even today many hymns and contemporary praise courses take their words verbatim from the Scripture; for example, "*How Great Is Our God*," by Chris Tomlin, is taken from 2 Chronicles 2:5. The course to the hymn "*I Know Whom I Have Believed*" quotes 2 Timothy 1:12 in the KJV.

Unquestionably, then, the Scriptures aid the worshipper to reflect on and to enact with the elements of the salvific drama, and embody their response to God's grace. At the same time, we believe it is important that worshippers comprehend the biblical passages that are presented, or that are being alluded to. In some uses of the Bible, which we will consider next (preaching and teaching), the goal will be to help hearers discover the meaning and significance of the texts incorporated in the worship service. In using the wealth of liturgical forms, those who lead music find ways to help participants understand what they are hearing or doing within each element. "The Bible contains no magical charms. People need to understand what it says to profit from its message."[8]

Using the Bible for Preaching and Teaching

The preaching and teaching ministry in the church is considered applied hermeneutics and therefore comes under the discussion of the practical use of the Bible. The basic theory of the ministry must be understood if the correct practice of the ministry is to be carried out faithfully. Whether one is a preacher or a teacher, the one who performs this role is a minister of the Word of God. He is not a person who is free to "sermonize" before a group of people without any restraint or obligation. If he is a true minister of God, he is bound to the ministry of the Word of God. He has only one claim to the right to preach and demand decision, and that is he is declaring the truth of God. It is impossible to separate the man from his calling, but as much as possible the minister must realize preaching/teaching is not his opportunity to express his religious views or to promote some personal agenda. His fundamental task in preaching/teaching is not to be clever or even to be profound, but to faithfully and accurately minister the truth of God.

The preaching ministry has as its essence the need for proclamation. Believing that the Bible is God's revelation to the whole world, Christians seek to proclaim its message to all who are willing to listen. By its very nature, preaching attempts to convey biblical information and to persuade people to respond to it in appropriate ways. The origin of preaching goes as far back as the prophetic ministry (cf. 2 Peter 2:5). In the book of Jeremiah, God condemns false prophets for speaking their own thoughts and visions instead of the Word of God: "And the Lord said to me, 'The prophets prophesy lies in My name. I have not sent them, commanded them, nor spoken to them; they prophesy to you a false vision, divination, a worthless thing, and the deceit of their heart'" (Jeremiah 14:14). A prophet's calling—like a preacher's today—was to faithfully proclaim all that God had revealed, and nothing else. Jesus followed a similar track when He sat atop a hill and preached to a gathered crowed in the open air—the Sermon on the Mount (Matthew 5–7). Accounts in the book of Acts provide additional examples of early Christian preaching (e.g., 2:14–41; 13:16–41).

When true to their calling, preachers possess the great privilege and awesome responsibility of comprehending the ancient text and conveying its significance to people in their own time and culture—that they may apply it appropriately to their everyday lives.[9] Thus, preachers serve as intermediaries who take the truth of God revealed in the Bible and transmit it to their respective audience.[10] The sermon itself may follow closely to the actual structure of the biblical text (sometimes called expository preaching), or it may gather biblical data from various places in a topical arrangement. What is important, however, is that biblical sermons find as their chief significance the proclamation of Scripture. We cannot stress too strongly, then, the importance of sound hermeneutics within the preaching process. When people listen to the preaching of the Word, they want to hear "a word from God." They want to hear something meaningful that will help guide them in living responsibly and courageously as Christians, or merely how to survive in a moment of crisis. They want to know what God thinks about their situation and how He might help. At times such as these, the self-help of human wisdom will never suffice.

Of course, not everything that alleges to be "preaching" follows what has just been set forth. Sadly, many loyal parishioners regularly subject themselves to all kinds of topical sermons or political orations that have little to do with the Bible. Or perhaps they frequently encounter speeches that start with a Biblical quotation but then proceed to change trajectory, leaving the Bible behind as only a distant memory. They may receive only psychology-oriented sermons, a clever list of "how-tos" or other human wisdom. This kind of preaching fails to take seriously the biblical message, and this, in our estimation, seriously violates the preacher's assignment. To use the Bible for one's own agenda, or for the purpose of human interest, constitutes a reprehensible abuse of both the preaching ministry and the Bible. Biblical preaching invites people to hear God speak and to obey His voice by responding to His will for their lives. Since the Bible reliably records His Word to all, only a faithful proclamation of the Bible's message fulfills the preacher's calling.

Much of what we have asserted about the preaching ministry will equally apply to the teaching ministry of the church. Indeed, we must not press too strictly a distinction between preaching and teaching, for good teaching always calls those who have been taught to respond in some way. But for our purpose here, let us refer to teaching as the training or instruction in matters of Christian beliefs and practice. Since the Bible in many ways functions as the believers' "textbook," God's people have always needed teachers who can educate and train them from that book.

In the time of Ezra, for example, God's people needed someone to give them the "sense" and to help them "understand the reading" of God's Word (Nehemiah 8:1–8). Thus the narrator explains the occasion of how Ezra the scribe stood on a high wooden platform (v. 4), opened and read from the book of the Law (vv. 5, 8), and proceeded to explain what he had read so the people could understand its meaning (v. 8). The result was an occasion of great rejoicing because they now understood the words that had been made known to them (v. 12).

Today the church needs teachers who consciously seek to teach accurately the Christian faith against the competing "truth" claims of other false belief systems and "New Age" thinking. Both Testaments attest to the perverse human tendency to stray from the Lord into false religions, heresies, and apathy. But as the objective standard of truth, the Bible serves as a guidepost for keeping believers on course. While the views of cults and other false religions represent major challenges to biblical Christianity, it may be that "nominal Christianity" poses the greatest threat of all. Many within this group are those who have grown up as "Christians." Yet, while they identify themselves as a Christian, the Bible plays virtually no significant role in their values or actions. Many others have been advised on some occasion simply to "receive Christ" without any accompanying instructions about what true discipleship demands. Certainly, the teaching role requires responsible hermeneutics and courageous proclamation to provide believers with an accurate understanding so that they may "contend earnestly for the faith which was once for all delivered to the saints" (Jude 3).

Biblical teaching, however, must go beyond defending orthodoxy—correct beliefs. It should encompass orthopraxy—correct living. Living in a Christian manner requires personal and dedicated training. Believers need to know and understand Christian doctrine, as well as what it requires of them in practice. The biblical writers, in providing instructions to their original readers, supplied both correction and guidance for all their successors in the faith. Both Testaments contain numerous examples of Israelites and early Christians who were misinformed or stubborn about what they were to believe or how they were to live. The Israelites supposed that their many sacrifices would please God, but Micah informs them what qualities God really sought in their lives: "He has shown you, O man, what is good; And what does the Lord require of you? But to do justly, To love mercy, And to walk humbly with your God" (Micah 6:8). Similarly, James informs his readers: "Pure and undefiled religion before God and the Father is this: to visit orphans and widows in their trouble, and to keep oneself unspotted from the world" (James 1:27). With sobering words Jesus warned "Not everyone who says to Me, 'Lord, Lord,' shall enter the kingdom of heaven, but he who does the will of My Father in heaven" (Matthew 7:21).

Traditions, cultural values, and false teachings draw many Christians today into a false sense of what God expects of them, as if He is simply smiling down upon whatever behavior or attitudes they adopt. Christian teachers need to understand what the biblical directives meant when first written and then explain how believers can fulfill God's expectations for their own individual lives. Bible instructors need to advise believers on how to serve Christ in the church and in the world. If we are to be biblical Christians, we must obtain our agenda from God's Word. Skillful hermeneutics, again, guides our quest for what is truly God's will for His people. Thus, it is necessary that the teacher preserve the delicate balance between being faithful to the intent of Scripture and allowing at the same time the Scripture to give perspective and guidance on the practical issues and problems we face today. We conclude this section with a few common violations frequently made through preaching or teaching:[11]

1. *Taking a phrase from a text because of its attractive wording.* The preacher does not actually expound the meaning of the text, but uses the fallacious wording of it as the basis for his own sermonizing. As Broadus says, "This is not preaching Scripture, but merely the words of Scripture."[12] A perfect example of this is how many sermons have focused entirely on the wording "dead in trespasses and sins" (Ephesians 2:1) without any consideration of its use

within a wider context. One cannot assume that "spiritual death" in every point relates to physical death (physically dead people cannot sin)! Rather, the words must be understood within the contextual intent of the author. No matter how literary the expression or how catchy to the ear, a phrase must not be estranged from its content and preached upon with no real interpretation of its meaning. Whatever else, this is not preaching the Word of God.

2. *Choosing a text but rather than explaining it, sermonizing on it.* The remarks in a sermon need not be as narrow as the text, per se, but if a text or passage is employed then the preacher is under holy obligation to explain its meaning. In this case, either the preacher ignores the text, save for the topic it suggests, or else he misinterprets it all together. This is not a willful perversion of Scripture but a negligent or careless treatment of the inspired text. Broadus again offers wise and pointed remarks: "It is a mournful fact that Universalist, Romanist, Mormons, can find an apparent support for their heresies in Scripture, without interpreting more loosely, without doing greater violence to the meaning and connection of the sacred texts than is sometimes done by orthodoxy, devout, and even intelligent men."[13]

3. *"Spiritualizing" a text or a passage and so imposing a meaning on the text that is not there.* This is usually done under the sincere pretense that the preacher is seeking a deeper meaning of the Bible. The unnecessary force of an allegorical or typological meaning on a text, usually for the purpose of "gospelizing" its meaning, only stands as a testimony to one's own imagination—"for such preaching is too often only building castles in the air."[14] For principles that can be used for identifying legitimate typology within Scripture, see pages 247–254.

Using the Bible to Provide Pastoral Care

In times of sorrow or affliction, God's Word has always proven to be a source of comfort and consolation for His people. Jesus Himself stated, "In this world you will have trouble" (John 16:33). He was not being unreasonably negative or overly pessimistic; His words simply state the reality of our human condition, not only for His disciples, but also for humanity as a whole. Life is filled with all kinds of trials and difficulties. Moreover, as if that were not enough, the world is often especially hostile to Jesus's followers. Yet Jesus added a crucial and comforting assurance to that verse: "Be of good cheer! For I have overcome the world." What comfort or support exists for strugglers in the midst of life's trials and tragedies, not to mention its doubts and dilemmas? For these answers we must look to the Word of God for help.

Whether a trusted pastor or councilor, a family relative or close friend, the Christian has many resources available to help when others are in need of spiritual guidance. Yet the Bible stands as the primary resource that empathetic helpers may use to provide relief for suffering believers. Using the Scriptures, we can remind those who despair or grieve, who are lonely or in agony, that God does care for them; He Shepherds them through their dark valleys (Psalm 23:4); He is a refuge for them in times of trouble (Psalm 9:9). As we encounter the Scriptures, we find in them teachings about God's love and provision, relevant stories of men and women of faith who had faced and overcome difficulties, and songs of comfort and prayers for deliverance. Hannah's example of persevering prayer in the mist of childlessness (1 Samuel 1–2) and Job's trust in God's character despite his painful plight not only speaks to the troubles of today, but they testify of a sympathetic God who cares and gives comfort to His people.

When dealing with the raw edge of human emotion, caregivers naturally want to give as much hope as possible. In such situations they may be tempted to abuse the Bible; so, we must insist on responsible hermeneutics as much here as in all our uses of the Bible. We deeply want to assure a parent grieving over a wayward child that all will be well. Therefore, we may be tempted to turn the well-known proverb into a definitive promise: "Train up a child in the way he should go, And when he is old he will not depart from it" (Proverbs 22:6). However, sound hermeneutics forbids such an error because proverbs state general truth, not specific promises. Furthermore, we may hope to encourage a person who is going through financial hardships, but we cannot quote Jeremiah 29:11 "For I know the thoughts that I think toward you, says the Lord, thoughts of peace and not of evil, to give you a future and a hope" as a specific promise of financial gain or success. This passage refers to God's unique plans for Israel's return from exile; we cannot apply this to every situation. Though God indeed seeks to prosper His people, we dare not read in the adverb "financially." Other sections of the Bible suffer similar misuse in our well-meaning attempts to provide guidance or comfort. Indeed, such an exploitation of the Scripture is all too common. For example, some mistreat the story of Jesus calming the storm on the Sea of Galilee. Matthew surely intended the story to highlight the authoritative power of Jesus. It seeks to call attention to Christ and elicit faith in Him as Lord of all. Yet we hear people treat the story as if it taught, "God will calm the storms of your life." This may be a true sentiment, but surely, it does not emerge in any hermeneutically defensible way from this passage.

Again, we can only provide comfort from the Bible by stating the promises and truths that God has in fact intended to say. "A responsible system of hermeneutics will restrain well-intended but misguided help. Caregivers dare not take text out of context or make them say what God never intended [them to] say. [We] subvert the function of God's Word when we make false promises or give false assurance in the name of God and the Bible. When such mistaken words prove to be empty, those in need of help may come to discount the [true] value of the Bible or, worse, become disillusioned with God Himself."[15]

In summary of this chapter, the Bible serves many purposes and communicates to us in various ways (as we have just reviewed). But if the Bible is to keep its integrity and maintain its divine potency as God's communication to His people, we must accurately understand the intended meaning of its message. We must not settle for muddled messages or, worse, impose our own meaning on the Sacred Text. Consequently, only sound hermeneutical methodology gives us confidence that we have understood God's message correctly. Only after we come to know the meaning of the Bible's message can we expect that meaning to perform what God intended. That God may work through or even in spite of faulty interpretations does not invalidate the relevance of hermeneutics. If a child asks to play with a gun and her mother instead hands her a piece of gum, things may turn out well in that instance, but we dare not argue that to understand the correct meaning of the words "gun" and "gum" is irrelevant. So it is in the application of the Bible: correct meaning is paramount. We must always affirm that the best outcome results from the most accurate interpretation.

16

APPLYING THE BIBLICAL MESSAGE

Theoretical knowledge of the Bible's content, while absolutely indispensable, does not in itself automatically guarantee spiritual growth. More is needed—namely, a responsive heart and willingness to appropriate the truth of the Scriptures into one's own life. As Sterrett has well stated, "The Bible has spiritual dimensions that can be grasped only when the will responds to what God says, not simply when the mind analyzes the language."[1] Thus many people, having begun the process of Bible interpretation, fail to finish the task by neglecting to apply the Scriptures (where appropriate) to their own daily experiences. This approach to the Bible reduces God's Word to an academic exercise and restricts the Scriptures to being only a sourcebook of information with little regard for its life-changing relevance.

This biblical deficiency is one of the greatest problems facing Christianity today. Many people desire to acquire more Bible facts and obtain more spiritual knowledge, as the sales of home Bible study materials will attest. Yet many Christians with extensive knowledge of the Bible are not putting that knowledge into action. They "know more than they show," which borders on hypocrisy. Moreover, without such a personal appropriation of the truth of God's Word, the Christian life remains sterile and fruitless.

Spiritual growth in one's life comes not merely from hearing, but from hearing and doing! This is precisely the point James was making when he wrote, "But be doers of the word, and not hearers only, deceiving yourselves" (James 1:22). If a person only hears or reads the Bible and does nothing in regard to its implications for their attitude and conduct—while thinking they have somehow fulfilled their obligations—they are only deceiving themselves. Whereas deception comes from neglecting to heed the Word, blessing comes from putting it into practice: "But he who looks into the perfect law of liberty and continues in it, and is not a forgetful hearer but a doer of the work, this one will be blessed in what he does" (James 1:25). "If you know these things, blessed are you if you do them" (John 13:17). The Bible emphasizes that head knowledge, although crucial to the spiritual life, is not enough. Continual obedience is required; both the progressive spiritual development of our inward man and our outward conformity with God's standards are commanded. The New Testament, for example, frequently encourages Christians to walk in a manner that is pleasing to God (Romans 13:13; Galatians 5: 16–25; Ephesians 4:1; 5:2, 8; Philippians 3:16; Colossians 1:10; 2:6; 4:5; 1 Thessalonians 2:12; 1 John 1:7; 2:6; 2 John 6; 3 John 4). Those who "profess to know God" yet deny Him by their actions are strongly rebuked (Titus 1:16). Scriptural depth is measured by a demonstration of "good conduct . . . in the meekness of wisdom" (James 3:13), not in the extent of one's knowledge of Scripture. This is why Ezra had not only "prepared his heart to seek the Law of the Lord," but also "to do it" (Ezra 7:10). Since we are "[God's] workmanship, created in Christ Jesus for good works" (Ephesians 2:10), Christians ought to be zealous for good works (Titus 2:14) and careful to maintain them (Titus 3:8). As Luther wrote, "The Bible is not merely to be repeated or known, but to be lived and felt."[2]

Furthermore, application is necessary because without it true learning has not taken place. As Zuck explains,

> Pupils have not necessarily learned if there is only a mental apprehension of truth without an actual experiencing of the truth, appropriated to their lives by the Holy Spirit. Facts not perceived, skills taught in isolation, and verbalisms presented to passive, unmotivated pupils fall short of effectuating genuine spiritual growth. Learning is the process in which a pupil modifies his behavior, through the Spirit's enabling, to conform more to the will of God and the image of Christ.[3]

This does not mean that we will find a personal application in every phrase or sentence in Scripture, however, and the amount and kind of application of a passage will vary from genre to genre. We must interpret and apply each text in its context (as part of a larger, meaningful linguistic utterance). Didactic or epistolary texts may place demands on our lives in virtually every phrase and clause. At the other end of the spectrum, we may need several chapters of genealogical material before finding much of relevance, and even then only broad principles about God's providence, His plan of salvation, His concern for individuals, and so on. But every sentence, indeed every verse, appears as part of a larger, coherent unit of thought that has some relevance for us, and it is the fundamental task of the interpreter to determine its relevance.

The Misapplication of Scripture

Despite the importance of application, few modern evangelical scholars have focused on this topic. In fact, most hermeneutic textbooks give it only brief coverage, and many major commentary series only mention application with passing remarks. Perhaps many assume that sound application is more "caught than taught." At some level this may be true, but sound application often seems hard to find, much less to catch! Fortunately, recent studies are helping to rectify this error of omission. Several recent commentary series are working more self-consciously and with greater sophistication to meet the need for application (e.g., The NIV Application

288

Commentary Series and The Zondervan Exegetical Commentary Series). Nevertheless, much more work remains, for Christians today still encounter widespread misapplication of Scripture. Though many more can undoubtedly be found, we will point out three of the most common here.

The Total Neglect of Context. When it comes to finding guidance for their lives, many Christians unfortunately use the Bible in a way we might term as the "Magic 8-ball" approach. Those who want to base their decisions on the will of God may be tempted to use the Bible as if it were a magical book. For example, often after a prayer for divine help someone might open the Bible at random and take the first verse they come to as God's answer for the decision they are making. While God might conceivably accommodate a sincere but misguided Christian through this method, He never promises to do so; consequently, serious mistakes with damaging consequences inevitably occur when people persist in this approach.

The Partial Neglect of the Literary or Historical Context. Fortunately, most Bible readers usually avoid the extreme errors of the Magic 8-Ball approach. Much more common, however, is the proof-texting error that is often encouraged by Bible memory systems and devotionals that focus primarily on individual verses. To their credit, those who use this approach at least read entire sentences and meaningful units of thought, but often they fail to observe the larger context that appears to limit the application in important ways. Philippians 4:13, for example, suffers regular abuse from Christians who quote *ad libitum* "I can do all things through Christ who strengthens me" to reassure others or themselves that they can succeed in some undertaking (of which they may or may not be qualified). Subsequent failure leaves them distraught with God as if He had broken His promise! But had they read verses 11 and 12, they would have seen that the application of this passage is limited to one's contentment to the Lord regardless of their economic state.

In other instances, such readers miss important contextual and historical-cultural insights. Psalms 127:3–5, for example, reads,

Behold, children are a heritage from the Lord, The fruit of the womb is a reward. Like arrows in the hand of a warrior, So are the children [sons] of one's youth. Happy is the man who has his quiver full of them; They shall not be ashamed, But shall speak with their enemies in the gate.

This passage is frequently misread by Christians to mean that God requires, or at least prefers, married couples to have large families. Those who do need to look more carefully at the historical context. "Contending with their enemies in the gate" refers to legal actions or financial disputes (which took place at the city gate; see Ruth 4). The point being, God's blessing in preserving the well-being of a family is seen in the fruitful provision of children, who would be able to defend their parents' honor or financial interests. Furthermore, the language here is exclusive: "sons" does not include "daughters" because in ancient Israel girls could not act as legal representation. In an age when infant and child mortality rates were high, large families ensured that sufficient "sons" would survive to care after the well-being of aged parents in their declining years. While there is at least one clear principle in this passage that Christians can apply (e.g., the need to care for one's elderly parents, cf. 1 Timothy 5:8), Christians dare not use this verse to assert that all couples must have large families.

The Use of Insufficiently Analogous Situations. One of the more subtle misapplications of Scripture occurs when readers correctly interpret a passage in its literary and historical context but then wrongfully apply the text to current situations in which it simply does not apply. A clear example of this sort of violation is provided by none other than Satan himself. During Christ's temptation, Satan, using a cunning ploy, quotes Psalm 91:11–12 to challenge the Lord, saying, "If You are the Son of God, throw Yourself down. For it is written: 'He shall give His angels charge over you,' and, 'In their hands they shall bear you up, Lest you dash your foot against a stone'" (Matthew 4:6). By having the Lord throw Himself from the pinnacle of the temple, Satan here is tempting Christ to "prove" He is the Son of God and display God's miraculous ability to preserve His life. His challenge is being made on the basis that the psalmist states that God promises safety and protection to anyone who dwells in the shelter of the Most High (Psalm 91:1). Certainly, Jesus had such power. The problem here is that the devil's challenge confuses the psalm's reference to "accidental stumbling" from high places with taking a deliberate jump. The psalmist's intent here is not that we test God's faithfulness to His Word by manufacturing situations in which we try to force Him to act in certain ways. Rather, it points out His providential care for His children. Jesus does refute the devil with another text of Scripture that strictly forbids presuming on the grace of God (v. 7; cf. Deuteronomy 6:16). No passage of Scripture can be casually or carelessly applied to any and every situation.

Principles for Discovering Legitimate Application

The very nature of application, which varies from individual to individual in ways that meaning does not, indicates that we probably cannot create a comprehensive list of foolproof principles; however, we can formulate some general and workable guidelines.

Recent evangelical analysis has come to a consensus that the key to legitimate application involves what many writers call "principlizing." Principles, often latent in the text itself, serve as bridges between interpretation and application. They often establish the essence of a Bible passage in terms that are applicable to a broad spectrum of readers and situations. Without such a bridge, a passage would only serve to relate the interests of what God had done or said in the past. The principlizing bridge spans the gulf between the past and the present, with a truth that is relevant to both. Ramm describes this concept as follows: "To principlize is to discover in any narrative the basic spiritual, moral, or theological principles. These principles are latent in the text and it is the process of deduction which brings them to the surface. It is not an imposition of the text."[4]

A principlizing bridge, then, serves to give the relevance of a passage, as well as the implication a passage might have on a reader today. What is important, however, is that a principle is derived directly from the meaning of the text and is thus inherent in that meaning. Ramm gives several examples of principles drawn from Biblical narratives:

> When David repeatedly refused to slay Saul we see the principle of obedience to powers that be. When Saul was not patient with God's prophet we see the principle of disobedience. When Isaiah prays for the shadow to retreat on the sundial we see the principle of great spiritual courage. In truth, Hebrews 11 is a magnificent example of principlizing. The great faith of a multitude of men is set before us as the true principle of their lives.[5]

The principle or general truth pertaining to Ramm's example of Saul and Samuel may be stated in this way: "Believers should be obedient to the Lord, for impatient disobedience might result in devastating consequences." Individuals may be challenged to respond to that principle in various specific ways, depending on their unique situation.

Furthermore, application must be based on elements the reader shares with the original audience. Sometimes the audience to which a passage of Scripture was initially addressed will have direct similarities with the reader of today. For example, Paul's words to Euodia and Syntyche to be of the same mind (Philippians 4:2) has important implications for any Christian today that is quarreling with another believer. Other times the audience to which a passage of Scripture was initially addressed, such as Israel in the wilderness, is rather dissimilar to present-day audiences. In this case the general relevance of the principle might differ substantially from its original situation.

Applying to our day the scriptural admonitions, commands, council, and instructions, given to the Bible's initial audiences requires finding a point of commonality between them and the modern reader. The point in common between the Corinthians, for example, who were commanded to do "all things to the glory of God" (1 Corinthians 10:31), and

Christians today is that both groups are members of the church, the body of Christ. This makes the instruction to the Corinthians immediately relevant for today. The point in common, however, with Paul's injunction to the Corinthians to refrain from eating meat sacrificed to idols in order to avoid causing other Christians to stumble (1 Corinthians 8:7–13) is a situation that is not current now. The first example of a point in common involves direct application and the second indirect application. Therefore, application requires determining what aspects of those situations may be parallel to present circumstances. When it comes to Noah building the ark, the parallel idea is not for Christians to build an ark, too, but to obey God when there is no visible evidence for doing so. Likewise, in the case of eating meat sacrificed to idols, the parallel is to avoid involvement in any practice, innocent in itself, which may cause others to sin. Wilson stresses the importance of determining the theological intent of the passage (the principles) and its correlation to a current audience: "If we fail to discover the theological intent, we may make a good application from the wrong text. On the other hand, if we fail to ask the question of audience correlation, we may make a valid application, grounded in the theology of the text, but to the wrong audience."[6]

This process illustrates that applications possess different levels of authority. The closer the modern application corresponds to the application in the biblical text, the greater the degree of confidence we can have that our application is legitimate. Usually, the specific application will be close to the text only if the broader principle it teaches specifically incorporates elements from the text. More general truth, like the ark example above, will not regularly yield specific, contemporary applications that closely resemble the original ones. We cannot, therefore, always assert with the same level of confidence that we have correctly applied a passage. How confident can we be? First, if we can employ the originally intended response in our situation with little or no change, and that response validly applies the timeless principle in the passage, we have the highest level of confidence that our application is valid. When we can derive a broader principle only, whose application incorporates greater or fewer particular elements in the passage, then we have the next level of confidence that our application is legitimate. But we have to be sure we have derived a valid, timeless principle from the text. Finally, when we move to the level of applying more general truths from a passage, our applications may well reflect good things to do, but we cannot be confident that they are actually applications of the specific text at hand. As Millard Erickson nicely phrases it, we should "look for principles of the maximum degree of specificity that meet the criteria of generalizability."[7]

Another issue that arises with principlizing involves the question of cultural relativity—that is, how do we determine what in the Bible pertains only to those cultural situations and therefore has little direct relevance on the present, and what in the Bible pertains to present as well as past cultural settings? This involves ascertaining which Bible passages are "culturally conditioned" and which ones are "transcultural." It is evident that some commands in the Scriptures are a reflection of local customs. Jesus said, for example, "Carry neither money bag, knapsack, nor sandals; and greet no one along the road" (Luke 10:4). As Sproul has observed, "If this is transcultural, then evangelists should preach in their bare feet!" He adds, "Obviously, the point of this text is not to set down a perennial requirement of barefooted evangelism."[8] Though we could offer other guidelines for differentiating cultural-bound from transcultural principles and commands, here we point out five for consideration:

1. Always look for any reason(s) given for a biblical principle. For example, the principle that we are to love one another is established on the basis that God first loved us (John 4:19). That we are not to love the world and its values is mandated because love of the world and love of God are mutually exclusive (1 John 2:15). If a principle is established on the basis of God's eternal attributes— His love, His grace, His holiness, His created order—it is doubtful that the principle is culturally-bound.

2. When a transcultural principle is embodied in a form that was part of the common cultural habits of the time, the form may be modified, even though the principle remains unchanged. For example, Jesus demonstrated the transcultural principle that we should have an attitude of humility and willingness to serve one another (Mark 10:42–44) by washing the disciples' feet (John 13:12–16), a familiar custom of the day. We retain the principle, although there are other ways to express that principle more meaningfully in our culture. In other words, we may give a hearty handshake instead of a holy kiss; we may set up inexpensive food banks instead of leaving our fields to be gleaned; and we should be concerned about the effect of consuming alcohol in the presence of recovering alcoholics, even if we are never faced with a dilemma of whether or not to eat meat sacrificed to idols. If there is no cultural equivalent, it might be worthwhile to consider creating a new cultural behavior that would meaningfully express the principle(s) involved.

3. When a practice that was an acceptable part of pagan culture is forbidden in Scripture, it is most likely to be forbidden in contemporary culture as well, particularly if the command is grounded in God's moral law. Examples of practices that were an acceptable part of pagan culture but were forbidden in Scripture include fornication, idolatry, and divorce, to name a few.

4. It is important to define the intended recipients of a command and to apply the command discriminately to other groups. If a command was given to only one church or one individual, this may indicate that it was meant to be a local rather than a universal practice. For instance, in 1 Corinthians 16:1–3, Paul issues an order of procedure for collecting and distributing a financial offering on behalf of the poor saints at Jerusalem. Yet few readers of this text have felt the need to collect an offering for this occasion. Clearly,

the mandate was given exclusively to the church at Corinth and no longer applies directly to today's readers.

5. If a cultural mandate is frequently repeated, and is in harmony with what is universally taught elsewhere, then it is most likely to be a transcultural practice. Fee discusses this guideline: "For a biblical precedent to justify present action, the principle of the action must be taught elsewhere, where it is the primary intent so to teach . . . Where there is ambiguity of models, or when a practice is [stated] but once, it is repeatable only if it appears to have divine approbation or is in harmony with what is taught elsewhere in Scripture."[9]

In summary, interpreters seeking to make application of any text should first determine five things: (1) The original audience of the text. In other words, who was the writer/speaker addressing? (2) The purpose for any principles or commands in a text. Particularly, is the desired application based on cultural interests or moral precepts? (3) The original application(s) intended by the passage. In other words, how would the original reader(s) or hearer(s) apply the text? (4) What level of commonality do we have with the original audience? (5) How does the original situation of the text parallel to our present circumstances?

Second, we must evaluate the level of specificity of those applications to their original historical situations. If the original specific applications are transferable across time to other audiences, we must apply them in culturally appropriate ways. Therefore, after we have found the principles that lead to the specific application "back then," we must seek to translate the principles into appropriate and corresponding applications for today.

Finally, if the original applications are not transferable, identify one or more broad cross-cultural principles that the specific elements of the text reflect. For example, J. B. Phillips suggests that "greet one another with a hearty handshake" may be a good American cultural equivalent to "greet one another with a holy kiss."[10]

In conclusion, everything we have taught in this book falls short of the intended goal if interpreters do not simultaneously pray and rely on the Holy Spirit to guide them in the hermeneutical task. Yet, as we pointed out earlier, an appeal to the Spirit is no substitute for sound interpretive methodology. The six crucial elements for proper interpretation and application are as follows: (1) salvation, (2) diligent study habits, (3) proper interpretive methods, (4) logic, (5) a humble dependence on the Spirit for discernment, and (6) spiritual maturity. While (3) and (4) have been our primary focus, we hope this book has demonstrated the necessity for all six of these elements. If we have stimulated your desire for reading the Bible more, for tackling some of the more difficult or lesser-known portions of it, or if we have heightened your awareness of the kinds of questions to ask of the text as you read and how to identify subtle, yet meaningful interpretive clues, then we have accomplished a great deal of what we set out to do. Nevertheless, our labor is in vain if we have not awakened a greater zeal to obey the Scriptures more, once they are understood, and to know and love the God who inspired them. So, we conclude this focus on application by encouraging you to put into practice the principles we have outlined in this book. As you do this you will strengthen your ability to handle correctly the Word of Truth (2 Timothy 2:15). Read the Word, study it, meditate on it, and, as God enables you, live it!

APPENDIX

A Summary of the Processes Involved in Interpreting and Applying a Text

I. **Gather pertinent background information of any book under study:**

    A. Determine the four "As": identify the *author, audience, aim* (the author's purpose for writing), and *age* (date) of any book. If possible, determine the historical background and situation that might explain the purpose and/or goal the writer had for writing the book.

    B. Determine the relationship between the writer and the readers that might help explain the book's subject matter.

        1. Note any explicit statements or repeated phrases that might establish the author's purpose for writing.

        2. Observe any issues that are directly mentioned in the text that might clarify the historical situation or occasion for writing.

        3. Discern the spiritual condition of the audience.

II. **Familiarize yourself with the overall context and theme of the book, as well as sub-themes, and natural breaks that occur in the book:**

A. Read the book in its entirety (preferably more than once) before studying any passage in depth. Write a topic sentence for each of the major divisions of the book. Pay close attention to any major theme(s) that are repeated throughout each section.

B. Determine how the various topics of a book relate to the central theme of the book. It may be helpful to consult Bible survey and introduction books at this point. However, it is essential that each Bible student back-checks the information that is presented in these books.

III. **Identify the general literary form or genre of the book, as well as any sub-genres within the book:**

A. Apply the interpretative methods and principles for each genre carefully.

B. Determine if a book has a high probability of using figurative, metaphoric, or symbolic language.

C. Identify any literary devices that a writer is using within a book and any purpose they might have for using them.

IV. **With points I–III in mind, study each passage**

A. according to its surrounding context and pay close attention to how an author's train of thought comes together to reveal the main idea of any passage;

B. according to the entire book context and determine how any passage might relate to the general purpose and/or theme of the book;

C. according to the context of the entire Bible and carefully determine any parallel passages that might shed light on other passages in a book. It is important to consider any books written by the same author before consulting other books written by different authors.

D. Determine the single meaning intended by the author in a given context.

V. **Seek to understand the grammatical structure and lexical analysis of any text (to interact with the original Hebrew and Greek,**

interpreters might want to utilize appropriate lexicons and other word study resources):

A. Identify the connecting words within the paragraphs and sentences and how they aid in understanding the author's progression of thought.

B. Identify the multiple meanings a word possessed in its time and culture, and select the definitions that best support the immediate context of the passage.

C. Identify the grammatical use of each word in a sentence: nouns, verbs, adjectives, adverbs, etc.

VI. **Determine the historical-cultural significance of any passage. Use Bible dictionaries, Bible history books and references, background commentaries, maps, and other cultural and archeological resources when necessary:**

A. Identify and explain any historical or cultural reference in any passage.

B. Be aware of cultural circumstances and social norms that add meaning to given actions or statements.

C. Identify the location of all geographical references within a passage, as well as any significance it might have in understanding that passage.

VII. **Determine the theological contribution a passage might have on the book from which it originates, as well as the Bible as a whole:**

A. Determine the theological significance a passage would have had to its original audience.

B. Identify any additional knowledge we have in light of later revelation that helps us understand the theological significance of any passage.

C. Determine how a passage supports, challenges, or broadens your view of the central theme of Scripture.

D. Determine how a passage supports, challenges, or broadens your view of a particular doctrine or practice.

VIII. **Compare your interpretation with that of other interpreters. Commentaries on individual Bible books will usually serve as the most helpful aid in this endeavor:**

    A. Determine the hermeneutical legitimacy of each interpretation.

    B. Modify, correct, or expand your interpretation as appropriate.

IX. **Determine the appropriate application of the passage:**

    A. Based on the author's intended meaning (what he meant to convey to his original readers), as well as the theological significance the passage has on Scripture as a whole, ascertain by deductive study (1) the principle(s) that are explicit in the text, or (2) the principles (descriptive truths) illustrated within the passage that remain relevant to the modern Christian. It is especially important to discern as accurately as possible the principle behind any command.

    B. Determine the transcultural transmission of any biblical command.

        1. Determine whether a principle is transcultural or culturally conditioned by examining the reason given for a principle.

        2. If a principle is transcultural, determine whether the same behavioral application in our modern culture will express the principle as adequately and accurately as the original application of a biblical principle.

        3. If the behavioral expression of a principle is no longer relevant in our culture, consider whether a cultural equivalent behavior will express the God-given principle behind the original command.

X. **Pray. Throughout the entire process, one should pray that the Holy Spirit would guide them in their quest for understanding and that He will give them a willing and wise heart in appropriately applying His Word to their everyday lives.**

ENDNOTES

PART 1: THE NEED FOR HERMENEUTICS

[1] Virkler and Ayayo, *Hermeneutics: Principles and Processes of Biblical Interpretation*, 18–19.

[2] This list, as well as some of the verbiage, is taken from Zuck, *Rightly Divided: Readings in Hermeneutics*, 21.

[3] Ibid., 21.

CHAPTER 1: THE GOAL OF INTERPRETATION

[1] Robert H. Stein, *A Basic Guide to Interpreting the Bible*, 7.

[2] Ibid., 7.

[3] Ibid., 11–12.

[4] Ibid., 16.

[5] Ibid., 16.

[6] Ibid., 17.

[7] Ibid., 17.

[8] Ibid., 19.

[9] Ibid., 24.

[10] See pp. 26–27, Stein, *A Basic Guide to Interpreting the Bible*.

[11] Ibid., 26.

CHAPTER 2: THE TASK OF THE INTERPRETER

[1] See Klein, Bloomberg and Hubbard, *Introduction to Biblical Interpretation*, 136–138. Some of the material found on these pages is paraphrased in this section.

[2] H. G. C. Moule, *Veni Creator: Thoughts on the Person and Work of the Holy Spirit* (London: Hodder & Stoughton, 1890) 63

[3] Bernard Ramm, *Protestant Biblical Interpretation*, 14.

[4] Klein, Bloomberg and Hubbard, *Introduction to Biblical Interpretation*, 143.

[5] Ibid., 143.

[6] McCartney and Clayton, *Let the Reader Understand: A Guide to Interring and Applying the Bible*, 79.

[7] Ibid., 80.

[8] Ibid., 80.

PART 2: THE RULES OF INTERPRETATION

[1] Klein, Bloomberg and Hubbard, *Introduction to Biblical Interpretation*, 213.

CHAPTER 3: CONTEXTUAL ANALYSIS

[1] This illustration is borrowed from Klein, Bloomberg, Hubbard, *Introduction to Biblical Interpretation*, 216.

[2] Ibid., 216.

[3] F. F. Bruce, *The Books and the Parchment* (London: Pickering & Inglis, 1950), 118.

[4] Klein, Bloomberg and Hubbard, *Introduction to Biblical Interpretation*, 217.

[5] Ibid., 222.

[6] Ibid., 223.

[7] Ibid., 223.

[8] Ibid., 225.

[9] Ibid., 225.

[10] Ibid., 226.

[11] Ibid., 226.

[12] Ibid., 227.

[13] Ibid., 228.

[14] Ibid., 229.

[15] Ibid., 229.

CHAPTER 4: HISTORICAL-CULTURAL ANALYSIS

[1] Klein, Bloomberg and Hubbard, Introduction to Biblical Interpretation, 229.

[2] R. Spittler, "Scripture and the Theological Enterprise: View from a Big Canoe," *The Use of the Bible in Theology/Evangelical Options*, ed. R. K Johnston (Atlanta: John Knox, 1985), 56–77.

[3] Klein, Bloomberg and Hubbard, *Introduction to Biblical Interpretation*, 232.

[4] For further commentary on this verse, see Osborne, *Revelation* (ECNT), 207–208.

[5] Klein, Bloomberg and Hubbard, *Introduction to Biblical Interpretation*, 238.

CHAPTER 5: LEXICAL-SYNTACTICAL ANALYSIS

[1] Klein, Bloomberg and Hubbard, *Introduction to Biblical Interpretation*, 241.

[2] Example borrowed, Ibid., 241–242.

[3] See D. A. Carson, *Exegetical Fallacies*, 52–53.

[4] Klein, Bloomberg and Hubbard, *Introduction to Biblical Interpretation*, 245.

[5] Ibid., 245.

[6] McCartney and Clayton, *Let the Reader Understand: A Guide to Interpreting and Applying the Bible*, 121.

[7] Louw, *Semantics of New Testament Greek*, 27.

[8] Klein, Bloomberg and Hubbard, *Introduction to Biblical Interpretation*, 259.

[9] Example borrowed, Ibid., 266.

[10] Ibid., 270.

[11] Ibid., 272.

CHAPTER 6: HISTORICAL NARRATIVES

[1] McCartney and Clayton, *Let the Reader Understand: A Guide to Interpreting and Applying the Bible*, 224.

[2] Ibid., 224.

[3] Ibid., 224.

[4] See Ibid., 224.

[5] Fee and Stuart, *How to Read the Bible For All Its Worth*, 91.

[6] Ibid., 92.

[7] Ibid., 92–93.

[8] Ibid., 93.

[9] Ibid., 105.

[10] Ibid., 105–106.

[11] These characteristics, along with many of the examples found in the story of Joseph, are provided by Fee and Stuart in their book, *How to Read the Bible for All Its Worth*, pp. 93–98.

[12] Ibid., 94.

[13] Ibid., 94.

[14] Ibid., 95.

[15] Ibid., 95.

[16] Ibid., 95–96.

[17] Ibid., 96.

[18] Ibid., 97.

[19] For a more critical treatment of these, see Robert Alter's *The Art of Biblical Narrative*.

[20] Fee and Stuart, *How to Read the Bible for All Its Worth*, 98.

[21] Ibid., 98–99.

CHAPTER 7: LAW

[1] Dan McCartney and Charles Clayton, *Let the Reader Understand: A Guide to Interpreting and Applying the Bible*, 227.

[2] Ibid., 227–228.

[3] Ibid., 228.

[4] Fee and Stuart, *How to Read the Bible for All Its Worth*, 163.

[5] Ibid., 163.

[6] Dan McCartney and Charles Clayton, *Let the Reader Understand: A Guide to Interpreting and Applying the Bible*, 228.

CHAPTER 8: POETRY

[1] Ross, *A Commentary on the Psalms*, 143–144.

[2] Fee and Stuart, *How to Read the Bible for All Its Worth*, 214.

[3] Ibid., 223.

[4] Ibid., 223.

[5] R. Alter, *The Art of Biblical Poetry*, 168.

[6] Klein, Bloomberg and Hubbard, *Introduction to Biblical Interpretation*, 387.

[7] Osborne, *The Hermeneutical Spiral*, 226.

[8] Fee and Stuart, *How to Read the Bible for All Its Worth*, 238.

[9] Klein, Bloomberg and Hubbard, *Introduction to Biblical Interpretation*, 394.

[10] Fee and Stuart, *How to Read the Bible for All Its Worth*, 245.

[11] Ibid., 245

[12] Ibid., 247–248.

CHAPTER 9: PROPHECY

[1] Osborne, *The Hermeneutical Spiral*, 258.

[2] Stein, *A Basic Guide to Interpreting the Bible*, 137.

[3] Virkler and Ayayo, *Hermeneutics: Principles and Processes of Biblical Interpretation*, 170.

[4] Osborne, *The Hermeneutical Spiral*, 274.

[5] Pentecost, *Things to Come*, 46–47.

[6] Payne, *Encyclopedia of Biblical Prophecy*, 383.

[7] Caird, *The Language and Imagery of the Bible*, 186–91.

[8] Kaiser, *The Old Testament in Contemporary Preaching*, 111–114.

CHAPTER 10: APOCALYPTIC LITERATURE

[1] Osborne, *The Hermeneutical Spiral*, 276.

[2] Ibid., 283.

CHAPTER 11: PARABLES

[1] Fee and Stuart, *How to Read the Bible for All Its Worth*, 152.

[2] Ladd, *A Theology of the New Testament*, 96.

[3] Osborne, *The Hermeneutical Spiral*, 307.

[4] Ibid., 308.

[5] Bloomberg, *Preaching the Parables: From Responsible Interpretation to Powerful Proclamation*, 25.

PART 4: SEEING THE BIG PICTURE: THE THEOLOGICAL ANALYSIS OF SCRIPTURE

[1] Kaiser and Silva, *An Introduction to Biblical Hermeneutics: The Search for Meaning*, 263.

[2] Ibid., 260.

CHAPTER 12: THE PATTERN OF REVELATION

[1] Lambert Dolphin, "The Tower of Babel and the Confusion of Languages."

[2] Goldsworthy, *According To Plan: The Unfolding Revelation of God in the Bible*, 124.

[3] Stuart, *Exodus*, NAC, 87–88.

[4] Curid, *A Study Commentary on Exodus*, 59

[5] Mackey, *Exodus: A Mentor Commentary*, 47.

[6] Schreiner, *New Testament Theology: Magnifying God in Christ*, 29.

[7] Dyer and Merrill, *The Old Testament Explorer: Discovering the Essence, Background and Meaning of Every Book in the Old Testament*, 58.

[8] Goldsworthy, *According To Plan: The Unfolding Revelation of God in the Bible*, 152.

[9] Ibid., 153.

[10] Ibid., 153.

[11] Ibid., 160.

[12] Ibid., 160.

Chapter 13: THE PATTERN OF REVELATION (PART 2)

[1] Goldsworthy, *According To Plan: The Unfolding Revelation of God in the Bible*, 164–171. Some of the material found on these pages is paraphrased in this section.

[2] Goldsworthy, *Gospel and Kingdom*, 89.

[3] Ibid., 92.

[4] Ibid., 99.

[5] Schreiner, *The King In His Beauty: A Biblical Theology of the Old and New Testaments*, 543.

[6] Kaiser, *Unity of the Bible*, 125.

[7] Schreiner, *The King In His Beauty: A Biblical Theology of the Old and New Testaments*, 578.

Chapter 14: Doing Theology

[1] Osborne, *The Hermeneutical Spiral*, 365.

[2] Bright, *The Authority of the Old Testament*, pp. 209–10.

[3] McCartney and Clayton, *Let the Reader Understand: A Guide to Interpreting the Bible*, 162–172. Some of the material found on these pages is paraphrased in this section.

[4] Cited by McCartney and Clayton in *Let the Reader Understand: A Guide to Interpreting the Bible*, 162–163.

[5] Ibid., 164.

[6] Godet, *Typos: The Typological Interpretation of the Old Testament in the New*, 151–152.

[7] McCartney and Clayton, *Let the Reader Understand: A Guide to Interpreting the Bible*, 164.

[8] Ibid., 170.

[9] Michael Steier, "Rationale for Catholics Reading the Old Testament," United States Conference of Catholic Bishops, www.uccb.org.

[10] Woudstra, "Israel and the Church: A Case for Continuity," in J. Feinberg, *Continuity and Discontinuity*, 228.

[11] Waltke, "Kingdom Promises as Spiritual," in J. Feinberg, *Continuity and Discontinuity*, 263, 274.

[12] Ryrie, *Dispensationalism*, 57–64.

[13] Kaiser, "Kingdom Promises as Spiritual and National," in J. Feinberg, *Continuity and Discontinuity*, 295–298.

[14] Saucey, "Israel and the Church: A Case for Discontinuity," in J. Feinberg, *Continuity and Discontinuity*, 295–298.

[15] Ware, "The New Covenant and the People of God," in Blaising and Bock, *Dispensationalism, Israel and the Church*, 68–97.

CHAPTER 15: USING THE BIBLE FOR SPIRITUAL GROWTH

[1] Zuck, *Rightly Divided: Readings in Hermeneutics*, 268.

[2] Carson, *For the Love of God: A Daily Companion for Discovering the Riches of God's Word*, vol. 1 (Wheaton:Crossway, 1998), x.

[3] Klein, Bloomberg and Hubbard, *Introduction to Biblical Interpretation*, 452.

[4] Ibid., 452.

[5] Ibid., 454.

[6] Ibid., 455.

[7] Ibid., 455.

[8] Ibid., 456.

[9] Ibid., 467.

[10] Ibid., 467.

[11] This list, as well as some of the verbiage, is taken from Zuck, *Rightly Divided: Readings in Hermeneutics*, 276.

[12] Broadus, *A Treatise on the Preparation and Delivery of Sermons*, 33.

[13] Ibid., 47.

[14] Ibid., 52.

[15] Klein, Bloomberg and Hubbard, *Introduction to Biblical Interpretation*, 471.

CHAPTER 16: APPLYING THE BIBLICAL MESSAGE

[1] Sterrett, *How to Understand Your Bible*, 171.

[2] Martin Luther, cited by A. Skevington Wood, *The Principles of Biblical Interpretation*, 80.

[3] Zuck, *Rightly Divided: Readings in Hermeneutics*, 285–286.

[4] Ramm, *Protestant Biblical Interpretation*, 199–200.

[5] Ibid., 200.

[6] As quoted by Roy B. Zuck, *Rightly Divided: Readings in Biblical Hermeneutics*, 292.

[7] Erickson, *Evangelical Interpretation: Perspectives on Hermeneutical Issues*, 65.

[8] Sproul, *Knowing Scripture* (Downers Grove: InterVarsity, 1977), 106.

[9] Cited by Zuck, *Rightly Divided: Readings in Biblical Hermeneutics*, 292.

[10] Wight, *Manners and Customs of Bible Lands*, 74–75.

BIBLIOGRAPHY

Abernethy, Andrew T. *The Book of Isaiah and God's Kingdom: A Thematic-Theological Approach.* NSBT. Downers Grove: InterVarsity Press, 2016.

Achtemeier, Paul J. *The Inspiration of Scripture: Problems and Proposals.* Philadelphia: Westminster Press, 1980.

Adams, J. McKee. *Biblical Backgrounds.* Nashville: Broadman, 1934.

Alter, R. *The Art of Biblical Narrative.* New York: Basic Books, 1983.

Alter, R. *The Art of Biblical Poetry.* New York: Basic Books, 1987.

Arnold, B. T. and Beyer, B. E. *Readings from the Ancient Near East: Encountering Biblical Studies.* Grand Rapids Baker, 2002.

Baker, David W. *Two Testaments, One Bible: A Study of the Theological Relationship between the Old and New Testaments.* 2nd ed. Downers Grove: InterVarsity Press, 1991.

Beasley-Murray, G. R. *Jesus and the Kingdom of God.* Grand Rapids: Eerdmans, 1986.

Berkhof, Louis. *Principles of Biblical Interpretation.* Grand Rapids: Baker, 1950.

Bright, John. *The Authority of the Old Testament.* Nashville: Abingdon Press, 1967.

Bright, John. *The Kingdom of God: The Biblical Concept and its Meaning for the Church*. Nashville: Abingdon Press, 1981.

Black, David A. and D. S. Dockery. *Interpreting the New Testament: Essays on Methods and Issues*. Nashville: Broadman & Holman, 2001.

Blaising, Craig A., and Darrell L. Bock. eds. *Dispensationalism, Israel and the Church: The Search for Definition*. Grand Rapids: Zondervan, 1992.

Blaising, Craig A., and Darrell L. Bock. *Progressive Dispensationalism*. Grand Rapids: Barker, 1993.

Bloomberg, Craig L. *Preaching The Parables: From Responsible Interpretation to Powerful Proclamation*. Grand Rapids: Baker Academic, 2004.

Bloomberg, Craig L. and Mariam J. Kamell. *James*. ECNT. Grand Rapids: Zondervan, 2008.

Broadus, John A. *A Treatise on the Preparation and Delivery of Sermons*. 30th ed. New York: Hoddard & Stoughton, 1899.

Brooks, Phillips. *Lectures on Preaching*. London: H. R. Allenson, 1877.

Brown, F. Driver, S. R. and Briggs, C. A. *A Hebrew and English Lexicon of the Old Testament*. Reprint. Peabody, MA: Hendrickson, 1996.

Brown, Raymond E. *The Sensus Plenior of Sacred Scripture: A Dissertation*. Baltimore: St. Mary's University, 1955.

Brown, Raymond E. *The Critical Meaning of the Bible*. New York: Paulist, 1981.

Bullinger, E. W. *Figures of Speech Used in the Bible: Explained and Illustrated*. Grand Rapids: Baker, 1968.

Caird, G. B. *The Language and Imagery of the Bible*. Philadelphia: Westminster, 1980.

Carson, D. A. *Biblical Interpretation and the Church: The Problem of Contextualization*. Nashville: Thomas Nelson, 1984.

Carson, D. A. *Evangelical Fallacies*. 2nd ed. Grand Rapids: Baker, 1984.

Carson, D. A., and John D. Woodbridge, eds. *Hermeneutics, Authority, and Canon*. Grand Rapids: Zondervan, 1986.

Carson, D. A., and John D. Woodbridge, eds. *Scripture and Truth*. Grand Rapids: Zondervan, 1983.

Chafer, Lewis Sperry. *Dispensationalism*. Rev. ed. Dallas: Dallas Seminary Press, 1951.

Clines, D. J. A., ed. *The Dictionary of Classical Hebrew*. Sheffield: Sheffield Academic Press, 1993.

Cole, R. Alan. *Exodus: An Introduction and Commentary*. TOTC. Downers Grove: InterVarsity Press, 1973.

Cook, Stephen L. *The Apocalyptic Literature*. Nashville: Abingdon, 2003.

Currid, John D. *A Study Commentary on Exodus*. vol. 2. Darling: Evangelical Press, 2000.

Dodd, C. H. *The Parables of the Kingdom*. New York: Scribner's, 1961.

Dyer, Charles, and Gene Merrill. *The Old Testament Explorer: Discovering the Essence, Background and Meaning of Every Book in the Old Testament*. Nashville: Word, 2001.

Erickson, M. J. *Evangelical Interpretation: Perspectives on Hermeneutical Issues*. Grand Rapids: Baker, 1993.

Fairbairn, Patrick. *The Typology of Scripture*. 2 vols. 1845–47. Grand Rapids: Zondervan, 1967.

Fee, Gordon D., and Douglas Stuart. *How to Read the Bible for All Its Worth: A Guide to Understanding the Bible*. 3rd. ed. Grand Rapids: Zondervan, 2003.

Feinberg, John S., ed. *Continuity and Discontinuity: Perspectives on the Relationship between the Old and New Testaments*. Westchester, IL: Crossway, 1988.

France, R. T. *Jesus and the Old Testament*. Downers Grove, IL intervarsity, 1971.

Fuller, Daniel P. *Gospel & Law: Contrast or Continuum? The Hermeneutics of Dispensationalism and Covenant Theology*. Reprint. Fuller Seminary Press, 1982.

Gentry, Peter J., and Stephen J. Wellum. *Kingdom through Covenant: A Biblical-Theological Understanding of the Covenants*. Wheaton: Crossway, 2012.

Girdlestone, Robert B. *Synonyms of the Old Testament*. 1901. Reprint, Grand Rapids: Eerdmans, 1948.

Goldsworthy, Graeme. *According to Plan: The Unfolding Revelation of God in the Bible*. Downers Grove: InterVarsity Press, 1991.

Goldsworthy, Graeme. *Gospel and Kingdom*. Crownhill: Paternoster Press, 1981.

Godet, Leonhard. *Typos: The Typological Interpretation of the Old Testament in the New*, trans. D. H. Madvig. Grand Rapids: Eerdmans, 1982.

Green, Joel B., ed. *Hearing the New Testament: Strategies of Interpretation*. 2nd ed. Grand Rapids: Erdmans, 2010.

Grudem, Wayne, C. John Collins, and Thomas R. Schreiner. *Understanding the Big Picture of the Bible: A Guide to Reading the Bible Well*. eds. Wheaton: Crossway, 2012.

Guelich, Robert A. ed. *Unity and Diversity in New Testament Theology*. Grand Rapids: Erdmans, 1978.

Hafemann, Scott J. and House, Paul R. *Central Themes in Biblical Theology: Mapping Unity in Diversity*. Grand Rapids: Baker Academic, 2007.

Hamilton, Victor P. *The Book of Genesis*. 2 vol. NIC. Grand Rapids: Eerdmans, 1990

Harrison, Roland K. *A History of Old Testament Times*. Grand Rapids: Zondervan, 1957.

Heaton, E. W. *Everyday Life in Old Testament Times*. New York: Scribner, 1956.

Hirsch, E. D. Jr. *Validity in Interpretation*. New Haven: Yale University Press, 1967.

Horton, Michael. *Introducing Covenant Theology*. Grand Rapids: Baker, 2006.

House, Paul R. *Old Testament Theology*. Downers Grove: InterVarsity, 1998.

Howard, David M., Jr. *An Introduction to the Old Testament Historical Books*. Chicago: Moody Press, 1993.

Jeremias, Joachim. *Parables of Jesus*. Rev. ed. New York: Scribner, 1956.

Johnson, Elliot E. *Expository Hermeneutics: An Introduction*. Grand Rapids: Zondervan, 1990.

Johnston, Robert K. ed. *The Use of the Bible in Theology: Evangelical Options*. Atlanta: John Knox, 1985.

Kaiser, Walter C., Jr. *A History of Israel*. Nashville: Broadman & Holman, 1998.

Kaiser, Walter C., Jr. *The Old Testament in Contemporary Preaching*. Grand Rapids: Baker, 1973.

Kaiser, Walter C., Jr. *The Uses of the Old Testament in the New*. Chicago: Moody, 1985.

Kaiser, Walter C., Jr. *Toward an Old Testament Theology*. Grand Rapids: Zondervan, 1991.

Kaiser, Walter C. Jr., and Moises Silva. *An Introduction to Biblical Hermeneutics: The Search for Meaning*. Grand Rapids: Zondervan, 1994.

Kantenwein, Lee L. *Diagrammatical Analysis*. Winona Lake, IN: BHM Books, 1979.

Kidner, Derek. *The Proverbs: An Introduction and Commentary*. Chicago: InterVarsity Press, 1964.

Klien, William W., Craig L. Blomberg, and Robert L. Hubbard Jr. *Introduction to Biblical Interpretation*. Rev. and updated ed. Nashville: Nelson, 2004.

Kraft, Charles. "*Interpreting in Context.*" Journal of the Evangelical Theological Society 21 (1978): 357-67.

Ladd, George Eldon. *A Theology of the New Testament*. Grand Rapids: Eerdmans, 1974.

Ladd, George Eldon. *The Gospel of the Kingdom*. Grand Rapids: Eerdmans, 1959.

Lampe, G. W. H., and K. J. Woollcombe. *Essays on Typology*. Naperville, IL: Allenson, 1957.

Larkin, William J., Jr. *Culture and Biblical Hermeneutics: Interpreting and Applying the Authoritative Word in a Relativistic Age*. Grand Rapids: Baker, 1988.

Longman, Temper, III. *How to Read the Psalms*. Downers Grove: InterVarsity Press, 1988.

Longman, Temper, III. *The Book of Ecclesiastes*. NICOT. Grand Rapids: Eerdmans, 1988.

Longman, Temper, III. *Literary Approach to Biblical Interpretation*. Grand Rapids: Zondervan, 1987.

Louw, Johannes P. *Semantics of New Testament Greek*. Society of Biblical Literature, 1982

Ludwigson, R. *A Survey of Biblical Prophecy*. 2nd ed. Grand Rapids: Zondervan, 1975.

Mackay, John L. *Exodus: A Mentor Commentary*. Ross-shire: Christian Focus Publications, 2001.

Marshall, I. Howard. *The Epistles of John*. NICNT. Grand Rapids: Eerdsmans, 1978.

Marshall, I. Howard, ed. *New Testament Interpretation: Essays on Principles and Methods.* Grand Rapids Eerdmans, 1991.

Matthews, Kenneth A. *Genesis.* 2 vol. Nashville: B & H Publishing, 1996

McCartney, Dan, and Charles Clayton. *Let The Reader Understand: A Guide to Interpreting and Applying the Bible.* 2nd ed. Phillipsburg: P & R Publishing, 2002.

McKnight, Scott, ed. *Introducing New Testament Interpretation: Guides to New Testament Exegesis.* Grand Rapids: Baker, 1990

Mcknight, Scott. *The Letter of James.* NICNT. Grand Rapids: Eerdmans, 2011.

McQuilkin, J. Robertson. *Understanding and Applying the Bible.* Chicago: Moody, 1983.

Mounce, William D. *The Analytical Lexicon to the Greek New Testament.* Grand Rapids: Zondervan, 1993.

Mounce, William D. *The Morphology of Biblical Greek.* Grand Rapids: Zondervan, 1994.

Meyer, Jason C. *The End of the Law: Mosaic Covenant in Pauline Theology.* NAC. vol. 6. Nashville: B & H Publishing, 2009.

Osborne, Grant R. *The Hermeneutical Spiral: A Comprehensive Introduction to Biblical Interpretation.* Rev. and expanded ed. Downers Grove, IL: InterVarsity, 2006.

Osborne, Grant R. *Revelation.* ECNT. Grand Rapids: Baker Academic, 2002.

Pate, C. Marvin. *The End of the Age Has Come: The Theology of Paul.* Grand Rapids: Zondervan, 1995.

Payne, J. Barton. *Encyclopedia of Biblical Prophecy.* New York: Harper & Row, 1973.

Pentecost, J. Dwight. *Things To Come.* Grand Rapids: Zondervan, 1958.

Ramm, Bernard, ed. *Hermeneutics.* Grand Rapids: Baker, 1971.

Ramm, Bernard, ed. *Protestant Biblical Interpretation*. 3rd rev. ed. Grand Rapids: Baker, 1970.

Reisinger, Ernest C. *The Law and the Gospel*. Phillipsburg: P & R Publishing, 1997.

Robinson, Haddon W. *Biblical Preaching: The Development and Delivery of Expository Messages*. Grand Rapids: Baker, 1980.

Ross, Allen P. *A Commentary on the Psalms*. 3 vols. Grand Rapids: Kregel, 2011.

Ross, Allen P. *Creation & Blessing: A Guide to the Study and Exposition of Genesis*. Grand Rapids: Baker Academic, 1996.

Ryrie, Charles C. *Dispensationalism*. Rev. and expanded. Chicago: Moody, 1995.

Sailhamer, J. H. *Introduction to Old Testament Theology: A Canonical Approach*. Grand Rapids: Zondervan, 1995.

Scofield, C. I. *Rightly Dividing the Word of Truth*. 1896. Reprint, Grand Rapids: Zondervan, 1974.

Schreiner, Thomas R. *Covenant and God's Purpose for the World: Short Study in Biblical Theology*. Wheaton: Crossway, 2017.

Schreiner, Thomas R. *New Testament Theology: Magnifying God in Christ*. Grand Rapid: Baker Academic, 2008.

Schreiner, Thomas R. *Interpreting the Pauline Epistles*. 2nd ed. Grand Rapids: Baker Academic, 2011.

Silva, Moises. *Biblical Words and Their Meaning: An Introduction to Lexical Semantics*. Rev. and expanded ed. Grand Rapids: Zondervan, 1994.

Sproule, R. C. "Controversy at Cultural Gap." *Eternity*, May 1976, 13-15, 40.

Stein, Robert H. *A Basic Guide to Interpreting the Bible: Playing by the Rules*. 2nd ed. Grand Rapids: Baker Academic, 1994.

Stein, Robert H. *An Introduction to the Parables.* Philadelphia: Westminster Press, 1981.

Sterrett, T. Norton. *How to Understand Your Bible.* Rev. ed. Downers Grove, IL: InterVarsity, 1974.

Stott, John R. W. *The Epistles of John.* TNTC. Grand Rapids: Eerdmans, 1964.

Stuart, D. *Old Testament Exegesis: A Primer For Students and Pastors.* Philadelphia: Westminster Press, 1980.

Stuart, D. *Exodus.* NAC. Nashville: Broadman & Holmes. 2006.

Terry, Milton S. *Biblical Hermeneutics.* 1883. Reprint, Grand Rapids: Zondervan, 1974.

Trench, Richard C. *Notes on The Parables of Our Lord.* 1886. Reprint, Grand Rapids: Baker, 1948.

Vanhoozer, Kevin J. *Is There a Meaning in This Text? The Bible, the Reader, and the Morality of Literary Knowledge.* Grand Rapids: Zondervan, 1998.

Vanhoozer, Kevin J. ed. *Dictionary of Theological Interpretation of the Bible.* Grand Rapids: Baker Academic, 2005.

Vine, William E. *Expository Dictionary of New Testament Words.* Old Tappan, NJ: Revell, 1940.

Virkler, Henry A. and Karelynne Gerber Ayayo. *Hermeneutics: Principles and Processes of Biblical Interpretation.* 2nd ed. Grand Rapids: Barker, 1981.

Waltke, Bruce K. and O'Connor, M. *An Introduction to Biblical Hebrew Syntax.* Winona Lake, IN: Eisenbrauns, 1990.

Walton, John H. *Ancient Israelite Literature in its Cultural Context: A Survey of Parallels Between Biblical and Ancient Near Eastern Texts.* Grand Rapids: Zondervan, 1989.

Walton, John H. *Genesis.* NIVAC. Grand Rapids: Zondervan, 2001.

Ward, James M. *Thus Says the Lord: The Message of the Prophets.* Nashville: Abingdon, 1991.

Weingreen, J. *Practical Grammar for Classical Hebrew.* 2nd ed. New York: Oxford, 1959.

Wellum, Stephan J., and Brent E. Parker. eds. *Progressive Covenantalism: Charting a Course Between Dispensational and Covenantal Theologies.* Nashville: B & H Academic, 2016.

Wight, Fred H. *Manners and Customs of Bible Lands.* Chicago: Moody, 1953.

Wood, Arthur S. *The Principles of Biblical Interpretation as Enunciated by Irenaeus, Origen, Augustine, Luther and Calvin.* Grand Rapids: Zondervan, 1967.

Wood, L. *The Prophets of Israel.* Grand Rapids: Baker, 1979.

Wright, G. E. *God Who Acts: Biblical Theology as Recital.* London: SCM Press, 1952.

Wuest, Kenneth S., *Word Studies in the Greek New Testament.* 3 vol. Reprinted. Grand Rapids: Eerdmans, 1999.

Young, B. *The Parables: Jewish Tradition and Christian Interpretation.* Peabody, Mass: Hendrickson, 1998.

Zuck, Roy B. *Basic Biblical Interpretation: A Practical Guide to Discovering Biblical Truth.* Colorado Springs: Victor Books, 1991.

Zuck, Roy B., ed. *Rightly Divided: Readings in Biblical Hermeneutics.* Grand Rapids: Kregel, 1996.